Wandering, Not Lost

Wandering, Not Lost

ESSAYS ON FAITH, DOUBT, AND MYSTERY

Barry L. Casey

Foreword by
Alisa Williams

WIPF & STOCK · Eugene, Oregon

WANDERING, NOT LOST
Essays on Faith, Doubt, and Mystery

Copyright © 2019 Barry L. Casey. All rights reserved. Except for brief quotations in critical publications or reviews, no part of this book may be reproduced in any manner without prior written permission from the publisher. Write: Permissions, Wipf and Stock Publishers, 199 W. 8th Ave., Suite 3, Eugene, OR 97401.

Wipf & Stock
An Imprint of Wipf and Stock Publishers
199 W. 8th Ave., Suite 3
Eugene, OR 97401

www.wipfandstock.com

PAPERBACK ISBN: 978-1-5326-9118-8
HARDCOVER ISBN: 978-1-5326-9119-5
EBOOK ISBN: 978-1-5326-9120-1

Manufactured in the U.S.A.   SEPTEMBER 27, 2019

Excerpt from "Entirely" from *Collected Poems* by Louis MacNeice, copyright © 2013 by Faber and Faber Limited, London. © Estate of Louis MacNeice, reprinted by permission of David Higham.

"Ich glaube an Alles noch nie Gesagte/I believe in all that has never yet been spoken," "Ich bin auf der Welt.../I'm too alone in the world . . . ,"and "Gott spricht zu jedem . . ./ God speaks to each of us . . ." from *Rilke's Book of Hours: Love Poems to God* by Rainer Maria Rilke, translated by Anita Barrows and Joanna Macy, translation copyright © 1996 by Anita Barrows and Joanna Macy. Used by permission of Riverhead, an imprint of Penguin Publishing Group, a division of Penguin Random House, LLC. All rights reserved.

"The Spanish Trilogy" from *Selected Poetry of Rainer Maria Rilke* by Rainer Maria Rilke, edited and translated by Stephen Mitchell, translation copyright © 1980, 1981, 1982 by Stephen Mitchell. Used by permission of Random House, an imprint and division of Penguin Random House, LLC. All rights reserved.

Excerpts from "Emerging," "Nuclear," and "Pilgrimages" *from Collected Poems 1945–1990* by R. S. Thomas, copyright © R. S. Thomas 1993. Used by permission of Orion Publishing Group, London.

All Scripture quotations, except where otherwise noted, are from the New Revised Standard Version (NRSV), copyright © 1989 by Division of Christian Education of the National Council of the Churches of Christ in the United States of America. Used by permission. All rights reserved.

To the Believers and Doubters class,
with whom many of these ideas were brought to light,

and

to Joy, my muse and delight,
for reading them all with love and uncommon sense

*There lives more faith in honest doubt,
believe me, than in half the creeds.*
—ALFRED LORD TENNYSON, *IN MEMORIAM*

Table of Contents

Foreword by Alisa Williams xi
Preface xiii
Acknowledgments xv

1. Wandering, Not Lost 1
2. Faith at the Between Places 5
3. Being with Thomas 9
4. A Loneliness that Hears 11
5. Forgiveness Perpetual 15
6. Beauty and Terror 19
7. Welcoming the Child 23
8. Not for This Life Only 27
9. For To Give 31
10. Understanding Backwards 34
11. Another Homecoming 37
12. Real Facts 40
13. Attention Deficit 44
14. Marching to a Different Drummer 49
15. A Path We Can Imagine 53
16. A (Very) Brief History of Silence 58
17. Our Fathers, Ourselves . . . 64
18. Life Becomes a Dark Saying 67

19. Augustine and the Word of Love 72
20. When a Bowl Is Not a Bowl 76
21. A Necessary Candle 80
22. Practicing the Grace We Have Received 84
23. First Church of Common Mysteries Now Open 88
24. A Single Step . . . 92
25. Imagine That 96
26. The Grace of Simple Things 100
27. Resist and Love 103
28. Devotional Doubt 105
29. Lane Walkers 108
30. Three Degrees of Success 111
31. The Stories We Become 115
32. Sing, and Keep Walking 120
33. Wisdom for the Contingent World 125
34. In Wildness the World Preserved 130
35. Abundance in the Midst of Plenty 133
36. Outrage and Longing 138
37. The Mystery of Iniquity 142
38. Consider the Lilies 146
39. Rooted Sideways 150
40. Can a Leper Change His Spots? 155
41. Our Infinite Choice 159
42. Hear the Pennies Dropping 163
43. The Hope in Shame 167
44. Our Moment at Jabbok 171
45. On the Boundary 175
46. This Is Only a Test 179
47. The Acts of the Disciples 183
48. My Bibles, My Life 187

49. The Worlds We Make 191
50. The Eyes of Your Heart 195
51. No Guarantees 199
52. The Light Coming into the World 203
53. Seeing Things 207
54. A Scandal We Can Live For 211
55. The Edge of Innocence 215
56. Unveiling Reality 220
57. Jonah's Bad Trip: A Lenten Meditation 224
58. Planks and Sawdust 229
59. The Doubtful Pilgrim 233
60. Cross-Purposes 237

Bibliography 241

Foreword

When I was young, I lived in a house situated rather precariously on the edge of a wooded ravine that overlooked a lazy creek. During the summers I'd spend long days down by that creek, my two dogs as my only companions, the sun filtering through the trees and the water laughing merrily as we played in its shallows.

On those expeditions, as I balanced on slippery rocks and fallen trunks, one foot carefully set in front of the other, I didn't know my destination, but I knew my purpose. My journey was undetermined, but not aimless. The smell of rotting wood, clay between my fingers, a rainbow trout skimming past bare legs, and the splash of dogs in joyful pursuit—these were the treasures I found without knowing I had been searching for anything.

I feel that way about my faith journey, too. God is bigger and more mysterious than I could ever wrap my mind around, but there is joy in the unknown, there is purpose in the adventure, and discovery awaits the patient, persistent traveler.

When I first read one of Barry Casey's essays, I had the same feeling I did as a kid navigating the creek bed. Here, I thought, is a fellow wanderer, who knows not his destination, but has made a life of the journey. Barry has since become one of my favorite storytellers. Whether he's bringing a biblical tale to life or sharing a personal narrative, light shines through his writing, revealing ideas and themes that I had never thought of before, but won't soon forget.

In Barry's essays, there is boundless faith in a loving God, creator of everything from the tiny creek to the greatest galaxy. There is doubt, too, but in Barry's hands, doubt is not something to be ashamed of or to shy away from. Rather, doubt is in a delicate balancing act with faith, two equal parts of the same whole. And, of course, there is mystery—a glorious celebration of our mysterious Creator, who is both known and unknowable.

Author Barbara Brown Taylor said, "I will always be at sea, steering by stars."[1] Barry's essays are like that. They are the stars in the night sky, an invitation forward when all around us is endless sea. I am grateful for the invitation, and for the company on this voyage. There's room for you, too. There's room for everyone.

Alisa Williams, managing editor of SpectrumMagazine.org

---

1. Taylor, *Learning to Walk in the Dark*, 140.

Preface

FAITH AND DOUBT HAVE always been my companions on my spiritual wanderings. I suspect that is true for many people. And thanks to the encouragement I have received from others for a thoughtful doubting, it is a companion I have come to cherish.

It wasn't always that way. I learned at an early age to keep my doubts about God, faith, evil and suffering, and many other things to myself. Getting entangled in arguments wasn't worth the trouble, and it almost never led to any kind of clarity on the subject. Besides, by the time I had formulated a question during public discussions at church or in classes, the ship had already sailed. I watched it drop over the horizon and lowered my hand.

In college, there were some professors who blanched at doubt, especially about religious matters, and others who seemed to see it for what it was—sincerity seeking a breathing space to consider how faith and facts were going to live together. I came across Pascal's saying, "The heart has its reasons that reason knows not," and it seemed entirely reasonable to me. Courageous, too.

Doubt lives in question form and questions shape our learning. The questions we hold form the mold for the faith that is produced. I marveled at Socrates' ability to drill down through our unquestioned assumptions to shake the foundations. In graduate school, studying Barth, Tillich, Niebuhr, and especially Jürgen Moltmann, Bonhoeffer, and the liberation theologians, I saw that doubt is not to be feared. In fact, if we have no doubts about our assumptions and our knowledge, we are in danger.

In the course of teaching religion, philosophy, ethics, and communications, I found that students could have the confidence to think for themselves if they could bring their doubts out into the light. Not just doubts about God or Jesus, but about themselves, about their own ability to sort through tough issues and arrive at some answers and actions, tentative though they might be at first.

Now, my certainties are few. One of them is that, inexplicably, God has chosen, at great cost, to love us. There are times when I have my doubts about God's bet on us; as a species we don't seem very promising, mucking up our relationships and fouling our own nest. But then I'll see someone's quiet strength in living for others, and I'll think, "Ah, there's a flashpoint for God's work in the world," and my hope will be strengthened. Faith, I've learned, is more done than said; too much saying about it can become a substitute for the doing of it.

The interplay of faith and doubt is a mystery, one that can enliven the heart with the reasons it alone can express.

Acknowledgments

I AM GRATEFUL TO Bonnie Dwyer and Alisa Williams, editor and managing editor, respectively, of *Spectrum Magazine*, in which most of these essays first appeared, and to the Adventist Forum, a force for good in the world. Bonnie made it possible for me to be published and to meet publishers, and Alisa edits my column from week to week with a sharp eye and a soft touch.

Dr. Lyn Bartlett and Dr. Mike Pearson have been boon companions on this journey, questioning, inspiring, and encouraging me. I hold them both in special regard as friends and mentors.

Although they don't know it, Thomas Merton, Parker Palmer, Jürgen Moltmann, and Paul Tillich have taught me much about faith and hope. I write under the influence—from afar—of Barbara Brown Taylor, Rowan Williams, Christian Wiman, Michael Mayne, and John Jeremiah Sullivan. One can always aspire.

Finally, I am grateful for the assistance and direction of the team at Wipf & Stock, especially Rodney Clapp, Acquisitions Editor, who first took an interest, and Matt Wimer, Assistant Managing Editor, whose steadiness throughout was reassuring.

1

Wandering, Not Lost

I believe in all that has never yet been spoken.
I want to free what waits within me.
so that what no one has dared to wish for
may for once spring clear
without my contriving.[1]

DURING MY YEAR OF college in England in the early seventies, I hitchhiked as often as I could. The roads were less crowded then, I dare say it was safer, and students wearing their college colors could almost always get a ride with lorry drivers and other travelers. On a fine autumn afternoon, I set out from my college near Windsor for Stratford (as in Shakespeare), a short hop of less than fifty miles. I was used to getting a ride within half an hour, but I grew impatient as the afternoon waned. So, I crossed the road to the opposite direction and got a lift within five minutes. The driver was headed south and west, whereas I had been heading north. But that was alright, so I went along.

The protocol for conversations ran along fairly predictable lines. I would lean in, the driver would ask where I was going, he or she would state their destination, and I would jump in. Often, the next set of questions would be, "Where are you studying?" or "What are you studying?" or more generally, "What brings you to this country?"

---

1. Rilke, *Rilke's Book of Hours*, 58.

After I replied that I was studying religion, the driver glanced over at me and gave a short laugh. He looked to be in his fifties, wearing jeans and a jean jacket, short graying hair, a ruggedly handsome face.

"I wonder if you can help me," he said. "My marriage is breaking up—my third marriage—and I don't know what to do. I have a cottage out in Cornwall"—he paused, "and I guess I'll stay there until I figure something out. You're religious: what should I do?"

I was a sophomore in college, nineteen years old, unschooled in the ways of the world, and near the bottom of the list for reliable marriage counseling. But I did have malpractice insurance and it was this: I had made a pact with God that if I got a lift I would speak of my faith in Christ as the opportunity presented itself. I added a rider to the agreement that only if the driver initiated the subject would I witness of my faith. I'd had enough experience of roaming packs of overenthusiastic Christian youths in Berkeley and San Francisco to know that imposing or tricking people into listening to a witnessing spiel was not for me.

So here it was: my cue to speak. I should also mention that the final clause in the agreement was that I be given the words to say. Not asking too much, I reasoned, given the stakes. So, we talked, or rather I talked, and he listened as we puttered along in his little Citroen. He listened intently, with a question or two now and then, or he smiled and nodded. Finally, up ahead was Stonehenge, where I had decided to get out, and with the stones silhouetted against a blazing sunset we coasted to a stop by the road. We sat for a moment, gazing in wonder at the sight. Then he turned to me with tears in his eyes and said, "Will you pray for me?" "Of course," I said, and opened the door to get out. "No, I mean now," he said, and put a hand on my arm. "Here, right now." I gulped, and then I prayed with him. We shook hands, I got out, he drove off. And I stood there with a full heart and a mind full of questions.

Here's the thing: when I got out—and even in the days that followed—I couldn't remember anything of what I'd said, except that at one point I recited 1 Corinthians 13 in its entirety—a passage I had never memorized to my knowledge. Now, over forty-seven years later, with a memory I no longer trust out of my sight, that recitation is still all I can remember saying. I don't know what happened to that man; I hope his life turned around. I know mine did. Theory turned into practice, hoped-for faith into action. It was enough.

We often describe our youth as lost, when they may just be seeking a site from which to launch. If you don't have a destination you can't be lost. It's only when we set a goal or a time limit or a linear point that we become concerned about losing our way. But on many of our life journeys we don't know the final destination and we may not even know the way. Our lives are moving illustrations of faith as a rolling wave, traveling in a general direction without a specific shoreline.

✶✶✶

Somewhere in his many writings Kurt Vonnegut sardonically tosses out the fact that the universe is expanding in every direction, whistling past our ears outward at thousands of miles per second. Everything else, he intimates, pales beside that. By contrast, Northrop Frye says in his classic, *The Great Code,* that our default demand for unity and integration, for drawing reality in around us, can only rise as high as our finite imagination.

We choose our metaphors, but before that they somehow choose us. Our descriptions of our paths through life spring from the images of what draws us onward through certain points in our journey. They may change as we change; the important thing to remember is that we adapt to live up to them.

For many people today, their life metaphor is exile and homelessness. Even if they live in the Hamptons, Aspen, or Palm Beach, they feel themselves to be adrift. Another group, evangelical Christians, revel in the faintly militaristic strains of "We're marching to Zion," and though the route ahead runs off the edge of the map they plunge ahead with confidence. Still others, as advanced in years as they are free to be both curious and experienced, will see their lives as a guided wandering, neither aimless nor predetermined.

We need to wander until being "lost" doesn't matter.

We need to wander until our reference points are behind us.

We need to wander without fear or assumptions.

But how long can you travel before it's too far to return?

Frye says that if we *really* want to see past the event horizon, we need to follow a way or direction until we reach the state of guided innocence symbolized by the sheep in the twenty-third Psalm.

> Even though I walk through the
> darkest valley,
> I fear no evil;
> for you are with me.[2]

2. Ps 23:4.

Frye goes on to note that Jesus was a wanderer and that the diffusion of early Christianity "is symbolically connected with the progress of man back to the garden of Eden," the "wandering but guided pastoral world of the twenty-third Psalm."[3]

The "wandering" motif runs against our linear, goal-driven, deadline-clutching lifestyle, and while there may be a place for all of that, there can also be time for unfettered curiosity and the blessedness of wandering *without* necessity or obligation.

Try it sometime: take a stroll through the Gospels or the Prophets or the Psalms, finding a text that lights up the imagination and following its references and associations until you reach a place you've not been to before. What do you find? Who is there? What do they smile or frown about? What makes them laugh and what are they completely serious about?

Try on a new idea or flip an old one around and see what difference it makes. Imagine that God is in search of us; that your coworker poses no threat but is struggling to get through her life; that a good word in due season is on the tip of your tongue; and that truth still really matters.

I look back on those hitchhiking days and I marvel sometimes. I would set out with no money and a light heart, sleeping in fields, trudging through the rain, alone on some country road with no traffic for miles—but it was all good. Countless times there were strangers who protected me; friends who gave me shelter, warmth, and a cuppa; country churches and city cathedrals that opened their arms to me; fields and meadows that welcomed me—there was delight in adversity.

What I didn't know freed me, what I was learning strengthened me, what there was to learn lured me onward. Be it ever so.

---

3. Frye, *Great Code*, 159.

2

Faith at the Between Places

We are beginning to see . . .
in everyday life
it is the plain facts and natural happenings
that conceal God and reveal him to us
little by little under the mind's tooling.[1]

"Midway in our life's journey, I went astray/from the straight road and woke to find myself/alone in a dark wood."[2] So said Dante and so echoed I, if not in word then in experience. But Dante woke to find himself there; I stumbled into it with my eyes wide open. Dante had his Virgil—and his Beatrice—to guide him through what lay ahead. I had Rainer Rilke, Jürgen Moltmann, the Gospels, and U2.

With my life at a standstill, trying to write a dissertation for a degree I wasn't at all sure I would have the chance to use, I woke to who I was—and wished I could sleep again. There is much about ourselves that we sense is just behind us, but we're too afraid to look. There is still more that we don't know until a fissure opens and we fall into the depths. Once there, every shadow is menacing, every sound unnerving, every thought doubling back on itself in an endless loop. We wonder if we were ever who we thought we were, and we are sure that everyone sees us more starkly and completely than we see ourselves.

---

1. Thomas, "Emerging," in *Collected Poems*, 355.
2. Alighieri, *Divine Comedy*, 16.

Trying to write a dissertation about hope and suffering and the mystery of evil when one has little hope becomes an ordinance of humility. The suffering we cause, when named and owned, is first a fire that sucks up all the air, and then a cleansing flame that scours away our pretense.

Down in the depths there is nothing to be gained by plugging in the formulae that others assure us we will need for peace of heart. What is needed is clarity, a fierce honesty that stops down the aperture of our soul for a convergent beam of light.

***

I visited my father once when he was working in research for a major defense contractor. He asked if I'd like to experience a sensory deprivation chamber. He promised to let me out after a few minutes, since I would have no sense of the passage of time. That was a darkness that seemed to atomize my body. Although I could touch my hand, I could not see it no matter how close I held it to my eyes. And although I shouted as loudly as I could there was absolutely no sound. None. It was like a mini-death, but I felt no panic, only a pang of loss, as if I could no longer remember my name or my face.

***

When we long for the presence of God, of a word we can hold in front of us like a candle, we feel the limits of our faith. How is it, as Christian Wiman ruefully admits in *My Bright Abyss,* that he can wake up as a Christian and go to bed an atheist? Why should we expect, as people of faith, that the path before us will be cleared of all obstacles before we touch a foot upon it? Why do we imagine that our faith in that which is eternal will be satisfied once for all? Why do we expect that the flame that is lit between ourselves and the Spirit will burn steadily from that moment onward?

Rilke was there with his angels, those terrifying angels, and the grandeur he uncovered in the spaces between prayers. He gave syllables to the breath within me that could just utter the name of God without choking up. I finished the dissertation in due course, defended it, and reinvented myself. I began to see hope in the crucified God and to turn my face toward the garden of the resurrection.

> It is not that he can't speak:
> who created languages
> but God? Nor that he won't;
> to say that is to imply
> malice. It is just that
> he doesn't, or does so at times
> when we are not listening, in
> ways we have yet to recognize
> as speech.[3]

There are days when we put on the brave face and speak of faith to others and pray that they don't see the desperation in our eyes. Doubt and faith journey together; when one falls behind the other pauses patiently to wait. Thomas became my patron saint, I his twin brother. When he exclaimed, "My Lord and my God!" he had seen through the familiar figure of Jesus to the God within. I wondered if I could see that God in the pale and fastidious Jesus of religious media.

"Christian faith teaches that the One whom we are to love most is the one whom we can never fully possess," writes Mark Oakley in *The Splash of Words*. "It means that our faith's language will be inevitably infused with desire, ache and search. The One we long for most finally eludes us."[4]

I learned that faith grows in the "between" places, and if I could not bear the potted version that provided contentment for many, God would generously—with patience and good humor—meet me where I stood, defiant but uncertain.

Oakley says, "we are not seeking *relevance* but *resonance*—not the transient ideas of today that can convince for a time but the truths that address the deepest longings of a human life and a fragile world."[5] Our faith weakens "when we think we somehow have captured God or contain God. This is when certainty more than doubt becomes the opposite of faith."[6]

Someone said—perhaps Rumi—that every morning we may say, "Now I begin!" If we can believe it, God starts anew with us every

---

3. Thomas, "Nuclear," in *Collected Poems*, 317.
4. Oakley, *Splash of Words*, xxx.
5. Oakley, *Splash of Words*, xxxi.
6. Oakley, *Splash of Words*, xxx.

moment; each breath may be our untainted first. Because we carry our memories and our guilt with us, and because we are creatures of time, we think in linear fashion: first this must happen, then that, and finally this will be the result. God, unbounded and beyond all constraints of time, sees us as we were, and are, and shall be evermore in every moment.

"As a Christian," Oakley says, "I believe that God has given us all a gift. It is our being. God asks for a gift in return—our becoming, who we become with our being. Because our gift back to God is lifelong and continually shifting and changing, it means that any language that is to be true to this spiritual adventure of being alive needs equally to resist closure, to protest at black and white conclusions and fixed meanings."[7]

We are *unfinished* beings, mercifully limited by space and time, and blessed with curiosity and imagination. If we believe that the One who started this good work in us will continue in our renewing, perhaps we will have the courage to see beyond the dark wood.

---

7. Oakley, *Splash of Words*, xxvi.

3

Being with Thomas

Whoever seeks to catch Him and hold Him loses Him. He is like the wind that blows where it pleases. You who love Him must love Him as arriving from where you do not know and as going where you do not know.[1]

I WOULD HAVE BEEN with Thomas in that upper room. Never an early adopter nor a joiner, I would have held back to watch others, see their reactions, imagine myself in their place until the resistance I felt toward the new had reduced its charge.

It's a question of how we know what we know and whether what we know can be verified. It's a question of how much you trust your senses and whether your rational faculties can puzzle it through. Mostly, it's about whether you're willing to look foolish in pursuit of truth.

Thomas gets the rap as the doubting one, forever holding out until he can touch and feel and see with his own eyes. Like it had never occurred to the rest of them that maybe this kingdom of God business was just too good to be true. Like all the other promises made that had not so much been broken as had not materialized beyond the promising stage. But with Thomas, it was never skepticism about the nature of Jesus' intentions. Nor was it cynicism about the possibility of goodness in the world. There was plenty of goodness, and beauty also, and where goodness and beauty live truth must be in the neighborhood somewhere.

---

1. Merton, *Seeds*, 125.

No, what Thomas knew about himself, with the clarity that comes from aloneness, is that he lacked the courage to commit himself to another.

It hadn't always been this way. After all, he was Thomas—Didymus—aka "the Twin." There had been another, his brother, older by two minutes and stronger twice over. They had been inseparable, each the other half of the other, together as one, but not the same. He had led, Thomas had followed. Thomas was thoughtful, holding back, his brother plunging ahead with a shout. Thomas had read and questioned, his brother had acted. They had talked and argued late into the night about politics, religion, freedom. His brother joined a group; they were armed. He was adamant: "Better to die trying than not to try at all." Later, after he was crucified with the others, the soldiers had come round for Thomas. By that time, he had gone into the night. Keeping to the back roads, he had traveled north to Galilee alone.

And now here he was amongst a band of brothers, younger than most, the first to ask, the last to step forward. When he had met Jesus, it was as if he had seen his brother again; all the strength, but without the recklessness. And now he was gone, crucified like his twin; another one taken, promises dashed.

So, he might be forgiven, Thomas reckoned, for standing back when the others told him, breathlessly, that they had seen the Lord. "The door was shut, we were afraid, and then there he was!"

"I see," said Thomas, but he didn't really. "He asked about you," they said. "He said he'd be back."

"I'd have to see that for myself," said Thomas dryly. Peter smiled. "He figured you'd say that."

Eight days later he was with the others, the door locked and bolted, voices lowered. And then he was there, smiling, in their midst, and looking Thomas in the eye. "I'm real," he said. "Touch me. Act on it! Believe."

All this was a long time ago, but set down this. Set down this: I came to faith, finally, by acting as if it were there. And then it was—and is and will be, if I but act.

> For we are saved by hope:
> but hope that is seen is not hope:
> for what a man seeth,
> why doth he yet hope for?
> But if we hope for that we see not,
> then do we with patience wait for it.[2]

2. Rom 8:24–25, KJV.

4

A Loneliness that Hears

We do not have to discover the world of faith; we only have to recover it. It is not a terra incognita, *an unknown land; it is a forgotten land, and our relation to God is a palimpsest rather than a* tabula rasa. *There is no one who has no faith.*[1]

"Be here now. Be some other place some other time. Is that so difficult?"

That is my recollection of a quote I heard several years ago attributed to Ram Dass, an American guru in the Hindu tradition. It's no wonder we find it difficult to be in the present moment: we can't see its edges. It's a Venn diagram, rather than a line or a point. Yet thousands of years of spiritual tradition and writings insist that this is where God is—here, in the present moment.

"Just as clairvoyants may see the future," says Abraham Heschel in *God in Search of Man*, "the religious man comes to sense the present moment."[2] Is this an extrasensory perception? Something that only one in a hundred is born with, those with second sight, the fortunate few who travel always in the assurance of being surrounded by the divine? "It is primarily, it seems, an enhancement of the soul," says Heschel, "a

---

1. Heschel, *God in Search of Man*, 141.
2. Heschel, *God in Search of Man*, 142.

sharpening of one's spiritual sense, an endowment with a new sensibility . . . Things have past and a future, but only God is pure presence."[3]

***

There is a Native American perspective that when we talk to one another we are surrounded by everyone and everything that has brought us to that moment. Our ancestors hover over and behind us; our past experiences and actions are melded into our bone marrow; our thoughts and words spring from the rivers of tradition and culture that water our singular desolation at times when we feel most alone. I have mentioned this to my students in ethics courses as a way of suggesting our links to our past and our debts to those who have gone before us.

When we speak, then, it is our entire experience of life to that point that shapes our responses to the person in front of us. Sure, we're processing the signals we encounter, decoding while we encode, taking in the feedback—both verbal and nonverbal—and trying to see the moment through the eyes of our partner; all of this in the wider context of our social, political, and psychological sensitivities. That we do all of this in seconds, without even breaking a sweat, is testament to the commonplace extraordinariness of communication between humans, surely one of the most complex aspects of our species. But that's just the baseline, something that most of us take for granted, like gravity or sneezing with our eyes closed. To recognize who we are as a result of our past can give us a wider understanding in order to be fully present in that moment.

When it comes to communicating with or even sensing God, though, we feel knocked back on our heels. Theories abound, well meaning, but ultimately trite and foolish. We try: we adjust the parameters of our experiments in reaching God, taking notes when something seems to work, discarding methods like junk mail with hardly a glance. At prayer we try not to put our own desires forth, somehow thinking that if we refuse to acknowledge the very thing we so desperately need, that God will be good enough to give it to us. It all becomes ridiculous after a while, akin to superstition or sorcery—prayer as incantation. So, we drop it in disgust or regretfully move on or determine to go it alone.

I was in Winchester Cathedral with friends. We had come for Evensong on a summer's afternoon, making our way from the Hospital of St.

---

3. Heschel, *God in Search of Man*, 142.

Cross and the twelfth-century Almshouse of Noble Poverty, through the quiet backstreets, past Winchester College, following the roofline of the cathedral in the near distance. When we arrived and slipped inside I had a déja vu moment reaching back four decades to when I had hitchhiked there as a student. I remembered it as one of the holiest moments of my life, in which I had encountered God in the echoing stillness of an afternoon as I knelt near the altar. There were no prayers, no words, no conjuring up of any images. The soaring windows above the nave and the transept, the light pouring in through the clerestory, were enough to lift me and awe me to my knees.

"Only those who have gone through days on which words were of no avail," comments Heschel, "on which the most brilliant theories jarred the ear like mere slang; only those who have experienced ultimate not-knowing, the voicelessness of a soul struck by wonder, total muteness, are able to enter the meaning of God, a meaning greater than the mind."[4]

I knew nothing of that then, only that the sheer immensity of a hovering and sheltering Being was there, a Real Presence that transcended and shattered all sectarian rigidity. The fact that the building was designed to evoke such a response did not detract from the experience, nor does the recognition that my recent visit, while spiritually uplifting and inspiring, did not overwhelm me in the same way as my first encounter—none of that diminished my sense of God's presence therein.

Abraham Maslow's little book *Religions, Values, and Peak Experiences* offers insight into these things. Maslow compares and contrasts the "plateau-experience" with the "peak-experience," and suggests that the former "is serene and calm" rather than the climactic response to "the miraculous, the awesome, the sacralized, the Unitive" that we get in peak experiences. Whereas the peak experience is almost purely emotional, the plateau experience *always*, says Maslow, "has a noetic and cognitive element . . . It is far more voluntary than peak-experiences are." As we age and begin to make our peace with death, we are more likely to cherish, with sweet sadness, the contrast between our own mortality and the "eternal quality of what sets off the experience."[5]

Perhaps most important, says Maslow, is to realize that plateau-experiencing can be learned, achieved, practiced, and continued throughout life. There are no shortcuts to this, however, and, as Maslow notes,

---

4. Heschel, *God in Search of Man*, 140.
5. Maslow, *Religions, Values, and Peak-Experiences*, xiv.

there isn't any way of "bypassing the necessary maturing, experiencing, living, learning. All of this takes time."[6]

We don't—and can't—live on the peaks continuously. Indeed, Maslow cautions that those who put the peak experience before everything else can become the nastiest, meanest, least compassionate people around. Furthermore, their constant pursuit of ecstasy triggers, the compulsion for an escalation of stronger spiritual stimuli, easily slides over into magic, the anti-rational, the obsessive.

Some of the greatest spiritual adepts have had their "dark night of the soul," when God cannot be found or even sensed. Most of us only have our gray days of the spirit, when our spiritual pulse is barely flickering. In those times we call upon our memories of the vistas we *have* seen from the peaks we *have* scaled.

"The most precious gifts come to us unawares and remain unnoted," says Heschel. "God's grace resounds in our lives like a staccato. Only by retaining the seemingly disconnected notes do we acquire the ability to grasp the theme."[7] In those gray days, and especially in the dark ones, we connect the dots looking back in order to be fully here in the Now.

There will be days when God seems not to answer, not to be found. God is not a pearl deep in the ocean, warns Heschel, as if we could, through our skills and intelligence, dive deep to discover him. We *can* take the initiative—in fact, we must not be passive—but without God's response and aid, we cannot come close to him.

There is an aloneness that is solitary, yet not abandoned. I felt it upon leaving Winchester Cathedral, and have felt it since. But there are times when the peaks are enshrouded in fog, when even the plateaus are beyond our reach, when the valleys are the only possible route forward. In those times, declares Heschel, "There is a loneliness in us that hears. When the soul parts from the company of the ego and its retinue of petty conceits; when we cease to exploit all things but instead pray the world's cry, the world's sigh, our loneliness may hear the living grace beyond all power."[8]

---

6. Maslow, *Religions, Values, and Peak-Experiences*, xvi.
7. Heschel, *God in Search of Man*, 142.
8. Heschel, *God in Search of Man*, 140.

5

Forgiveness Perpetual

I grew weary of sinning
before God grew weary of forgiving my sin.
He is never weary of giving grace,
nor are his compassions to be exhausted.[1]

I'VE NEVER BEEN FOND of the poem "The Hound of Heaven." Somehow, the image of God on the trail with cold intent to pursue me until I find myself with my back to the wall, nowhere to go, and thus *must* yield to his designs—that image instills fear rather than love. I don't deny that some people respond favorably to this and similar images. I'm just saying that in the vast repertoire of metaphors we have for God that one is way down the list for me.

But in a sense, it doesn't matter all that much what I think about God; whether I think God resembles a hunting dog or a lover or a rock or a fountain of everlasting water. These are educational toys pointing, sometimes distractedly, toward a Being who breaks all categories and metaphors, simply because he/she/they cannot be contained in our refracted lenses.

What really matters is what God thinks of me. For starters, God hates the sins that I manifest so effortlessly. Absolutely, unequivocally, irrevocably, and any other "lys" we'd like to conjure up. This is the case for a couple of reasons.

1. Teresa of Avila, *Santa Teresa*, 400.

First, our sin rends the beautiful creation God has provided us. There is a thread running through world faiths that sees a clear causality between human arrogance toward the created world and the fracturing of that world. Back behind the science of climate change are the fables, stories, parables, and straight-out testimony for thousands of years that say we are inextricably intertwined with our world. Because we have command of so many tools, our impact on the environment is far out of proportion to our physical size.

We change our world simply by our presence on the planet. Like all other beings, we take our place in time and space. But we can minimize our unintended harm and work to eliminate our deliberate havoc. That is sin, and it tears through the perfect circles of interdependence that God set up.

But the second reason God hates sin is what it does to us. How it distorts our perception, calcifies our empathy, teaches us cruelty and contempt, makes us mock the innocent and destroy the beautiful. How it places us beyond contrition and in contention with compassion, stretches our patience to the breaking point and snaps our attention, glorifies violence and belittles peace, derides those who listen and castigates those who are honest. The list goes on, but we get the point. All of this, in God's way of thinking, is not who we are, and though we find it difficult to separate the gold in others and ourselves from the dross, God sees both and draws the distinction.

Despite our expertise in sinning, our development and refinement of its methods, the thousands of ways we have devised to ruin a beautiful world and to break each other, somehow God is able to see through the sin to the sinner. And the sinner in all of us—incredibly—is what God loves.

We are the pearl of great price that Jesus the Holy Diver plucks from the bottom of the ocean. We are the treasure in the field, buried in a rusty old tin box, that the fellow with the metal detector finds while skimming back and forth across the furrows. We are the lost and forgotten masterpiece picked up at a yard sale and restored to its former beauty, the coin wedged in a grate in the gutter.

But what of those who cower before God, those who keep to the backroads to avoid being seen, the ones who run for their lives if God appears because of the shame and fear of their sinning? Like a dog beaten and abandoned, who limps off when people approach, we see danger in the one who only wants to help.

Soren Kierkegaard tells a parable of the king who woos and weds a lovely peasant girl. The king loves her deeply and truly, but anxiety grows within him because she responds to him as the king, not as her companion, husband, and lover. Their difference in status calls up admiration in the girl, but not confidence. To appear in all his majesty before her would overwhelm and further distance her, for she thinks herself not his equal. Despite their love for each other, there is an unbridgeable gap between them. Neither really understands the other.

Kierkegaard suggests this is God's dilemma. Since we could not be elevated to a level where we could fully understand God, God would take on himself the form of a servant so that God could understand us.

But perfect fear casts out love, and if we have been told that nothing short of perfection in this life will satisfy God, it's no wonder that so many run in the opposite direction from the One who comes with healing. God's persistence looks like deadly intention; his moves to reach and bandage us we see as seizing and shackling us. In desperation and in fear we plunge on through our wilderness.

He tracks us by the blood on the trail, the pain our acts cause for others and ourselves. That which separates us from God and condemns us—sin—becomes the very means through which Christ finds the cancer and excises it. As Dante shows us, Christ follows our sins down to hell in order to liberate us, not to condemn us. The very presence of our sins leads to confession and repentance, and finally to absolution and reconciliation.

Complications arise. According to our usual reading, God's forgiveness of us is a contractual arrangement: if we forgive others, then God can forgive us. If we can't forgive, then God won't either. The rules are clear, there's no ambiguity. We go first, then God reacts. We read it this way because we're used to relationships that involve some type of transaction, that are functional, that include a payoff or a return on investment.

But this is not how God looks at forgiveness. He doesn't wait for us to reach out, to make the first move. God's ego is not tender. He is not easily offended.

Those who are forgiven can forgive. Forgiveness received can become forgiveness extended to others, but it does not work in reverse. We cannot forgive if we have not experienced forgiveness as an extension of God's unfathomable love.

The woman who crashed a private party for Jesus at Simon the Pharisee's house wept for joy because she had been forgiven. Perhaps she and Jesus had had an encounter before this that convinced her of God's unconditional love and forgiveness. Perhaps she had grown weary of the trap of her sins. As Luke quotes Jesus, "Her sins, which are many, are forgiven, for she loved much; but he who is forgiven little, loves little."[2] Perhaps because of this she could even forgive the men who had enjoyed the use of her and then condemned and shamed her for it.

Paul Tillich, in a sermon in *The New Being*, points out that if we fear God and feel rejected by him, we cannot love him. But if we can see—and feel—that God's love is without limit, then it truly is a new world. He says, "We cannot love unless we have accepted forgiveness, and the deeper our experience of forgiveness is, the greater is our love."[3]

As Jesus says, "Who needs a doctor: the healthy or the sick? I'm here inviting outsiders, not insiders—an invitation to a changed life, changed inside and out."[4] Whatever hellish darkness we find ourselves in, whatever pain we are carrying, we can be assured of this: only those with a pre-existing condition will be accepted into this universal health care plan.

---

2. Luke 7:47.
3. Tillich, *New Being*, 10.
4. Luke 5:31, Message.

6

Beauty and Terror

He said to them, "Take nothing for your journey, no staff, nor bag, nor bread, nor money—not even an extra tunic."[1]

WHEN HE CALLED US together finally, it was in order to send us out together alone, without him. We had been with him long enough to know that he did not stand on protocol. In fact, he did not stand on much except faith in the ineffable Spirit of God, a gossamer thread that was subject to stress with us, but was a linked chain of cast iron for him. So, when he said he was sending us out with power and authority to throw out demons and heal diseases and generally talk up the good news of the kingdom, it was a release of the breath we had been holding since we first met him.

I'll be honest with you: I remember that moment with crystalline clarity because I was terrified. He was asking us to go out into the hills, where people had been out of work for months, where opioids opened some doors and closed others forever, and where a gun in the hand was worth two in the cabinet. Demons and diseases, devils and dust—there was scarcely an upside to this.

But I went. We went, Andrew and I, and the others, two by two. What the hell, I thought, it's time to take him at his word.

There is a lightness in just going, nothing in hand, and no clear plan for the end of day. At the first town off the interstate that we came to, we

---

1. Luke 9:3.

headed for the 7-Eleven and asked who might be sick in town. It took persistence.

"Are you doctors or something?" asked the kid behind the counter. He didn't bother to get up.

"Not exactly," said Andrew, "but we can help." The kid didn't say anything. He looked out the window at the pickup next to the pumps.

"Talk to Roy," he said finally. "His mom's been laid up for months. You want some buffalo jerky?"

I shook my head.

"Heh Roy," said the kid, "these guys can help your mom." I turned as a tall man with a scraggly ponytail came through the door.

"Why you talking about my momma, Craig?"

"These guys said they could help."

"That true?" he asked. "Here's ten for the gas." He dropped the bill on the counter and stepped back.

"Yes," said Andrew, "it's true." He looked at Roy steadily. I held my breath.

"Are you doctors or something? Preachers? 'Cos we've had enough of preachers up here. Can't trust 'em."

"I know it sounds crazy," Andrew said, "but we've been given power to heal."

"I don't have that kind of money," said Roy. "Not interested."

"It's not about money," I said. "We want to help. It's about the kingdom."

"No kingdom around here," laughed Craig. "What you talking about, 'kingdom'? Jesus!"

"In a manner of speaking, yes, it's about Jesus," said Andrew quietly.

"Okay, then," said Roy, after a moment. "Get in the pickup. We'll go see her."

I sat in the bed of the truck, while Andrew sat up front. I didn't feel like being crowded as three men in a space for two. Besides, I wanted to savor the strangeness of the moment: how was I in the back of a pickup truck high in the hills of Appalachia near sundown to find some woman with God knows what illness and to heal her? And then what?

We turned off the main road after ten minutes and jounced down a dirt track beneath an arch of trees and vines. At the end was a stained double-wide trailer in a clearing with a wooden hut nearby and a rusting 1981 Ford truck up on blocks. Roy braked to a stop and switched off the engine. We got out.

"I don't know how she is today," said Roy. He looked down. "I talked to her yesterday. She doesn't take well to strangers."

I tried to imagine her life here, how she waited for her son to come by, maybe watched television and smoked in the evenings. There were cigarette butts everywhere on the ground around the steps.

"Shall we go in?" said Andrew gently. Roy rapped on the door.

"Momma," he called. "It's me, Roy. I've brought a coupla friends by. They want to meet you."

"Is that you, Roy?" came a voice from inside. The door opened a crack and then wider.

"It's me, Momma," said Roy, and he swung the door open enough for us to see the woman inside. She stood, clutching the door frame with one hand, the other pulling a robe together across a thin chest. She wore jeans and slippers and a Batman T-shirt that was frayed and dirty. Her hair was long and gray, with yellow streaks, and hung limply around her shoulders. She looked right through us and put out a hand.

I realized she was blind when Roy gently touched her shoulder and turned her to the inside. "Come in," he said to us. "You can sit over there." He pointed to a table in the back with a built-in window seat and two folding chairs. He guided her to the table and steadied her as she sat down and slid behind it. He stood awkwardly next to her.

I sat down in one of the chairs. Andrew made as if to sit down but then straightened again. "I'm Andrew," he said, "and this is Thomas."

The woman across from us put out her hand. "I'm Suzanne," she said. "How do you know Roy?"

Andrew took her hand in his. "We met just now at the 7-Eleven. We'd like to help you."

She didn't pull away, but her back stiffened. "With what? How?" she said. "Roy, what's this about?"

There was a pause. Roy looked at Andrew and then at me. "Well . . . ," he said hesitantly.

"You're blind and we can help," I cut in. I realized how that sounded, but I rushed on. "We can heal you if you'll give us a chance. Really," I added lamely.

She laughed bitterly. "And how much is this going to cost me?"

"No, no!" I said. "It's nothing, it's not about money, it's about . . ." I paused and looked at Andrew.

"It's a gift from God," said Andrew simply. "Just that. We know someone."

There was silence. Roy shifted uneasily.

"Well," she said at last, "I suppose it's worth a shot." She held out her other hand to me. "What are you going to do?"

I took her hand in both of mine. The skin felt dry and cold, cracked across the knuckles and reddened in places. I licked my lips; I was sure my voice would break.

I glanced at Andrew. He nodded. I took a breath and looked up . . .

* * *

I must have drifted for a moment because when I came to myself he was saying, "Look, now I am sending you out. I'm giving you authority over demons—all of them, and power to heal and to announce to people that the kingdom of God is here." He smiled: "Bring them peace and travel light. If they don't want you, leave and go to the next town. We're not in the business of forcing anyone."

Later that afternoon, before we left, I took out the battered copy of Rilke's *Book of Hours* that I always carry in my backpack and read this:

> God speaks to each of us as he makes us,
> then walks with us silently out of the night.
> These are the words we dimly hear:
> You, sent out beyond your recall,
> go to the limits of your longing.
> Embody me.
>
> Flare up like flame
> and make big shadows I can move in.
>
> Let everything happen to you: beauty and terror.
> Just keep going. No feeling is final.
> Don't let yourself lose me.
>
> Nearby is the country they call life.
> You will know it by its seriousness.
> Give me your hand.[2]

---

2. Rilke, "Gott spricht zu jedem nur, eh er ihn macht."

7

Welcoming the Child

Then he took a little child and put it among them; and taking it in his arms, he said to them, "Whoever welcomes one such child in my name welcomes me, and whoever welcomes me welcomes not me but the one who sent me."[1]

JESUS CALLED A CHILD to him. I am that child. Or was. That was many years ago and now I have a child of my own. I remember him that day, how he smiled at me, and touched me on the shoulder as I was playing. He drew me to him and put his arms around me. I looked down at his tanned hands, the fingers interlaced across my chest. When he spoke to the men around me, I could feel the resonance of his voice rumbling through his face next to mine.

I knew these men. They were friends of my father and my father was one of them. I was glad that day because my father was at home, finally, and I hoped that he would stay for a few days this time, before he and the others and Jesus went off again.

I liked Jesus. He was kind to me, and he listened to me. Sometimes he would carry me on his shoulders down by the lake and he would tell me stories as we skipped rocks. But sometimes, when we were sitting by the lake, he looked sad. I knew children weren't supposed to ask grown-ups questions about themselves. "You don't want to pry into other people's business," my mother always said, but it made me sad to see him that way.

1. Mark 9: 36-37.

> At that time the disciples came to Jesus and asked, "Who is the greatest in the kingdom of Heaven?" He called a child, set him in front of them, and said, "I tell you this: unless you turn round and become like children, you will never enter the kingdom of Heaven. Let a man humble himself till he is like this child, and he will be the greatest in the kingdom of Heaven."[2]

***

The grown-ups are acting like children, we say, when they squabble and bicker over who gets to be first in line. In the midst of this revolutionary experiment of living up to a higher plane, the disciples want to know, in all seriousness, who will be first in the kingdom of heaven. But Jesus does not react with impatience or astonishment. Instead, he draws a child to him and, encircling him with his arms, speaks of turning in the opposite direction, away from the door that the adults have crafted and toward a child's doorway, one that you would have to bend down to get through—that is, if you'd even noticed it.

Once again, Jesus reverses expectations with such abruptness that you can almost see the skid marks. "Become like children," he says, in a society in which children, while loved, were to be seen and not heard. Decisions were made *for* children, not with them. Children gazed upward, puzzled, as the adults vigorously debated the consequences of their behaviors and the perils of nonconformity over their heads. No one, having been a child, would want to return to that state.

To turn around on this track (the word is *metanoia*, to repent) means to recapture the difference between childishness and childlikeness, the latter of which picks up the simplicity and trustfulness of childhood. We cannot, knowing what we know as adults, simply reverse the tape and re-record our lives. Nor is there any goodness in a pious helplessness that refuses action without a direct command from God.

We don't chide children for being "childish." It's what we call people whose behavior doesn't match their age. But to be "childlike" is to suggest a sense of trust, of wonder, of innocence. When spoken of an adult, there is sometimes a tinge of pity, as if this naif was off picking flowers when he should have been reading up survival guides for the apocalypse.

---

2. Matt 18:1–5.

Sometimes you sense a bit of wistfulness for eyes that can see goodness in the world or in another person.

And then there is Paul:

> *When I was a child, I spoke like a child, I thought like a child, I reasoned like a child; when I became an adult, I put an end to childish ways . . . Brothers and sisters, do not be children in your thinking; rather be infants in evil, but in thinking be adults.*[3]

Except you become as a little child, you shall not enter into the kingdom of heaven.

Christ wants us to be childlike; Paul wants us to grow up.

It's a question of maturity and, as Reinhold Niebuhr suggests in *Beyond Tragedy*, "Childhood cannot see beyond its time and place. Maturity extends the range of its knowledge to larger areas of life and experience. Maturity is thus the fulfillment of the promise of creation. It represents a larger life than childhood."[4]

But maturity can also signal the atrophy of imagination and eagerness. Sincerity devolves into deviousness, "mere" honesty into becoming brutally honest. Maturity that has lost its anticipation of the new relies on the sighs of cynicism to carry the weight of authority.

The consciousness of childhood gives way to the self-consciousness of the youth, and the egotism of the adult. Every adult experiences the reality of the fall, over and over, in the course of life. Our rational freedom, a gift from God, opens possibilities to transcend our situation. But it's also reason that often sabotages our ability to achieve such harmony. Niebuhr warns that, "Therefore man is estranged from himself and discovers that there is a law in his members which wars against the law that is in his mind."[5]

Becoming as a little child again is not a promise of a recaptured innocence. "To repent and be converted," says Niebuhr, "cannot mean to achieve perfect honesty. It must mean to achieve the honesty of knowing that we are not honest."[6]

Paul sees spiritual maturity as the conscious evolution of the child in Christ. There's no condescension toward being a child: the child speaks,

---

3. 1 Cor 13:11; 14:20.
4. Niebuhr, *Beyond Tragedy*, 136.
5. Niebuhr, *Beyond Tragedy*, 138.
6. Niebuhr, *Beyond Tragedy*, 140.

thinks, and reasons as a child should. Rising to maturity, on the other hand, is not inevitable as one clocks the years. The very fact that Paul has to exhort the Corinthians suggests that becoming an adult involves a clear-eyed decision to take the long view over the short-term gratification of childishness.

"Be infants in evil," says Paul, "but in thinking be adults." Paul, of all people, is neither naive nor cynical. Don't be experts in the latest ways to do others in. Don't be sophisticated in your conspiracies against your enemies. Be innocent of evil and be grown up in how you think.

***

As I say, I remember Jesus from that day, the last time I would see him. He went up to Jerusalem. He was killed there, my father told us. Something else happened soon after. My father wouldn't say much about it, but every time he talked about it, he'd shake his head in wonder. A few years later someone read us a letter at our gathering that said, "Now we see in a mirror, dimly, but then we will see face to face. Now I know only in part; then I will know fully, even as I have been fully known."[7]

---

7. 1 Cor 13:12.

8

Not for This Life Only

*If for this life only we have hoped in Christ,
we are of all people most to be pitied.*[1]

PITY IS ONLY AS good as our capacity to rise above it. It's a natural response for most of us to the suffering of others, and it can open the door to something longer lasting, say empathy or understanding. But by itself pity doesn't lift or restore us. It usually drops us in our own estimation.

We want hope now, in this life. We need it. The paradox here is that our hopes for the future churn up our present and make us restless for a present that opens up the future. Most of us do not live in the present, despite the wisdom of the ages and the sages among us. We live with one foot in the past and we lean into the future, while the present is what happens to us as we stretch between the two. Somehow, we make it work.

We're not even sure what the dimensions of the present are. It depends on the context. If we're talking about the present in the historical flow of things, it could be this year and maybe part of last year, although so much seems to happen now in weeks and days that last year seems like an eternity gone.

Our own present flexes and stretches like an accordion. My present is that which is of interest and concern to me right now. The length and depth of the love I have within my family and friends, the books I'm reading, the words I am writing, the events I am reacting to. How I respond to

---

1. 1 Cor 15:19.

Christ in this moment, how honest I am with myself, or how I dodge the things that unnerve me.

We hear enough about living in the present from wise people in all ages and from all faiths in the world that we should pay more attention. Jesus asks us not to worry about the future because it has enough worries of its own. Paul suggests that we hold the past in memory and press on to the present. Both of them believe that God meets us in the present and promises us a future. God can't change our past, but he can help us to live with it.

But Paul is writing to the Corinthians, people whose community together is shot full of incest, drunkenness, and fighting. They are learning as they go, trying to rely on each other and on this mysterious Spirit, not at all sure they can leave behind what defined them in their past. Maybe that makes it harder to live right in the present, seeing as how some lines of habit are burned into their relations with each other.

But there's something else. The Christ that Paul has introduced the Corinthians to had been murdered by the Romans in a manner specifically designed to humiliate and terrify him and anyone who might have claimed to be his friend. State criminals like that were crucified and their bodies were thrown out on the ash heap, to be torn by dogs and left to the birds. This is not a person you want to claim as your god.

If the Corinthians only have hope in this life, Paul claims, they are most to be pitied, for the implication is that their god has played them for fools. Even pagan gods were immortal. And anyway, they wouldn't be caught dead on a cross at the hands of inferior beings like us. More likely, they would rain down fire and plague until we cried out speechlessly.

The theme that Paul riffed on—the extended guitar solo, if you like, soaring on the music of the oral traditions of Jesus in his time—was the battle that Christ had waged with the angels and principalities and powers of the universe. That battle had been won when Jesus died; the worst they could do to him turned out to be the burning fuse that eventually blew their powers to kingdom come. Along the way, these powers found common cause with those who were so anxious to perfect the path to God that they crushed the spirit of those who sought to find their way.

"When the 'religion of fear' finds its way into the Christian church," said Jürgen Moltmann, in *The Crucified God*, "those who regard themselves as the most vigilant guardians of the faith do violence to faith and smother it."[2]

---

2. Moltmann, *Crucified God*, 19.

The violent bear it away, *a la* Flannery O'Connor.

"This pusillanimous faith," continues Moltmann, "usually occurs in the form of an orthodoxy which feels threatened and is therefore more rigid than ever. It occurs wherever, in the face of the immorality of the present age, the gospel of creative love for the abandoned is replaced by the law of what is supposed to be Christian morality, and by penal law."[3]

The Corinthian Christians, along with all their bumbling relationships, were having a loss of confidence. Their neighbors and former confidants were trying to understand how anyone could fall for such a loser god. Because that man, Jesus, was crucified and he died, just as every Jew the Romans crucified died. The Romans scored 100 percent on the efficiency scale for all that. So, if these Christians had put their trust in that man, they deserved to be pitied (when they weren't being mocked) because a dead god was even less useful than a dead goat. Nobody could beat the Romans for mopping up all resistance and wiping out the political opposition.

They were efficient, but not effective: one man got through to the other side.

Oh, he died alright. But in some way that can't fully be explained, after crucifixion and a hasty burial in a sealed tomb, he showed up in Galilee on the beach, he entered a locked room in Jerusalem filled with terrified disciples, and he hiked the seven miles to Emmaus with two of his friends and then vanished over dinner. Peter saw him, the Twelve saw him, as did five hundred of his friends in Jerusalem, along with James, his brother, and his closest circle in Jerusalem. Lastly, in a weird kind of premature birth, he appeared to Paul, who made that singular experience the balance point of his spiritual gyroscope for the rest of his life.

Paul's message—the engine that kept him going over mountains, across seas, through the fires, in spite of whippings and chains—is that Christ, the one into whom all the fullness of God had been poured, the one who suffered a most humiliating death—that one had been raised from death to start human history up again with a new beginning.

As A. N. Wilson put it: "The young men, or angels, at the empty Garden Tomb in the different Gospels emphasise for the reader or hearer the same story: 'Why do you look for the living among the dead?'"[4]

---

3. Moltmann, *Crucified God*, 19.
4. Wilson, *Paul*, 73.

Buddhism says if you are shot with an arrow, don't get in a debate about the type of arrow, the composition of the arrowhead, and the trajectory that embedded it in you. Pull out the arrow.

We could argue for eternity how the resurrection could have happened, but without resolution. Because it isn't verifiable by our usual standards of empirical measurement. It isn't even comprehensible in a way that can be said without stuttering. What matters is the result of the message of the resurrection—a faith-filled community that infiltrated the world and stayed true, even unto death. That is power. The glory is still to come.

9

For To Give

Take heart, son; your sins are forgiven.[1]

THIS IS JESUS, BENT over, talking to a young man lying on a stretcher, the stretcher carried by his friends, sweating and shifting their grips from hand to hand as they come up alongside the Son of Man. And they haven't even said anything yet, but he sees their faith and says to this guy, "Your sins are forgiven."

This is a one-sided conversation that they've entered, but it seems to them like it's one that's been going on for some time—maybe all time—and while they don't want to interrupt there is, nevertheless, the fact that this man is standing right in front of them, the man who can heal at a glance, a once-in-a-lifetime chance for them and their friend, who, by the way, hasn't said a word, just looks, his hand curled like a claw, his arms like brown sticks, his fingers splayed like roots, chin covered in stubble, breath coming hard—no words—his eyes burning deep like topaz in the last light of the day.

And we, looking on, shift a bit and smile at nothing in particular. Sins! Not a word we've heard or used in quite a while, and truth be told, not something we can actually relate to, come to think of it.

---

1. Mark 2:5.

***

"Have you ever sought God's forgiveness?" asks the reporter. The candidate stops, puzzled. "I'm not sure I have ever asked God's forgiveness," he says. "I don't bring God into that picture... When I go to church and I have my little wine and my little cracker, I guess that is a form of forgiveness." He pauses, shrugs his shoulders. "Why do I have to repent or ask for forgiveness, if I am not making mistakes? I work hard, I'm an honorable person."

***

Actually, we'd be more comfortable if the conversation revolved around rights and obligations. We have respect for privacy; we believe everyone has the right to their own opinion, and who are we to say who has committed a sin or not. That's their business and not something that can really—or should really—be talked about, seeing as nobody has the right to tell me, or anybody else, what I should or should not be doing. I pay my taxes, I work hard, I try to help others out where I can, but in the end it's really my life and no one else's and I really don't—I mean, you know—you don't have a right to tell me what to do, you know?

This moment. This paralyzed man, his friends breathless, waiting, the crowd at our backs, the sun slanting into our eyes, a dry, coppery taste in our mouths. Jesus smiles and straightens. "I know what you're thinking," he says. "Why do you think such evil? What's easier, to say 'Your sins are forgiven' or to say, 'Stand up and walk?'"

***

We don't know what to say. They're just words; anyone could say them but that doesn't prove a thing. I mean, I could say that—not that I would—but if I wanted to I could say that, but what good would that do anyway? Nobody talks like that! Who talks like that, anyway?

Jesus turns. "Stand up," he says to the guy on the stretcher. "Go home."

And I do. I swing my legs down, set my feet on the ground and stand up, a little shaky at first, but I'm up.

"Thank you," I croak. I look down. My fingers ball up and I rub my arm. My friends stand paralyzed.

"Thank you," I say, and the people near me fall back.
"Thank you"—the words are stronger now—and I walk.

10

Understanding Backwards

It is perfectly true, as philosophers say, that life must be understood backwards. But they forget the other proposition, that it must be lived forwards.[1]

FOR A GOOD PART of my life I have seen religion as a duty that must be accomplished with dedication if not enjoyment. Since all people are sinners and sinners must seek salvation, it did not occur to me that some people might not see the point in all this religion business. "Oh, I'm not religious," some friends would say to me, as if it were genetically transmitted or perhaps an acquired taste. They would blithely go about their lives, unencumbered by guilt, enjoying their sins, and occasionally pausing to shake their heads at my dutifulness. "Why do you bother?" they would ask curiously.

For my part, I could not understand how religion could be regarded as an accessory. It was core, at the heart, deep inside, that which guided and prompted all that was good and pure and true. One could no more shuck it off and live a decent, upright life than one could see one's hand in a room without light. There was one way to salvation and that was through obedience to the rules, as inexplicable as they appeared sometimes. And yet I continued to meet people who claimed no religious allegiance, but seemed to me honest and good, the kind of people who would

---

1. Kierkegaard, *Papers and Journals*, 160.

take you in during a storm or give you a lift miles out of their way. It was disconcerting. Some of them even smoked.

So, I tried harder, tried to be dutiful, tried to be aligned without completely losing myself. But my self would slip out of my grasp at the most inopportune moments and do something embarrassing, like refusing to stand and go forward for altar calls. Even if I had made a clear and heartfelt decision years before to join the side of the angels, I squirmed in the pew when the preacher began his pitch. I felt that I owed it to the unchurched and the disbelievers in the house to stand yet again and be a living example. Despite my inner diatribe that religion was personal and that honesty demanded a consonance between motivation, belief, and action, I felt I was letting down the team.

And yet I was always fascinated by religion, or rather by the quest for God and transcendence. Growing up in California in the sixties, I was surrounded by those who sought a shortcut to enlightenment or at least bliss. I plodded along, waving as they roared past, secure that I had the safer path, if by far the slower one. If it was there, I thought, I'd find it eventually by dint of just keeping at it, one foot in front of the other. But I didn't.

I studied theology and philosophy of religion, eventually got a doctorate and taught religion for some years. I had no doubt I should be there and yet I constantly felt like an imposter. I could not be like my colleagues, men who had signed up for the church for life and who seemingly could overlook all manner of missteps and outright lies on the part of the church. I struggled to understand how to avoid the sin of self-righteousness while side-stepping hypocrisy. But pride goes before a fall—and I took a fall of my own making.

Years later I am seeing some things much differently. I am learning not to let the foibles of the official church body distract me from my own spiritual quest. I have met the enemy, like Pogo, and they are me. I know what I am capable of doing against my better judgment and where most of the fault lines appear in my foundations.

And I have learned, or perhaps discovered, that signing up for a set of beliefs is not the point. Some beliefs fall away over the years because they never really found a place because I never really believed them. Others simply don't make sense no matter how I've tried. But the vast majority of religious beliefs ought to be seen as practices. We practice them because in the practicing comes understanding and with understanding comes the willingness to live in grace, to be in God. "Religion is a practical discipline that teaches us to discover new capacities of mind and heart," says Karen Armstrong in *The Case for God*. "You will discover their truth—or lack of it—only if you translate these doctrines into ritual or ethical action."[2]

Orthopraxy over orthodoxy—right action over right belief—is how I see it, but with two important caveats. First, we do not earn our way through "right" action because this is not a contractual relationship. God is in the giving business, not the litigation business. Thus, I have nothing to fear from him; I have no need to protect myself. Second, belief is not abandoned, but made firm through action. "Like any skill," continues Armstrong, "religion requires perseverance, hard work, and discipline. Some people will be better at it than others, some appallingly inept, and some will miss the point entirely. But those who do not apply themselves will get nowhere at all."[3]

In the end—and in fact, in the beginning and in the middle—is grace. That is what makes this whole venture possible. Room to move, to experiment, to make mistakes and learn from them. Here is the mysterious presence of the Christ. And that is enough for the time being.

---

2. Armstrong, *Case for God*, xiii.
3. Armstrong, *Case for God*, xiii.

11

Another Homecoming

When we fall and when we get up again we are kept in the same precious love. In God's sight we do not fall: in our own we do not stand. I see both of these to be true. But God's sight is the higher truth.[1]

IN THE PARABLE OF the prodigal son, it's the prodigal who gets all the glory. It's an old story, played out across countless families, in every small town, to the tune of heartbreak in a million hearts. He's the badass boy that all the girls want, the one who brushes off the worshipful without a sideways glance, who gets his Vette with the money that's coming to him and roars out of town for the city.

He's every arrogant kid who struts into the stage lights, full of himself and full of life, aching to make his mark by sheer force of need, daring himself farther up above the abyss like some flaming Icarus, until desire cracks full force into indifference and he plunges.

I could have told you so.

I'm the one who stayed behind, the older brother whose diligence was mistaken for acceptance. The one who was expected—not in so many words—to pick up the slack and obediently plow the fields until sunset every day. Now that he was gone there was an understanding that

---

1. Julian of Norwich, *Revelations of Divine Love*, 208.

everything left would be mine when the time came. Until then it was mine to lose; if I didn't work it there would be nothing left to claim.

* * *

In Rembrandt's painting *The Return of the Prodigal Son*, the elder brother stands alone, isolated in a pool of light, his stiff resolve drawing him up and into himself. He stands on a platform, the diagonal of which bisects the plane and separates him from his father and brother. Although only a single step forward would put him on the same level as his brother, we sense there is no power that could induce him to any movement except to withdraw further into the darkness behind him. The eldest son is all verticals; the father and the prodigal are rounded, bent toward each other at awkward angles, the one falling into the embrace of the other and both in light. On the elder brother's face there is sorrow, hurt, and anger. This is the moment he has played out in his mind countless times; now that it is here, he is mute and paralyzed.

* * *

I know what the people in the town thought of me. They would tell you that I was the resentful one, angry because my brother took off to live for song and women in a far city. In this version, I would have been long gone—even before him—if I had had the balls. But that's not me.

The story has a life of its own now, and there is little I can do to change it in the minds of those who hear it. I am not a man of words. Even this is difficult to express, but I can only tell you honestly what I held in my heart all that time he was gone.

I loved my brother and I knew why he left. I knew he would leave, and I knew there was nothing any of us could do to make his leaving seem right. He would take his leave, to put it quaintly. He would take it and run with it and he didn't give a damn if anyone got hurt in the taking. But frankly, there was nothing for him here, and if he could play out his talents on a larger stage, well, more power to him.

When I'm working in the fields I'm always thinking. I'm thinking about Cain and Abel, Jacob and Esau, Castor and Pollux, James and John—the "Sons of Thunder," as Jesus called them. What I do you might not call prayer, but I think of my brother and I imagine him in his life.

I hope for his safety at the very least, and I hope for the enlargement of his spirit.

He returned in winter. The days were bitter and short; it was all I could do to get the chores done in the daylight. That year we had more snow than usual and more days of flying sleet and slosh. I was up to the hills out back, seeing to the sheep, when I caught a glimpse of a figure stumping along the road to the house. As I strained to see through the rain and sleet, I saw the old man in his peacoat hobbling up the road. They met in the road, their figures melding together in the gathering dark, and they turned toward the house. By the time I was down the hill and coming through the upper pasture, all the lights were on in the house and smoke was pouring from the chimney.

* * *

In Rainer Maria Rilke's retelling of the Parable of the Prodigal Son, the young man returns home to the welcoming embrace of his family. They hover, hanging on his every word, their faces shining, laughter quick in their throats. He retreats to his childhood room, tired and pressed on every side.

In the morning, before light, he gets up, quietly steals out the back door, and runs across the frosted fields as the sun comes up. We know he will not stay; he is drowned in love and has no defenses against it. He feels himself to be disappearing and knows he will lose himself if he doesn't leave.

* * *

His story came out over the days as we worked together in the fields and the barn. I didn't press him for the details. I knew he couldn't hold them back. Whatever my brother was feeling was written on his face and there was little in his actions that winter that I could not have predicted. So, when he came to me one night in the early spring, I knew he was leaving.

Now that our father has passed on, the farm is my responsibility. I could no more leave than my brother could stay. But I love the land; we each find our own level.

I'll be here when he returns.

12

Real Facts

The distinctive thing about real facts, however, is their individuality. Not to put too fine a point on it, one could say that the real picture consists of nothing but exceptions to the rule, and that, in consequence, absolute reality has predominantly the character of irregularity.[1]

OF ALL THE STRANGE things that happened to us that year, my walking on the water got the most laughs. Even today it's a cliché for magical thinking, the punchline about someone who thinks he's divine or just insufferably self-righteous.

I've always had impulse control issues. I load, I fire, I aim. I leap—and I look—all the way down.

I am Peter, aka The Rock, not because I am the foundation for the church, but because I am hard-headed. He knew that, of course; it was an inside joke between us. You put the least qualified in charge and see how it rolls. By beholding we become changed and all that. There is something to that, by the way, for I softened over the years. Not that I was weak, but rather I became deliberate. That was years away from the unfortunate water landing, and well after Jesus leaned into me one afternoon and said, "Someday they will bind you and take you where you do not want to go." Just that, and he held my gaze for a moment, stopping my quick retort.

---

1. Jung, *Undiscovered Self*, 9.

For once, I had nothing to say. I dropped my eyes then, for I was seeing myself on a stony path by torchlight, my hands bound in front of me, soldiers at my back and front.

I am the disciple, remember, who almost got it right about Jesus and then got it all wrong—all within an hour. He had asked one of his questions again; this time he wanted to know what people were saying about him. An odd question, until you realized that almost no one knew what he was. It wasn't enough that he was a man from Nazareth or even that he was the one who made a few loaves and fishes into a meal for thousands. The crowds only had a few superheroes they could imagine: Abraham, Moses, Elijah . . . oh, and John, recently beheaded by Herod. So, they thought he was another version of one of those.

He asked, "Who do people say I am?" and we all muttered one thing and another about Elijah and John. "Who do *you* say I am?" he said, and we all looked at our shoes. He really seemed unsure. It was as if he needed confirmation of something he desperately hoped was true —or was afraid was true.

You have to get these things right for him, and frankly, we weren't all that sure ourselves. But, as usual, I jumped in there with the answer we all wanted to hear. "You're the Messiah!," I blurted. There wasn't anyone else who it could be, even though he didn't seem to care much about the position. But this time he didn't deny it. Of course, he didn't admit to it either. He just told us to keep it to ourselves.

"Well, good," I thought, "things are looking up." But then he started in about going up to Jerusalem, and how the elders, and the chief priests, and the scribes would reject him. That wasn't a surprise: he'd been on the outs with them for a long time. The words were coming in a rush now, about how he would be killed and would live again three days later. He was very plain about it. That's when I pulled him away from the others. I lowered my voice, "What are you saying? We here *know* you are the Messiah. Take it! The Messiah doesn't die. Am I missing something here?"

At that he spun back to the others. "Get away from me, Satan!" he shouted. "You're counting on human plans, not divine ones!" He was speaking to them, but he meant me. I saw the shock on their faces at his words and then they glanced at me, horror stricken. Before I could reply, he was rounding on the crowd that was gathering.

"If *you* want to follow me, then take up your cross! If you want to *save* your life, you will lose it, and if you lose your life because of me and the gospel, you will save it." Clearly, this was crazy talk, but he wasn't through.

"What does it matter if you gain the whole world, but you lose your own soul?" He glanced around at them. "What could you give to get your soul back, eh?"

I am remembering all this because I have been trying to sort out how we who followed him understood him. When you're in the midst of it you just try to keep up. The understanding comes later, I found. And if we take up our cross to follow him, then at some point the cross becomes more than a symbol: it is a killing machine upon which we really do die. After all, the point of "taking up one's cross" is to realize that we carry our death with us daily. What I couldn't understand at the time is how that could ever be anything but suicide or treason.

At the time, I could not bear the thought that he would die in this way. I envisioned a deathless life for him. I saw him as the one who would change the architecture of our world so that the long shadow of this constant cruelty would vanish. I wanted him to open up the sky so we could stand in the sunlight as creatures of God, not as prisoners of Rome. If that meant pulling down the palaces and temples that blocked the sun, then let's get on with it.

But that's not what he was on about. He saw the world so differently than we did. I wanted to ask him, "When you look at the world what is it that you see?"[2] There were times when we were with him that something he said or did clicked into focus and we saw an expression that was so clear and so true that it changed the atmosphere when he walked into the room.

But I found that the clarity dissolved when he wasn't around. When we tried together to remember and explain it to each other later in that upper room, it refracted like a kaleidoscope. My unprayed thought back then, even before his death, was that I tried to be like him, I tried to feel the way he did, but without him it was no use.

I couldn't see what he saw when I looked at the world.

****

All these years later I am writing from this prison cell. As he said so long ago, my hands were bound, and I was led away.

---

2. U2, "When I Look at the World."

His death changed everything, of course. That was all, but it was everything. I carried my cross every day after that.

I betrayed him and he forgave me.

This is how we see the world like he does—through the lens of betrayal and forgiveness.

These are the real facts.

13

Attention Deficit

Men have no eyes but for those aspects of things which they have already been taught to discern.[1]

In April 1931, George Orwell wrote a short piece entitled "The Spike" for a magazine called *Adelphi*. In it, he describes time he spent as a tramp. He became a tramp, a homeless person, partly of necessity and partly because he wished to understand the particular forms of suffering that tramps go through. One virulent irritation was boredom. Orwell came to think that boredom was the worst of a tramp's burdens, worse than hunger and worse than the feeling of social disgrace. "It is a silly piece of cruelty to confine an ignorant man all day with nothing to do; it is like chaining a dog in a barrel," he said. "Only an educated man, who has consolations within himself, can endure confinement. Tramps, unlettered types as nearly all of them are, face their poverty with blank, resourceless minds."[2]

Today, Orwell would be accused of elitism and would be made to tweet an apology. But Orwell was nothing if not honest and having lived the life on the street could speak with authority. One need only pass through any metropolitan area to see the homeless on benches, median strips, near metro stations or on corners, many of them slumped against a wall, sleeping huddled against the cold or in a quiet corner of a coffee

---

1. James, *Psychology*, 235.
2. Orwell, *Facing Unpleasant Facts*, 6.

shop. Their days unwind with agonizing slowness, each minute trudging after the next. In this essay, Orwell recounts how he was saved from the ten hours of daylight boredom in the spike (homeless shelter) by the blessed reprieve of working in the kitchen. Even so, one suspects that with his powers of observation and his interests in literature, politics, and history, Orwell would not likely suffocate in boredom.

There are two elements at work here: memory and attention. Memory because we are hardly human without it, and attention because it is necessary to learning of any sort. William James devotes a chapter of his seminal work *Psychology* to attention, describing it as of two kinds. There is the effortless, involuntary, and passive kind, and there is the active and voluntary kind. Involuntary attention occurs when we follow a train of thought that is interesting as a means to an end or when the mere association with the thought burnishes us with a sense of satisfaction.

Active, voluntary attention is that which we make a determined effort to accomplish by bending our minds to it. James remarks that it is a feeling which everyone knows, but which is indescribable. We sense it when we try to discriminate between sensory experiences or attend to one voice near us against a babble of other voices. It is an effort whose accomplishment slips through our fingers like water. James says, "*There is no such thing as voluntary attention sustained for more than a few seconds at a time*" (his emphasis).[3] He describes a process that sounds like the building, layer upon layer, of a pearl around a grain of sand. The mind, finding something interesting, comes back to it, turns it over and over until the novelty wears off, then drifts away, only to return for the feeling of both familiarity and the stimulation of finding something new. And here is the sentence that lit up for me like a Jumbotron: "*No one can possibly attend continuously to an object that does not change*" (his emphasis).[4]

We pay attention to what matters to us, says James, in a statement that seems so self-evident as to be trivial. That is, until you realize what it implies: that so much of what we overlook, do not see—not to say, ignore—is a result of us just not caring enough.

Actually, that's not quite true: to say that we don't care is to suggest that we somehow rank the sensations and ideas coming to us on a scale from exciting to dull, and we jettison everything that doesn't bend the needle of our interest. But James's research led him to what one of his

---

3. James, *Psychology*, 224.
4. James, *Psychology*, 225.

sources called *preperception,* "the imagining of an experience before it occurs."[5] In other words, there must be a memory, an image, an association already in us in order for something to become the object of our willed attention. While shiny and colorful objects may momentarily grab our attention, such eye candy cannot hold us for long.

The kind of intellectual attention needed for concentrated study or contemplation seems to be a combination of external sensation and internal preparation that, comments James, "always partly consists of the creation of an imaginary duplicate of the object in the mind."[6] To put it another way, when we give our attention to an object of thought we hold an image of it in our mind going forward. Not only that, but the image remains as a hook to snag passing thoughts, perceptions, even emotions, so that we can take up ideas where we left them in memory because we have something almost tangible to return to.

When we form such an image and it fills our attention, we cannot un-notice it. James again: "But who that has once noticed the identity can fail to have it arrest his attention again? . . . Every bonnet in the street is momentarily taken by the lover to enshroud the head of his idol. The image in the mind *is* the attention; the preperception is half of the perception of the looked-for thing."[7]

We pay attention to what we have already been taught to discern. That is both good news and bad news. The good news is that what we've been taught has some chance, however slight, of catching our attention again. The bad news is: what would it take to have us care enough about what we don't know to pay attention long enough to form an image in our minds? In the end, this is an epistemological question, a question of how we know, what can be known, and what we do with what we know. Inevitably, it is a question of learning—and teaching.

"I see everything," says Robert Downey Jr., playing Sherlock. "That is my curse." But for most of us, our curse is not seeing enough of what we are paying attention to, narrow though that slice of life may be.

Attention must be paid! To *pay attention* reveals the cost of focusing with intention on something. When we focus on something, says Winifred Gallagher in *Rapt: Attention and the Focused Life,* we select some things and leave the rest as a blur. What we select literally becomes our

---

5. James, *Psychology*, 232.
6. James, *Psychology*, 232.
7. James, *Psychology*, 235.

reality so that in a very real sense I have my reality and you have yours. The fact that much of our realities overlap means that we can communicate with each other while experiencing reality from singular perspectives. But I digress...

We select that which stands out—a red cardinal flitting through the trees, a hissing snake—whatever is new or different in our environment. Gallagher calls this "bottom-up attention," the kind which keeps us in touch with what is going on in the world. It's necessary, sometimes crucial, for our survival, but it also includes a host of unnecessary distractions. Think of dogs and squirrels and you get an idea of what life would be like if this passive form of attention was all we had.

The other form of attention is the "top-down" intentional and focused variety in which we concentrate on what we want. This active attention requires hard work and energy, but despite our intense focus, it will likely quickly fade. That's the cost we pay for attention that can give us direction and purpose—a meaningful life rather than a jumble of confusing stimuli.

**

Given all this—given the fact that we have what Buddhists call "monkey mind," which flits from one thing to another like a monkey swinging through the trees—how do we focus our attention upon God? Every religious tradition has sought ways to quiet the mind long enough to hear the still, small voice within the hurricanes and tremors of daily life.

There are techniques for quieting oneself, methods of breathing, ways and means for being truly present that people have used for thousands of years in this pursuit of God. All of these have their place; my purpose here is neither to endorse them nor to diminish them. What I'm trying to grasp is how I might have the mind of Christ or pray without ceasing or meditate on the Lord both night and day. All of these states of being assume that we can still brush our teeth, put on our socks, drive our cars, and carry on conversations. Whatever it means to focus one's attention on God, it cannot necessarily mean that we isolate ourselves. "Christ comes alive in the communion between people," writes Christian Wiman in *My Bright Abyss*. "What this means is that even if you are socially shy and generally inarticulate about spiritual matters—and I say this as someone who finds casual social interactions often quite difficult and my own feelings about faith intractably mute—you must not swerve from the engagements God offers you."[8]

These may come in the form of people who do not look like God. We might not even see them because they are not usually within the scope of our attention. On the other hand, we may constantly be with people who seem wholly self-sufficient, confident, amiable enough—people much like ourselves—people for whom God is an article of belief rather than a mystery of faith. Nevertheless, those whom we meet are, in every case, an offer of communion from Christ.

God approaches us in the persons of others: "the least of these," the one-percenters, the strangers within our gates. Our attention, divided though it may be, honors God in this way.

---

8. Wiman, *My Bright Abyss*, 21.

14

Marching to a Different Drummer

Real generosity toward the future lies
in giving all to the present.[1]

WHEN WE ARE YOUNG, we cannot see the point in moderation. It strikes us as timid, cautious, a toadying to the powers that be. In any case, if we pull back or withhold our effort, we risk the derision of the socially graceful, those young gods whose spectacular failures are even more to be envied than their modest and expected successes. Thus, if you grew up in the sixties in an evangelical community, you were bound to hear thrilling stories of the dissolute life in a far country, the "coming to oneself" among the pigs, and then the trembling but resolute return to the family.

Those of us who listened to these stories and who never left home found ourselves split unequally in three ways: we were in part rejoicing with the father that the prodigal had returned; we were wistfully longing to *be* the prodigal; and we were, in some measure, the resentful older brother, dutiful and dull, in whose constricted craw the younger brother's tempestuous travails stuck like a bone.

It wasn't so much that we actually wished to smoke the holy weed that breathless news stories assured us was being consumed all around us, but that we lacked the *cajones* to step off the well-lit path and into the shadows. I had no hunger for drugs or alcohol—a deficiency I am

---

1. Camus, *Rebel*, 304.

now grateful for—mostly because I believed I had no brain cells to waste. Sometimes, with a tinge of envy, I listened to friends describe their trips, but for the most part my adventures were of the literary sort. Albert Camus, George Orwell, Tolkien, C. S. Lewis, Thoreau—these were my mentors.

I had a poster on my bedroom wall with a quote from Thoreau: "If a man does not keep pace with his companions, perhaps it is because he marches to a different drummer." I was pretty sure my drummer was different from the rest, although musically speaking he went by the names of Ringo or Ginger Baker or Crosby, Stills, and Nash, Joni Mitchell, James Taylor, Gordon Lightfoot, and Carole King.

I've always been grateful I grew up in the sixties, for it was one of those disjunctive moments in history that shakes everything up—art, music, politics, religion, mores, self-identity, national consciousness. But with all of that exploding around us, and living almost within sight of San Francisco and Berkeley, those of us raised as Christians—who at some point consciously *chose* to be Christians—learned to listen to some drummers and not to others.

Every generation has to leave home—sometimes in anger, sometimes with many a backward glance—but leave they must. It's not for nothing that the central metaphor in most wisdom traditions is the *path* or the *way*; the idea of life as a journey is so self-evident as almost to be trite. Yet, in looking back we believe we see a pattern to our wanderings that gives us comfort while it still surprises us. "You can't connect the dots looking forward," said Steve Jobs in his now-famous commencement address at Stanford. "You can only connect them looking backward."[2]

Can we choose our rebellions when we're young? I'd like to think we have the wisdom to sign up for the ones that have the longest half-life, but I doubt we can see that far. "It is perfectly true, as philosophers say," remarked Kierkegaard, "that life must be understood backwards. But they forget the other proposition, that it must be lived forwards."[3] While we may not have clearly seen the road ahead, there was still something that was drawing us on to take *this* path and not *that* one. Sometimes we acted with conviction and urgency, other times with a sense that we had no other choice but to follow this particular track. Only as we got far enough

---

2. Jobs, "You've Got to Find What You Love."
3. Kierkegaard, *Papers and Journals*, 160.

down the road that we could look back did we begin to make some sense of it. And by then, of course, it was too late . . .

So, while we'd like to be able to say to the young just starting out, "Try to live in such a way that you don't have to lie about where you've been," it's probably not going to be heard. We learn best by doing, not by memorizing, which is why history is still an important subject, because it's a way to connect the dots for those who are busy leaning forward.

In 1956 Albert Camus published his seminal essay *The Rebel*. Reviewers called it a "piece of reasoning in the great tradition of French logic," and noted that "here is the voice of a man of unshakable decency." In a shattered Europe after WWII, Camus had the courage to ask, "What is a rebel? A man who says no, but whose refusal does not imply a renunciation. He is also a man who says yes, from the moment he makes his first gesture of rebellion."[4]

No and yes—both were required. Yet, here was the dilemma I saw: unthinkingly joining up in a mass movement can lead to tragic results, while refusing to extend oneself can lead to moral and creative paralysis. But on the other hand, the only way we come to know who we truly are is to put ourselves in situations where we *are* tested. Some tests we will fail, and we can only hope that we will fail upwards and not fall by the way in the process.

We may not, with clarity, be able to choose our rebellions, but we can choose to rebel—against injustice, despair, fear. In the closing pages of *The Rebel* Camus' voice rises in eloquence, leaving behind the cool cadences of his logic and sounding a note prophetic and courageous.

"For twenty centuries the sum total of evil has not diminished in the world,"[5] he says. We might be tempted to turn away then and cultivate our narcissism. There are plenty who stand ready to help us indulge ourselves for a price. But rebellion, says Camus, can't exist without "a strange form of love."[6] It is a love that does not calculate and is unstinting in its gifts to those yet to come. "Real generosity toward the future," says Camus, "lies in giving all to the present."[7]

There is no future in the politics of resentment or retribution. To put aside the murderous impulses of power and history, Camus says, "a new

4. Camus, *Rebel*, 13.
5. Camus, *Rebel*, 303.
6. Camus, *Rebel*, 304.
7. Camus, *Rebel*, 304.

rebellion is consecrated in the name of moderation and of life."[8] Camus could not believe in the Church's kingdom to come nor could he devote himself to a secular utopia purchased through the blood of millions. "It is time to forsake our age and its adolescent furies,"[9] he says.

As a Christian, I couldn't agree more. This is a rebellion wide enough to embrace this earth, our home, while we choose to rebel in a thousand ways each day against injustice in the name of courage and decency. "Do not be conformed to this world, but be transformed by the renewing of your mind," says Paul, a rebel drummer worth marching with.[10]

---

8. Camus, *Rebel*, 306.
9. Camus, *Rebel*, 306.
10. Rom 12:2.

15

A Path We Can Imagine

As often as I think I am seeking other people out in order to get something for myself, the deeper truth is that I am hoping they will draw me out of myself.[1]

I BEGAN READING ABOUT Dorothy Day while a graduate student in philosophy of religion at Claremont Graduate School, in California. I had picked up a copy of *Catholic Worker* in Los Angeles, a newspaper published to highlight social justice issues in the Catholic tradition. It was started by Dorothy Day and Peter Maurin in 1933 and has been published continuously ever since. I was taking classes in liberation theology and social justice at Claremont, learning about the movements in Latin America by Catholic priests to educate the people and to teach them to read, using the Bible. Then later, when I came to Columbia Union College in Takoma Park, Maryland to teach, I contacted the Sojourners community in Washington, DC, met Jim Wallis, the editor and co-leader, and became aware of some of the networks of Christians in the metro area who were working with the homeless.

Eventually, I met Mitch Snyder, who was living and working out of a row house on Euclid Street in Washington, DC. He had been an adman on Madison Avenue before he dedicated his life to the homeless. He and some friends operated a soup kitchen in an abandoned garage across the

---

1. Taylor, *Altar in the World*, 91.

street. My students and I would go down on Sunday mornings to cut up vegetables for stew and often we'd come back to hand out meals in the evenings. We continued to work with Mitch and his community over the years, as they advocated and cared for the homeless. Always aware of the official studied neglect by governments of the homeless, he fasted to the brink of death until the city capitulated and opened the DC Shelter on 4th Street in Washington. Many students worked and helped out at the shelter over the years.

My friendship with Mitch continued even after we were no longer actively involved in the community. One evening, he asked if I'd like to go up to Baltimore and meet Dan and Phil Berrigan, the Catholic priests who had been in the vanguard of protests against the Vietnam War and had worked for decades in the civil rights movement. When we arrived, we were ushered into a row house filling with young people as well as grizzled veterans of the peace movement. As the sun was going down, light streaming into the windows, Phil Berrigan led us in a worship and prayer service for the homeless. For me, this was a golden moment, a revelation of the commonalities of Christian activism that begin with prayer and are sustained through worship.

My interest in the *Catholic Worker* movement had begun much earlier, when a friend from college decided to become a Catholic priest. We were graduate students together at Andrews University and, unbeknownst to me, he was taking catechumen lessons at Notre Dame University. The night before Easter Sunday he was baptized into the Catholic Church. We stood in for him as witnesses, since his family, staunch Seventh-Day Adventists in Southern California, had rejected him and his calling. He felt his calling was to work in East Los Angeles among the barrios, the poverty, and the gangs. His life, after baptism, was brimming with hope; his enthusiasm for the *Catholic Worker* movement and its mission to reach those in poverty led him to give up his comfortable upper-middle-class life and to enter a vocation that was open to the Spirit's leading in all parts of his life.

Witnessing his baptism and seeing his joy caused me to reflect on what had brought him from Adventism to Catholicism, from wealth to voluntary poverty. While he was one of the most intelligent people I've known, it was his single-minded direction toward Christian activism that stirred me.

Years before, as a teenager newly awakened, I was keen to witness. I wanted to fix the spiritual errors that I saw around me and to confront those, especially in the Catholic Church, whom I felt were perpetuating these errors. One of our high school faculty, our Bible and history teacher, invited a Catholic priest to his home one Sabbath so that some of us could learn more about Catholic beliefs and his friend's faith. I confronted the priest with all the bravado and ignorance that a fifteen-year-old on a mission from God could muster. He graciously answered my questions, parried my thrusts, and generally treated me with respect and interest. I came away feeling that I had made a holy fool of myself.

While at graduate school at Claremont I took a course in liturgies of the Church. We studied all the major liturgies and their history, from the time of Justin Martyr in 155 CE up to John Wesley's "Service of the Methodists in North America," written in 1784. One of the requirements of the course was to attend a worshipping community outside of our own faith for the semester. At that time, I was an active member of the North Hills Seventh-Day Adventist Church in Claremont, but I easily found an Anglican church in Ontario and began attending their Sunday services also.

I was immediately struck by two things. One was the homily delivered each week (without notes) by the priest. It was literate, deeply scriptural, and invariably opened windows into the life of discipleship. It brought together the liturgy, the Scripture, and current news in ways that set my imagination on fire.

The second thing was the compassion and respect shown toward the gay couple that attended from week to week. This was in 1977, not a particularly easy time for gays, and especially not the norm for the Anglican Church. But each week that they were there they were surrounded by people who obviously cared about them, who did not regard them as either a curiosity nor an abomination, and who did not shy away from sharing the cup with them during the Eucharist.

***

There is a sociological and communications theory known as symbolic interactionism, which counts among its strengths the idea that "Almost everything we do, we do in part in relation to others,"[2] as scholar Joel Charon puts it in his *Symbolic Interactionism*. Founded on the work of George Herbert Mead and extended by Herbert Blumer and others, symbolic interactionism says that we form our self-identity through

---

2. Charon, *Symbolic Interactionism*, 149.

interaction with others. We are social beings, said Mead, and we shape each other through our interactions. That may seem self-evident, but Mead believed that it is only through what he called "role-taking" that we can communicate, develop a self-identity, and become part of a society.[3]

Role-taking relies on imagination, a central characteristic of humans that makes it possible to put ourselves in the place of others. The ones who influence us the most are our *significant others*; they may be parents, friends, role models, heroic figures, people we emulate or admire.[4] They may even be people we fear. We imagine how our actions will affect them, and we imagine what they might be thinking, feeling, and understanding in certain situations. It's impossible to ever take on another's role with complete accuracy, but it's essential for everything that we do as human beings to try our best. As we grow more capable, we become more understanding of others, better communicators, more able to anticipate the expectations of others so that we can conform, rebel, choose, and exercise our will in relation to others.

Mead called another group of people our *"generalized other,"* a combination of several significant others who make up a group or a community, a society of sorts that we visualize as we act. We might think of "my friends," or "my family," or "my church," or even "my generation" and "my country." Another term for this is a *"reference group,"* a group of significant others we hold in our imagination.[5]

While we need to take others into account in almost everything we do, there are two exceptions to this: those who are extremely selfish and those who hold extreme power. Those who are almost totally self-centered may regard others as simply objects to be manipulated, and those who have extreme power may actually do so. Of course, by provoking fear or anger in others, such people can expect retaliation in kind, which generally reinforces their selfishness. As long as their power is intact, they are personal hurricanes of chaos. They lack the imagination and the social intelligence to take the role of anyone but themselves.

Symbolic interactionism gives us perspectives through which we can actively and consistently see ourselves and others in a new light. It provides a consciousness that can be turned to great good or to evil. We can learn to empathize with others or to manipulate them. It means that we go through our days with eyes wide open, continually attempting to

3. Charon, *Symbolic Interactionism*, 109.
4. Charon, *Symbolic Interactionism*, 76.
5. Charon, *Symbolic Interactionism*, 77.

see the world—and ourselves—through the eyes of those we are communicating with.

As a Christian, a person attempting to live in grace by faith, it helps me to visualize and imagine the lives of others. It helps me to learn from those with whom I interact. To try to see the world through the eyes of a person in the LGBTQ+ community or to try to imagine how a Protestant asking a Catholic about sexual abuse by priests must seem to a Catholic—those are exercises of the imagination worth attempting.

***

In later years I taught at two universities, both embedded in the history of the renegade order of nuns who came to America from France and established colleges for young women in the early twentieth century. My friendships with colleagues at both schools opened my eyes to larger issues of justice, education for the disadvantaged, and the power of a constant witness to biblical activism in the nation's capital. In a way, the ripple that began at the Basilica of the Sacred Heart at Notre Dame on that Easter many years ago has finally lapped against the shore. The sisters of Notre Dame de Namur, whom I got to know at Trinity, were once as young as my college friend. In their lives of devotion to scholarship, service, and compassion, I imagine the trajectory of my friend, now lost to me these many years. He moved me to question how fervent my faith was; the sisters' lives are testament to a steady will in a singular direction.

These kinds of moments might have come to me in other ways. Perhaps because of temperament, inclination, opportunity, and curiosity, I leaned this way instead of other ways. I needed work; they opened their doors; it turned out well for both parties. Going forward, I did not have a long-range plan. We rarely do in life. Nor did I determine to follow a specific course to meet people who understood and practiced faith in ways different than mine. Rather, I found myself responding to intuition, the promptings of the Holy Spirit, the openness of God to "strangers," and the curiosity that searches out how others worship and come to know God.

The experiences that we have and the people we meet may seem random, but there is reason to believe that the paths we cross with others can be seen, in time, as part of a larger pattern. God has a multitude of ways to meet us in unexpected places and to reveal the moments of grace we need in the midst of the mundane, the sublime, and the tragic.

16

A (Very) Brief History of Silence

The deepest level of communication is not communication, but communion. It is wordless. It is beyond words, and it is beyond speech, and it is beyond concept.[1]

Emma González, one of the last of the student speakers at the March for Our Lives, March 24, 2018, in Washington, DC, called out all seventeen names of the students murdered in the Parkland shooting, and then fell silent. As she gazed out over the enormous throng on the Mall, the minutes ticked slowly by. At first, the crowd thought she had been overcome with emotion, but although tears trickled down her cheeks, she did not waver. Three minutes went by and some in the crowd raised a cheer to fill the silence. Four minutes, and by now we understood that she had a purpose in mind. Many in the crowd around me bowed their heads and wept. Finally, she spoke again: "Since the time that I came out here, it has been six minutes and twenty seconds, the shooter has ceased shooting and will soon abandon his rifle and blend in with the students so he can walk free for an hour before arrest."

Silence can be a presence and a protest. Sometimes it's a cold absence. But it is never nothing. It can make a difference to one's spirit to know these silences.

In the Bible there is the silence of God's *darkness* in the Psalms, the main exhibit being Psalm 88; there is the silence of *fidelity* in Jesus'

---

1. Merton, *Seeds*, 65.

response to his captors; the silence of *endurance* of God toward Jesus' agony on the cross; and the silence of *awe* and *understanding* in Revelation 8 when heaven itself falls silent for half an hour.

***

The Silence of God's Darkness

N. T. Wright, in his book *Evil and the Justice of God*, has called Psalm 88 "the darkest and most hopeless of any prayer in Scripture."[2] The psalm is not a theological treatise; it's not interested in speculation. It's a brutal eyewitness account of what it's like to be a partner to a God who does not answer when the situation is dire.

Walter Brueggemann calls Psalm 88 one of the "psalms of disorientation" in *The Message of the Psalms*. These psalms speak of terror, the sense of forsakenness, the inexplicable silence of God. Brueggemann says, "The truth of this psalm is that Israel lives in a world where there is no answer."[3]

In verses 6–9, the Psalmist calls out in sorrow and anger. Not only has he descended to the Pit, but it's Yahweh who put him there. "You have made me a thing of horror." God doesn't come off well here. "Do you work wonders for the dead?" cries the Psalmist. "Are your wonders known in the darkness?" Of course not.

But the silence of God does not silence the speaker. There is no atheism here or rejection of God. The speaker redoubles his efforts to break through the silence and to force God to act. As Brueggemann says, "Yahweh must be addressed, even if Yahweh never answers."[4]

The psalm closes in desperation: "Your wrath has swept over me, your dread assaults destroy me."[5] You'd think some of this would rouse Yahweh to respond or even just to acknowledge the situation. But no. The psalm ends as it began—in darkness and silence, but this time a darkness that is brought on by Yahweh in contrast to the natural darkness of the night.

---

2. Wright, *Evil and the Justice of God*, 61.
3. Brueggemann, *Message of the Psalms*, 78.
4. Brueggemann, *Message of the Psalms*, 79.
5. Ps 88:16.

***

The Silence of Fidelity

Jesus' silence before those who mock him at his trial is *the silence of fidelity*, of staying true to his vision of God rather than escaping to fight another day. Even in captivity, Jesus regards his tormentors with assurance and humility. He will neither elaborate upon nor dumb down that which he has already revealed about the character of God and his kingdom in a multitude of ways over many encounters.

"When violent resistance to evil is renounced," says Jack Miles in his book *Christ*, "there is no guarantee that dignity or decorum will be retained."[6] When the righteous are mocked in the Psalms they complain, expecting the Lord to smash the wicked in the mouth. But here God is laughed at in the person of Jesus. Miles continues: "If God has not spared himself ridicule, his people cannot expect that he will spare them. The psalmbook has to be read in a new way. The servant, as he has reminded them, is not greater than the master."[7]

In his brief but pointed exchanges with Annas and Caiaphas, the high priests at his trial, Jesus refuses to engage them, while pointing out that he has taught openly in their synagogues and the temple. "Why ask me?" he says. "Ask my hearers about my teaching." And then calmly: "They know what I said."

"My kingdom is not of this world," Jesus says before Pilate. "So, then, you *are* a king." Jesus replies, "It is you who say that I am a king." Miles comments that "His confrontation with Pilate marks the birth of the Western tradition of nonviolent resistance."

In his silence toward his captors, Jesus fights for the greater cause and God's longer game. He may not have understood all the moves in this game, but he trusted that God had the upper hand in this cosmic battle. That is why Jesus could commend his spirit *to* God, even when he felt forsaken *by* God in his agony on the cross.

---

6. Miles, *Christ*, 227.
7. Miles, *Christ*, 227.

***

The Silence of Endurance

God's silence toward Jesus on the cross is *a silence of endurance.* "My God, why have you forsaken me?" Jesus cries, the prayer that God does not answer.

Jesus' agony on the cross is mirrored by God's agony of silence. In the Christian *mythos,* this is the culminating moment in cosmic history and God will not intervene. This is not about God requiring his pound of flesh in some legalistic payback scheme; it's about revealing the lengths to which God—and God in Christ—is willing to go to show that love wins in the end over hatred.

***

The Silence of Awe and Understanding

In the clangor and violence of the book of Revelation there comes a breathtaking moment: "When the Lamb opened the seventh seal, there was silence in heaven for about half an hour," verse 8:1 records. "On the whole," writes Sigve Tonstad in *God of Sense and Traditions of Non-Sense,* "Revelation depicts heaven as a noisy place. But silence is itself a distinctive category of response, the most spontaneous and intuitive form of reacting to the unexpected and the most trustworthy measure of the magnitude of the surprise."[8]

The breaking of the seventh seal rips a sharp intake of breath in heaven. There are no words. It is the sigh of understanding that all religions and faiths and peoples have longed for throughout the ages.

"After this I looked, and there was a great multitude that no one could count, from every nation, from all tribes and peoples and languages standing before the throne and before the Lamb, robed in white, with palm branches in their hands."[9] It is the culmination, at this stage, of what can be experienced of God by humans.

But this is also just the beginning of what the apostle Paul looked for, the revelation of which is to "know as we are known." For those caught

---

8. Tonstad, *God of Sense and Traditions of Non-Sense,* 404.
9. Rev 7:9.

up in God, *entheos,* the glass, so dark before, grows brighter moment by moment.

***

In the *Tao Te Ching*, the book of Taoism, emptiness has a place. "We shape clay into a pot, but it is the emptiness inside that holds whatever we want. We hammer wood for a house, but it is the inner space that makes it livable. We work with being, but non-being is what we use."[10]

Emptiness, silence—these elements in Taoism are regarded not as negation or lack, but rather a presence to be apprehended through intuition.

The Hebrew metaphysic is quite different. Emptiness and silence are to be resisted; they are an affront to the soul, a setback to the vigorous movement of the body through the obstacles strewn in our way in this life. God, having once spoken, is not allowed to remain silent, not even to take a breather out of sight in an adjacent room from the clamorous clanging of his errant children. The great Hebrew visionaries, the Psalmist among them, take their cues for meaning from the Creator: words bring objects into being and words create reality. Silence is dismissal, not conversation in another musical scale. For this we should be grateful, since it is through words that many of us live and move and have our being. What you cannot construct with your hands you can imagine with your mind and bring into being with your words.

Perhaps if it were not for the righteous fury of the prophets and the Psalmist in the silent darkness of God, we could not bear to hear from those in the Christian tradition who have learned to live in that silence—people such as St. John of the Cross, St. Therese of Avila, Thomas á Kempis, Thomas Merton, and C. S. Lewis. Like the Psalmist, they did not shrink from the plain reality that for us, too, God is often silent and clothed in darkness.

Until we see God face to face, we must take the dark with the light, and find in God's silence our memory and our future in faith. "Silence is the language of faith," says Christian Wiman. "Action—be it church or charity, politics or poetry—is the translation . . . It is also true that without these constant translations into action, that original, sustaining

---

10. *Tao Te Ching*, 11.

silence begins to be less powerful, and then less accessible, and then finally impossible."[11]

To see and understand in this way is the working out of our faith within the world's travails. But it is also the anticipation of a much deeper understanding of God through the *eucatastrophe*, the "good downstroke" or "breaking in," of God that will reveal the knower to the known.

---

11. Wiman, *My Bright Abyss*, 107.

17

Our Fathers, Ourselves . . .

> *Let him be whomever you wish. Like a fluttering candle*
> *into a stormlamp, I place myself there inside him.*
> *A glow becomes peaceful. May death*
> *more easily find its way.*[1]

WHAT DO WE KNOW of our fathers? They seem, through a child's eyes, almost as gods, striding purposefully through the world, shouldering aside doubt and uncertainty, magical in their strength, bending down from their great heights to lift us up higher than we could reach, but less than we imagined. At times, later, we think we've outgrown them, that perhaps the large hand on the bicycle we pedaled for the first time alone, which dropped away without us noticing, is not needed anymore. And still later, when we become adults, we may see them as persons, men in their own right, with admirable qualities, homely flaws, and modest hopes.

My father and I were different expressions of the same English-Canadian stock. In fact, we were raised by the same people: his parents, my grandparents. For reasons that do not need explanation for this story, I was taken in by my grandparents three years after my birth and after moving between families and countries and loving intentions, until at last I arrived on their doorstep, bewildered but grateful, embraced and

---

1. Rilke, *Selected Poetry*, 123.

welcomed as a second son. I remained—with times away in England—until I graduated from college and left their home in Northern California.

My father left home early, at eighteen or maybe nineteen, as near as I have understood, hitchhiking out of a small college town in Alberta, where both his parents were teachers and he was a campus kid. Perhaps the vice-like grip of loving concern in a church community grew unbearable—there were hints of a mistake on his part and harsh judgments rendered—but in any case he lit out for the world. It broke my grandmother's heart and brought a sadness to my grandfather's eyes.

He left; I stayed. He left the church; I am still in it. He became an engineer, thinking through his hands, whip-smart, a man of few words. I became a teacher, given to many words, uneasy around math and at home in the humanities. He was twenty when I was born; I was thirty-five when my son was born. He found his way through the world without a college diploma but helped to develop some of the most intricate technology of the computer age. I couldn't get enough of studying and resolutely worked my way through several degrees. He worked for IBM for many years; my first real computer was a Mac and I have never departed from the Apple orchard.

Thus, when he passed away after a long struggle with brain cancer, I was at a loss to know what to do. I cannot think of another way to put it except to say that my emotions were waiting at the door for permission from my rational nature to enter and be at home. It is typical to feel numb after such a loss and yet, on the contrary, I felt as if my senses were sharpened and enlivened. I saw myself, a man who had lost his father, and I wondered what made that man different from the one who had received the news hours before. The voice of a friend, tender with concern, moved me to tears; as I put down the cell phone it occurred to me that I had not wept until then. Was I moved to tears because another shared my grief? Or was it rather that his care for me called the leviathan Sorrow up from the depths? Was it self-pity I was feeling—see the poor fellow with the tears welling up in his eyes—or pity for my father who suffered in ways that all humans dread but must endure to the end?

Perhaps because I did not live with him as a child and had infrequent but vivid encounters with him as an adult, I lacked the emotional notation for that musical score—I would have to improvise. I was to begin teaching a course that evening at a nearby university, but I cancelled. I was wary, not at all sure I wouldn't be koshed from behind by a furtive emotion. This will be a process, so people assured me, and I will emerge from this experience a changed man. That's a fairly safe assumption since most of what we experience in life changes us.

The best counsel came from my sister, a person wise beyond her years and the one who guided her mother through the dark wood of my father's approaching night. She called this experience a sacred moment, a luminous experience, one to be opened by and lived through with all senses alert. I was reminded of Pascal's comment, "The heart has its reasons of which reason knows nothing,"[2] and realized that I had been granted a rare privilege: to view my father first as a man whom I loved and admired, and secondly as my father. Whatever our fathers are to us, they are always and simply themselves, a glory as mystifying as it is obvious. That night, walking home with a wisp of summer breeze, I saw the evening star: brilliant, benevolent, constant—and I was glad.

---

2. Pascal, *Pensées*, 154.

18

Life Becomes a Dark Saying

> *I don't know what it means to say that Christ "died for my sins"... but I do understand—or intuit, rather—the notion of God not above or beyond or immune to human suffering, but in the very midst of it, intimately with us in our sorrow, our sense of abandonment, our hellish astonishment at finding ourselves utterly alone, utterly helpless.*[1]

It is a curious thing to be a human being. There is in us a drive to be more than we are and also a drive to be that which we are not. These are not the same, and it's worth our time to make the distinction. But what we find most difficult is to be what we are. If we could truly know what we are, both in the aggregate and as individuals, we might not be so anxious to be something else. Even more to the point, we might not be so anxious.

"Be all that you can be," says the army's recruiting slogan, with the implication that whatever you are right now is not enough compared to what you *could* become with the proper training and motivation. It's a clever slogan, and it works for a lot of people, because most of us do not really know what we are but we're pretty sure we'd rather be *other* than what we are. Whatever that is.

---

1. Wiman, *My Bright Abyss*, 134.

So here is one way we're given to understand what we are. The basic message is: you're no good. The thing is that while a lot of advertising uses this technique, so do some iterations of Christianity.

The advertising arm of this approach is relatively benign. It says—sometimes loudly, sometimes softly—but always incessantly: You are deeply lacking in some crucial areas of life. But don't worry; there are people here who can help you, who want the best for you, and who *know* what's best for you. Toothpaste, cars, clothes, men's shaving razors (Harry's, I'm looking at *you*), lifestyles, attitudes, beliefs—anything can be commoditized and sold. It's a service we're proud to provide.

The Christian versions also begin with the claim that we are absolutely corrupted and there is nothing good in us. The more sadistic brands then justify beating the hell out of children and making sure the adults know what complete failures they are. The milder but more acquisitive forms counsel surrender to Christ in order to reap the rewards of victory. Having put our hand to the plow, we never look back; the furrow we cut through the world is straight and true because we have made it so. Victory is ours.

We are quick to say that all the glory goes to God. He is the one who has blessed us. As we warm to the subject, we rejoice in the fact that since everything belongs to God, and since he wants us to be happy, he can give us whatever our hearts desire. He does not want his children to be seen as poor. It brings shame upon the family name. God knows our needs and wants. Once we were blind, but now we see that God is our great investment banker: if we put ten dollars in the collection plate, he will multiply that and increase our goods tenfold, a hundredfold, beyond our wildest dreams. All things are ours if we are willing to believe that God will reward our faith.

It is a seductive message the prosperity gospel puts out. There is truth to it, but not in the ways the seduced would want to own. The first truth is that on our best days we're running a low-grade fever of illusion that we can scrub out all our imperfections if we just put our minds to it. The second truth is that on our bad days we're blaming everybody else for our failures. These things are so true that they whipsaw us back and forth until we demand a product that will put an end to the pain.

For some, the analgesic comes in the form of all that advertising sells. For others, the pain is dulled by a Jesus who promises a carefree life. The proviso is that our faith must keep that balloon aloft. The moment we stop huffing and puffing is the moment we plummet. Still others of us will attempt perfection because we think that is what Christ demands. We will fail. Christ's lawyers will tell us that we fell short, that we were out of compliance. Our weakness is our fault.

But here is another kind of truth:

> And when he had called the people unto him with his disciples also, he said unto them, "Whosoever will come after me, let him deny himself, and take up his cross, and follow me. For whosoever will save his life shall lose it; but whosoever shall lose his life for my sake and the gospel's, the same shall save it. For what shall it profit a man, if he shall gain the whole world, and lose his own soul? Or what shall a man give in exchange for his soul?"[2]

This has long been for me one of the most significant texts in the New Testament. It is paradoxical, upside-down thinking, literally about matters of life and death. Without blinking or turning away, Jesus calls us to one of the most barbaric forms of death in human history. Our eyes bounce and swoop over the words now, because for many the cross has become mere jewelry. Jesus' death on the cross is far, far back in history, the stuff of theological councils, a done deal. But this story, this ragged, gut-wrenching cry—this is a forewarning of what is to come.

Needless to say, this invitation will not draw the masses to the revolution. It isn't even a message that Jesus reserves for those most familiar with his rhetorical themes—his disciples. He might have drawn them quietly aside, cleared his throat, and said, "By the way, you'll want to be preparing for your eventual death on a cross. Do that and you'll live forever." Instead, he turns and speaks openly to the jostling people who are following him around, the ones just hoping to be healed or touched or listened to or in some real way seen for the first time in their lives. Did they hear him? Could they hear him? Is he trying to thin the crowd, to cut it down to the hard-core cell of those who would go to death for him and the cause?

He says all this knowing somehow that all of them will abandon him to his wild dreams as he breathes his last on the cross to the laughter of the soldiers who nailed him there. But he is serious, and we must take him seriously. We owe him that much.

(In time we will realize how utterly clueless that was, to think our debt to him could so easily be paid up by deigning to listen, politely leaning forward, our brow wrinkled in concentration, a half-smile on our

---

2. Mark 8: 34–37, AV.

lips that we hope will be taken as agreement but that barely hides the clanging of our hearts and the hot, racing pulse that suddenly is pounding so loudly in our ears that we cannot clearly hear what he is saying. And yet Jesus will not call us out on that. We will find it in our own time, consciousness dawning belatedly, gratitude welling up and dissolving our barriers to his gentle forgiveness.)

***

We have a soul and we can lose it, and we have a life, and we can lose that too. Actually, the way Jesus puts it here, we are ensouled; that's what we are as humans. To have life is to be a soul; to be a soul is to have life. There are lots of ways we can lose our ensouled life, but apparently only one way we can save it, and that is by taking up our cross and following Jesus. Each of us has a cross and our cross is as individual and unique as we are. Our job is to recognize it and to take it up, not just once, but every day.

Denying ourselves, we give up our panicked glances for the exits, and our half-remembered survival tips, and we trust that when it comes to it, when our last means of escape has been closed off, that we will know as we are known, and that that will more than suffice.

For an immigrant mother struggling in poverty to provide for her children, her cross might be the loneliness of fear and the grind of daily life—to bear it through the grace and strength of God. For another, his cross may be the wear and tear on his faith as he copes with the treatment of his cancer. A pastor struggling with opioid addiction, who must dull his pain while caring for others.

We don't choose our crosses, but we do find them in the course of our lives. For some of us it will be that which we cannot shake off, which haunts us at the edges of our peripheral vision. Some might call it the shadow, the deep part of ourselves we do not want to recognize, and which is capable of much mayhem within our souls.

I suspect that many of us will find a brother in the man who cried out to Jesus, "I believe! Help my unbelief." His first response is what he thinks Jesus wants to hear. His second response is his heart-cry, the desperate honesty of one who has no more options but cannot let go of his fleeting hope. In like manner, our faith will wax and wane, yet can be sustained by the one who says, "My grace is sufficient for you."

"Life is a dark saying,"[3] wrote Soren Kierkegaard. Yet, "it perhaps happened that your mind became more gentle and took to heart the words that had been planted in you and that were able to give a blessing to your soul—namely, the saying that every good and perfect gift comes down from above."[4]

We are curious creatures, we human beings. Early in life we think we know so much. Later in life, we find we know so little. Earlier in life we are making ourselves, but later in life we discover ourselves. Earlier in life we are taught to forgive other people. Later in life, we learn to forgive ourselves.

---

3. Kierkegaard, *Spiritual Writings*, 6.
4. Kierkegaard, *Spiritual Writings*, 8.

19

Augustine and the Word of Love

But let all of us who, as I acknowledge, discern rightly and speak truly on these texts, love one another and likewise love you, our God, the fount of truth, if truth is really what we thirst for, and not illusions.[1]

IN 387 CE, AUGUSTINE, the man who would become the greatest theologian of the early Christian church, was baptized by Bishop Ambrose in Milan, giving up a glittering career in the emperor's court and his renown as a celebrated teacher of rhetoric. A year later he and several equally distinguished friends returned to Thagaste, North Africa, where he was born. Settling there on his family's estate, Augustine began a life of writing and contemplation. But by 391 he was ordained to the priesthood and had moved to Hippo Regius, on the coast of Algeria, to found a monastery. Legend has it that one Sunday as he was attending services in the cathedral, the presiding bishop, Valerius, looked out in the congregation and cried out, "Stop that man! Do not let him escape. He is to be my successor when I die."

Four years later, in 395, Augustine was consecrated as bishop of Hippo Regius and remained its bishop until his death in 430. But in 397, a decade after his baptism and only two years into his bishopric, Augustine was forty-three, approaching middle age. In the midst of a busy life

---

1. Augustine, *Confessions*, 272.

of teaching, pastoring, and defending the faith, he wrote his *Confessions*, a remarkable work of intellectual and spiritual therapy set as a literary prayer to God which we are allowed to overhear.

Were we not already numbed by countless current memoirs that revel in self-deprecating "honesty," we might find his *Confessions* startling. Unlike so many ancient and medieval biographies, for instance, which depict their subjects as heroically exhibiting ideal qualities, Augustine reveals himself as a man whose past still resonates in his present. He is a bishop whose youthful sexual adventures still haunt him and whose memories are still painful. He underscores the force of desires that result in habits which become engrained and lock a person into paths not easily reversed. Long before Freud, Augustine understood that childhood experiences shape the adult. But unlike Freud he knew that change could only come from processes beyond one's control. His prayer is suffused with wonder and gratitude at God's intervention in his life.

The Confessions is comprised of thirteen books, what we would call chapters. In book 12, Augustine takes up a dispute over the meaning of the phrase "heaven and earth" in the Genesis creation story. It's an argument on whether God created *ex nihilo*, "out of nothing," or whether he used pre-existing material on hand in order to bring a new world to life. Within the intellectual and theological community of which Augustine was a member, this was, apparently, a matter worth coming to blows over.

He poses a number of interpretations for the meaning of the phrase and assesses their relative merits. Some make more sense than others, but Augustine asserts that any of them could be true, since we don't know exactly what Moses was thinking. What we *do* know is that what comes from God is truth.

Augustine believes that the interpretation he has arrived at is that which God prompted *him* to understand, but he holds that others may have arrived at different truths. His principle is to settle for one truth, "so long as it is firm and helpful, however many other truths may suggest themselves."[2]

When there are so many possibilities for interpreting Scripture, Augustine confesses that "I make my testimony on the understanding that if I have identified what your servant meant, that is the best and highest truth, the one I was bound to strive for."[3]

---

2. Augustine, *Confessions*, 310.
3. Augustine, *Confessions*, 310.

That would be the ideal, as difficult as that would be to reach. In humility, though, Augustine concludes that if he didn't reach that truth, "let me at least express what your truth willed me to take from the author's words, just as your truth willed what the author himself said."[4]

Apply your understanding through love, says Augustine: "So when one man says Moses meant what *he* means, and another says Moses meant what *he* means, I think it is more in the spirit of our love to say: Why cannot both be true?"[5] After all, why shouldn't we think that Moses intended *all* these various meanings?

God, states Augustine, "has suited his Scripture to readers who will find various truths when different minds interpret it."[6]

Augustine had come to realize that his earlier difficulties with understanding the Bible were because of spiritual pride; the Scriptures were only accessible to those who had rid themselves of conceit and self-importance. God spoke through images that we could understand, but even so we could never know the whole truth in this life. Language fails us, even in our relationships with others. How impossible, then, that we should be able to fully express the mystery of God in our own words. Wrangling and bitter disputes about the meaning of Scripture were futile. As Karen Armstrong puts it in her *The Bible: A Biography*, "Instead of engaging in uncharitable controversies, in which everybody insisted that he alone was right, a humble acknowledgment of our lack of insight should draw us together."[7]

Augustine had arrived at the insight of the renowned Rabbi Hillel and others: "Charity was the central principle of Torah and everything else was commentary."[8] For him, the rule of faith was not lodged in a doctrine, but in the spirit of love.

This would not be easy—Augustine rather ruefully begs for divine help in disputations:

> O my God... rain down gentleness into my heart, that I may patiently put up with such people, who say this to me not because they are godlike and have seen what they assert in the heart of your servant, but because they are proud, and without having

---

4. Augustine, *Confessions*, 310.
5. Augustine, *Confessions*, 309.
6. Augustine, *Confessions*, 309.
7. Armstrong, *Bible*, 122.
8. Armstrong, *Bible*, 123.

grasped Moses' idea they are infatuated with their own, not because it is true but because it is theirs.⁹

If we can each see some truth in what the other says, observes Augustine, where do we see it? "I certainly do not see it in you, nor do you see it in me; we both see it in the immutable truth itself which towers above our minds."¹⁰

Thus, we can arrive at a principle of Bible study: trust that if we open our hearts in humility to God's teaching through scripture, and if we do not claim to have the sole authoritative interpretation, then we can trust that we have been led into a truth which God has for us.

In Armstrong's felicitous phrase, this is "a compassionate hermeneutic."¹¹

What would such a hermeneutic look like in practice? We might, with charity toward all, apply it to our constant controversies. We have nothing to lose but our fear.

---

9. Augustine, *Confessions*, 266.
10. Augustine, *Confessions*, 267.
11. Armstrong, *Bible*, 229.

20

When a Bowl Is Not a Bowl

The most provocative of all realities is that reality of which we never lose sight but never see solely as it is.[1]

THERE IS A ZEN saying:

> Before enlightenment, a bowl is just a bowl.
> During enlightenment, a bowl is no longer a bowl.
> After enlightenment, a bowl is a bowl again.

More and more these days, this expresses much of how I perceive the paradoxes and puzzlements I face in life.

The saying refers to those moments when the host prepares the tea for his guest. Each step is carefully attended to, unhurried and calm. To hear the sound of the hot water being poured into the bowl and how the tone changes as the level rises, to hear the sound of the whisk briskly stirring, to see the steam rising from the surface and feel its heat through the bowl held in one's hands—these are each moments to be lived into with all our senses and to be remembered. In other words, the point is not to slurp down a cup of tea and rush out the door, but to see in the most common of moments a glimpse into the sacred beauty of life. It is also to grasp, with a shock of heightened awareness, that something we took for granted may be pointing us to a truth.

1. Stevens, *Collected Poetry and Prose*, 848.

Here is a mundane example of how our perceptions change in other realms of life: I buy a book that catches my eye. The subject is within the universe of interests that I carry, and I think I would like it. I read the front, the back, the introduction, scan the table of contents and the first paragraph. And I buy it. Fickle beast that I am sometimes, my interest wanes and I put it on the shelf. A decade later I take it down; memory has stirred curiosity and I am entranced. I wonder why I hadn't seen the riches of this book years ago. I study it fervently, underline and annotate it, commit passages to memory. In short, it has become one of the most cherished books in my library. Nothing has changed except my perception of its relevance and meaning to me—and that has made all the difference.

How does our perception change relative to the universals and the particulars? Jesus, in his suspension of the Sabbath law, teaches us to aspire to the universal (the love and care of others) over the particular (keeping the Sabbath commandment pure). How do we reconcile this? How should we work this out in practical terms? Do we ignore all Sabbath restrictions? Abandon the Sabbath altogether? What is the universal here? Is there a principle by which we can live?

We judge our theologies by several criteria. We ask if they are grounded in Scripture, by which we understand that the doctrine is not founded on a single verse, but multiple sources throughout the Book. We ask if they are carried by Christian communities down through the centuries, an argument from continuity and tradition. Sometimes they are not, like the Seventh-Day Sabbath, so we revert to the scriptural criterion.

But we also ask what any given doctrine reveals about God's character and, thus, how that knowledge affects our relation to God and to others. In short, we want to know if this belief will make a difference in our lives. What is the "cash value," as William James says, of our beliefs to our conduct and meaning for life?

The most basic universal principle from our side, the human response to God, is that freedom to choose to follow God is part of our learned spiritual behavior. In fact, we can say that freedom to *choose* is our human birthright. It's always been a principle part of our defining identity as humans, and people of faith are bold enough to say that it is God-given. It took the Enlightenment to bring this into the foreground, against the resistance of religious and political powers that had a fierce determination to bring about their ends through any means possible.

Now we are in a postmodern era in which the very idea of truth is vulnerable. Our economy of truth trades on facts—usually those of science—and the gathering, collating, dissemination and testing by facts is our major industry. Because determining what is factual is arduous and costly, we rely on experts who have the time, the skills, and the interest to uncover the truth in many areas of life. Although a good scientist's professional *modus operandi* is that current truth is only as good as its last iteration, when it comes to religion some seem to think that beliefs stated by committees should stand for eternity.

Part of the difficulty here is that theology—our human reading of God's ineffability—cannot be verified or proven false in the ways that scientific propositions are. As Richard Holloway puts it in his *Doubts and Loves*, "The reason theological dispute is so endless is that there are no empirical experiments we can appeal to that can obviously settle them, the way we might settle a dispute over the exact temperature of the boiling point of water."[2] And that is where religions pick up the weapons of coercion, guilt, and intimidation.

We return to the example of Jesus and the disciples, famished in a field on the Sabbath day. Raising the bodily needs above the ritual requirements, Jesus says nothing as the disciples pluck and eat the grains on their way. It's only when the Pharisees confront him (were they keeping the disciples and Jesus under surveillance?) that he responds, upsetting their carefully honed arguments. David, he said, allowed his soldiers to eat the consecrated bread, even though only the priest may do so. Then he adds the statement that relativizes our theological maxims: "The sabbath was made for the sake of man, not man for the sake of the sabbath. Thus, the son of man is lord even of the sabbath."[3]

What this seems to affirm is that when human needs come up against religious requirements, human needs must take precedence. If there's one thing that Jesus and God insist upon, it's the practical care of others. See that you care for the widows, the orphans, the poor, the disabled, says Jesus. Care for the children. I've come for the sick, not the healthy, he says. Of course, if we think we're healthy and wealthy and in need of nothing, then we're probably suffering from spiritual and social blindness—and we might not even know it if we're incapable of seeing beyond our feet.

---

2. Holloway, *Doubts and Loves*, 111.
3. Mark 2:27–28, Lattimore trans.

We have our particulars and they have their place. In religion, they help us pay attention to the details. Do we pray with hands raised and eyes closed? Do we tithe? Do we observe holy days and live modestly? Sweep away the details and we wobble from one religious fad to the next. But to make absolutes out of the details is to place formidable barriers between us and God. In those cases, God can still get through to us, but the question is: when we see the barriers falling will we realize we are being liberated or will we think we're being attacked?

***

So, in the end, after enlightenment, the bowl is just a bowl again. Once it was simply a means of holding the tea. Then it was the vehicle for clarity and insight, perhaps thought of as something miraculous because of it. Now, once again, it is a means of holding tea, not to be venerated but certainly respected for the part it played in opening one's eyes. Without the bowl there would be no drinking of the tea, but without the tea there would be no purpose for the bowl. The tea is the purpose of the bowl, the bowl is the means of the tea, and together they provide the moment in which to be fully present.

Let us say that the church, as *distinct* from our spiritual communities, is the bowl.

There is another aspect to this which is even more important: the means to the realization of any truths, as important as they may be, are not the truths. The map is not the territory; the symbol is not the reality to which it points; the law is not the gospel—in fact, even the gospel points beyond itself to the person of Jesus and the being of God. We too easily settle for that which can be categorized, quantified, and assessed. In the language of Paul Tillich, we turn the penultimate into our ultimate concern—whether it be the Bible, our personal faith, or our church. We look at the finger pointing at the moon instead of the moon itself.

Zen has a cure for that: if you keep returning to the bowl instead of going forward to the truth it's pointing to, then you need to drop the bowl.

21

A Necessary Candle

What has come into being in him was life, and the life was the light of all people. The light shines in the darkness, and the darkness did not overcome it.[1]

THE GOSPELS GIVE US many metaphors for the kingdom of God. They come at us like rapid fire: the pearl of great price, the treasure in a field, the mustard seed, the sower and the soil, the wheat and the weeds. They are often at the center of parables, those enigmatic bundles of meaning that Barbara Brown Taylor says act more like dreams or poems than as a code to be broken.

They are vivid images, some that resonate with our twenty-first-century sensibilities, others that stretch our imagination. And we get plenty of metaphors for Jesus, too. He gives us some of them: "I am the vine"; "I am the water of life"; "I am the good shepherd"; "I am the way." Others are ascribed to him, most famously the Word and the light of the world. They are contact points by which the veiled glory of his life and the courage of his death and the shocking eruption of his resurrection can jump-start our cold, dead hearts.

"To every age, Christ dies anew and is resurrected within the imagination of man," muses Christian Wiman in *My Bright Abyss*. He continues, "One truth, then, is that Christ is always being remade in the image of man, which means that his reality is always being deformed to

1. John 1:3–5.

fit human needs ... A deeper truth, though, one that scripture suggests when it speaks of the eternal Word being made specific flesh, is that there is no permutation of humanity in which Christ is not present."[2]

When we read the prologue to the Gospel of John, those first eighteen verses, they are like ancient tales spoken by bards in firelight. Their language and rhythm and repetition are mesmerizing; they speak of this world and time, and that which is beyond time, and of the creature not recognizing its Creator, and of the one who returns home from across the universe but is turned away by his own family.

Where does the story of Jesus begin? For John it does not begin with a virgin carrying the divine seed inside her, but farther back and higher up, with the Word that begins all creation, not with a bang but a whisper of supreme delight, "Let there be light!" That Word, that *Logos*, is now concentrated, distilled down, purified to its essence so that sound becomes light, both a particle in Mary's womb and a wave that carries everyone who sees: the Light has come into the world and the darkness will not overcome it.

John writes later, after the letters of Paul and Peter, and after the gospels of Mark, Matthew, and Luke are well established. John both synthesizes what is known of Jesus and transcends the day-to-day accounts by opening a portal for us to Jesus as the *Logos*, present at the creation and ever more as the present light that enlightens every person who comes into the world.

John may have known that in Matthew's story Jesus announces to those gathered around him, "You are the light of the world." These "lights" were a sorry lot by most standards. They were the lame, the blind, the ragged, the widowed and the orphaned, the restless and the rebellious, the defiant and the dumbfounded, the quarrelsome and the nearly invisible. And Jesus loved them all. Through the prism of eternal forgiveness Jesus looked on these sheep without a shepherd and saw them refracted into beams of light that carried the eternal weight of glory.

Where do we fit in? We might not have seen Jesus as someone we wanted in our neighborhood. He kept bad company, he was homeless, he had a sharp tongue for the respectable and the wealthy, he made us damn uncomfortable. He drew comparisons to bone boxes, made allegations of theft and cruelty toward the weak, and gave us slanderous names, like "slaves to sin" and "slayers of the prophets." It was all too

---

2. Wiman, *My Bright Abyss*, 11.

much. Something had to be done. And when it was done and dusted, and we could breathe again, there came word that he was inexplicably alive. The Light had not gone out after all.

Then along comes Saul, the living embodiment of the fanatic who is willing to kill for the glory of God and the sanctity of the Law. Breathing fire and threats, he terrorized those who had begun to carry the Light, taking names and rounding them up for a quick trial and summary executions.

And yet the Lord singled him out, considering him to be a pearl of great price, and broke through his armored heart to the pulsing flesh beneath, to the white-hot love of someone to whom he could give his all, even unto death.

This Paul, then, as sure now of the love of God in Christ as he had been of God's hatred of traitors to the Law, becomes the apostle of the new, assuring all who would listen that "if anyone is in Christ, there is a new creation: everything old has passed away; see, everything has become new!" And the newness in our human experience is that God is eternally, irrevocably, joyously on our side, closing up the abyss between us and God that we had dug. He is the great reconciler through Christ. "Truth," says Christian Wiman, "inheres not in doctrine itself, but in the spirit with which it is engaged, for the spirit of God is always seeking and creating new forms."[3]

Somewhere, Simone Weil says that God takes absence as God's form in the world, a saying that would be devastating if we did not know that against all odds God has chosen to appear to the world through those who carry the Light. "So, we are ambassadors for Christ," says Paul, "since God is making his appeal through us; we entreat you on behalf of Christ, be reconciled to God."[4]

We are living in times so full of bile and darkness that we are more certain of bitterness than we are of acceptance. Yet we have been called, all of us, any who wish to carry that Light, to be that necessary candle. "As people reconciled with God through Jesus," says Henri Nouwen in *Bread for the Journey*, "we have been given the ministry of reconciliation . . . So, whatever we do the main question is, "Does it lead to reconciliation among people?"[5]

3. Wiman, *My Bright Abyss*, 11.
4. 2 Cor 5:20.
5. Nouwen, *Bread for the Journey*, loc. 4079.

My friend Mike Pearson has given us a ladder of communication, each rung of which leads us to this reconciling work in the world.

- "Sometimes you have to settle for outcomes which are less than perfect in the name of maintaining relationships and forging community.
- You have to hope that your trust will inspire trust in others with the real risk that you may appear naïve and be open to exploitation.
- You have to use your imagination to find some fresh solutions.
- You have to listen truly and not simply wait deafly for your turn to speak."[6]

"We are not sent to the world to judge, to condemn, to evaluate, to classify, or to label," says Nouwen.[7] This sounds almost impossible, given that the way of the world is anything but nonjudgmental. "Only when we fully trust," he says, "that we belong to God and can find in our relationship with God all that we need for our minds, hearts, and souls can we be truly free in this world and be ministers of reconciliation."[8]

Bearing the Light in this world begins with us "accepting that we are accepted," in Paul Tillich's phrase, an experience so simple that it is difficult to grasp. It is the foolishness that leaps over the logic that would keep us in the dark.

---

6. Pearson, "Long Time in Politics."
7. Nouwen, *Bread for the Journey*, loc. 4097.
8. Nouwen, *Bread for the Journey*, loc. 4089.

22

Practicing the Grace We Have Received

Then the righteous will answer him, "Lord, when was it that we saw you hungry and gave you food, or thirsty and gave you something to drink?"[1]

WHEN I TOOK A group of students down to a homeless shelter in Washington, DC, some years ago, I fell into a conversation with a young man who was living and working there. His father was a professor at Yale and this fellow had grown up in ease, if not luxury, and had gotten an Ivy League education for free. I wondered what kept him there, working day in and day out, never getting a word of thanks from those he helped. I wondered because I had just witnessed a homeless man, clutching his coat around him in the January chill, roundly curse out my acquaintance as he served him soup in the gathering shadows outside the row house on Euclid St.

"Do they ever thank you?" I asked. Kevin stopped for a moment and thought, and then shrugged. "Not really," he said. "Why do you ask?" He leaned forward to ladle soup into an outstretched bowl.

"Because I wonder what's in it for you," I said. "Why do you stay, considering the kind of upbringing you had? You could be anywhere else, doing whatever you want."

---

1. Matt 25:37.

"I *am* doing what I want," he said. He frowned, puzzled. "It doesn't matter whether they thank me or not."

I persisted. "But you see the same people day after day. Nothing changes for them. Why do you keep at it?"

His answer was indistinct as he reached for a bowl to hand to the old woman in front of him. "Because they could be gods," I thought I heard him say. Or perhaps he said, "Because they could be God's."

The story Jesus tells in Matthew 24 is about Judgment Day. All the nations are gathered in front of the Son of Man, who sits upon his throne. He divides them up, some on his right side, some on his left. The writer calls those on the right side "sheep" and those on the left he calls "goats." Those hearing the story must have understood the analogy because there is no explanation why sheep are preferred over goats as moral exemplars. Since we probably derive most of what we know about sheep and goats from this and other stories in the Gospels, we have to find the meaning for ourselves. And there are two things that are intriguing in this story.

The first is that the list of good actions taken by the sheep is repeated—once with approval by the king and again in puzzlement by the sheep-people. In fact, when we get to the goat part the list is again repeated, this time as actions *not* taken by the goats (to the disapproval of the king) and their anxious query: Tell us again when we didn't do these things for you? The actions are important to the writer and to Jesus. Feeding the hungry and thirsty, taking in the stranger and clothing the refugee and the displaced persons, being with the sick and those forgotten in prison—these are the actions which separate the sheep from the goats.

This is what we are to do, all of us, from all the nations. Not just those from churches, mosques, and temples, but just people. They are designated not by religions but by nation-states and cultures. And what separates the nations is not creeds of beliefs or political ideologies or even economic prowess, but how well they take care of those pushed into the shadows and left behind.

The second thing that intrigues is the apparent blindness of both the sheep and the goats to their actions. Both are genuinely surprised at the judgments of the king. The sheep can't remember doing anything of the sort and the goats are anxiously raking through their memories, trying to think how they could have overlooked something so obviously to their advantage. Both were unconscious of their actions and therein lies the meaning of this tale.

✱✱✱

In intercultural communication studies there is a ubiquitous grid that shows the stages a person might go through as they grow aware of the complexity of communication. It is divided into four quadrants of communication competence.[2]

The first is *unconscious incompetence*, the stage in which we are blithely unaware of our rampaging incompetence. We don't even notice the trail of missed cues, trampled symbols, and outright weirdness on our part. Somehow, through the grace of God and the graciousness of others, we are spared the humiliation of being called out in public for our sins of commission and omission, and we live to err another day.

But then someone might kindly take us aside and clue us in to what we've missed and now, embarrassed but determined, we follow the actions of others like a cat on a laser pointer. We are focused and aware, but we still make mistakes that can only be lived through and learned from. We are *consciously incompetent*.

The third phase comes through practice, patience, and imagination as we become *consciously competent* in our communication with others. While our actions still demand our attention, we have the experience and the confidence to handle most situations that come our way.

In the final phase, rare but not impossible to attain, we are *unconsciously competent*. We have watched, listened, followed, and learned to the point where we no longer have to decide every action. The situation gives rise to our response. We act in the right way at the right time for the right reason and with the right result. It is so much a part of us that others may describe it as our "second nature."

This is what Aristotle called virtue, the habit of choosing the right action between the extremes of excess and deficiency. Finding the sweet spot between them is neither formulaic nor precise, he said. Ethics is not like mathematics and we should recognize this for ourselves and others. Cut some slack, he said, this kind of thing takes a lot of practice. It's not enough to self-consciously act appropriately one time and feel we've done our duty, for "one swallow does not a summer make."

This is what Confucianism and Taoism call *wu wei*, "actionless action," that which requires no effort on our part because we have practiced. The body and muscles retain memory, just as does our conscience. It is what Jesus calls "walking in the Way." Aristotle thought it would be best

---

2. Credited to Gordon Training International by its employee Noel Burch, 1970s.

if we started early in life on this, and Hebrew sages encouraged parents to train up their children in the way they should go so that when they were old (adults) they would not depart from it.

We do depart from it, of course, and quite frequently. Just as the sheep can learn the unconscious competence of virtue through practice, the goats can learn the unconscious competence of vice in the same way. This is what flares up into deadly force between people and roars up into wars. It's what turns economic policy into weapons against the poor and cuts off those who struggle to speak.

The habits of a lifetime become our character. None of us succeed at this without effort; all of us are capable of behavior that is grace filled.

23

First Church of Common Mysteries Now Open

> *Every human society is an enterprise of world-building. Religion occupies a distinctive place in this enterprise . . . All socially constructed worlds are inherently precarious. Supported by human activity, they are constantly threatened by the human facts of self-interest and stupidity.*[1]

RELIGION GETS ITS KNOCKS these days as the perpetrator of all things evil, the invention of adults who never outgrew their childish fears, the condemner of all that is spontaneous and upgrowing. Some of that is true, and when we who can still remember our childhood conscription into religion somehow find ourselves passing as adults and still floundering gracelessly around in the warm waters of the faith we were baptized into, we may be forgiven for our slack-jawed lack of defense. Some practices of religion, like manners and clothes, are a matter of habit. Habits smooth our way and free us up to think about important things, so we may be reluctant to drop those that, so far, have not resulted in serious injury or loss of footing.

But perhaps, like a man whose waist has outgrown his trousers, our boundaries to religion are too small, too much the skinny jeans rather than the comfort waist regular cut with a smoosh more room in the seat.

1. Berger, *Sacred Canopy*, 3, 29.

"Were we to limit our view to it," says William James in *The Varieties of Religious Experience*, "we should have to define religion as an external art, the art of winning the favor of the gods."[2]

Few Christians would admit to that, although their practices might. The *institution* of religion—its churches, ecclesiastical hierarchies, vestments, holy books, and, of course, the systematic theologies, commentaries, councils, and connections—all of that is the external manifestation of world building and world maintenance, as Peter Berger notes in *The Sacred Canopy*. It's a way of not only maintaining order in the world, but also, says Berger, "the audacious attempt to conceive of the entire universe as being humanly significant."[3]

We can't fault people for organizing a religion: that's what symbol and ritual lead to, after all. The first person to consciously repeat an action that had projected him into a holy and awesome experience was trying to recapture the moment. And it must have worked on some level or he wouldn't have passed it on to others. It's certainly not wrong to long for a repeat of something that moved us deeply, but no experience, however vivid, can fully be duplicated. In fact, the more vivid and detailed the experience, the less likely it can be reconstituted.

It's the generic expressions that translate best over time and culture: the movement of the body in dance and worship, the eating together in fellowship, the common prayer shared amongst a grieving circle, the reading of holy scripture in search of understanding.

All of this is religion, *religare*, from the Latin for "to bind." It's religion that binds us together through these rituals, these attempts to relive an experience of the past. There is nothing wrong with this. But we must realize we are trying to elevate a secondary reflection of someone's primary experience to a primary experience for ourselves.

What we retain is a reverence for the gesture, the word, the ritual—the "finger pointing to the moon" instead of the cool radiance of the moon itself. We feel a solidarity with the countless congregations through the centuries, gathered in glades deep in the forest, in huts and homes, in cathedrals and chapels, in temples, mosques, and tents.

We are reenacting a drama, reading from a script that by now is tattered and smudged from a thousand fingers tracing out the lines. The

---

2. James, *Varieties of Religious Experience*, 34.
3. Berger, *Sacred Canopy*, 28.

script itself becomes a holy object, passed reverently from hand to hand, as the players rehearse for a show that never ends.

Religion binds us together then, sometimes closer than we want, and sometimes in ways that seem to trap and fetter us. But there is another derivation of the word, this one from Cicero, who suggests that religion is connected to *relegare*, Latin for "to go through" or "over again as in reading, speech or thought." Still another rendering is that religion is related to the English *reck*, "to heed," or "to have a care for."

Religion as an activity that humans engage in is that which they care about, what they perform with care over and again from many different motives and with mixed results, to be sure, but at the very least with the hope that through this they will come into the presence of the divine.

Thus, the external symbols and rituals seek to penetrate to one's heart.

But the internal response, the deep inwardness that comes when we fall into a reverie waiting for the light to change—that is not to be trifled with nor ignored. "The relation goes direct from heart to heart," says James, "from soul to soul, between man and his maker."[4]

This is what we call "spirituality," the diffuse but real sense of the divine surrounding us. I suspect that part of its appeal to many is the fact that it is non-binding. The binding to the institution of religion, its *religare* function, may be more than some people can bear. Political evangelicals have already alienated many by their enthusiastic endorsement of Trump and his administration's actions in recent months. Their explicit support for these policies is a breaking point for many Christians.

But the power of spirituality lies in its first-order, primary experience with God. That's what people want, even those who are entrenched in rituals, week after week, that make no sense to them. They want to hunger after God, they want the numinous, the *mysterium tremendum et fascinans* that lifted Moses and Abraham and Jacob, Jesus, Paul, Martin Luther King Jr., and millions more. They desire meaning and purpose to their lives.

We have these holy moments of beauty; they drift up like dandelion seeds before us and we might not even see them, focused as we are on the flotsam of our days.

There is no inherent reason why spirituality and religion can't coexist. But it's clear that religion without spirituality is a valley full of dry

---

4. James, *Varieties of Religious Experience*, 34.

bones. And it's also clear that, as Karen Armstrong says, some people just don't have the knack for religion.

The capacity for spirituality is encoded in every person. It is not magic nor is it superstition. It is not unreasonable, nor does it depend on some secret instruction, *a la* Gnosticism. It is a capacity for wonder that we begin to lose early in life. It is a way of perceiving the beauty around us, despite what we have done to the natural world. It is a willingness to be released from the bonds that fetter us and narrow our vision. It is a prayer of grace and courage to live in this moment in the presence of Jesus.

We should ask ourselves a simple question: Do we want to see God's beauty in the world? Then attention must be paid, and spirituality as a practice provides the means. This is what grace gives us: the courage to notice the common mysteries of our lives.

24

A Single Step . . .

Let us remember: We never deal with reality per se, but rather with images of reality—that is, with interpretations.[1]

THOMAS MERTON (1915–1968) WAS a Trappist monk, a writer, and a peace activist who struggled continually with his place in the world. He was torn between committing himself to efforts to end the war in Vietnam and to following his vocation as a monk devoted to the solitary, contemplative life. On the one hand, almost anything he wrote (that made it through the censorship of his superiors) was eagerly published; on the other hand, his growing notoriety encroached upon his time and humility. "The creation of another image of myself—fixation on the idea that I am a 'writer who has arrived'—which I am," he writes in his journal. "But what does it mean? Arrived where?"[2]

His dilemma was not uncommon, but his circumstances were. Here is a man who seems the very embodiment of conflicting opposites. He is gregarious but seeks silence in order to communicate with his brothers through hand signals. He has spent most of his life running against the grain yet strives to submit to superiors whom he feels only want his submission for their ego's sake. He loves writing but comes to loathe the

---

1. Watzlawick, *Language of Change*, 119.
2. Merton, *Turning Toward the World*, 174.

process of being published—the interviews, the book tours, the attention that flatters him and fills him with horror.

His struggle is that of the private man called to a public role, the extension of oneself far out over the abyss in ways that most people are almost unaware of. He receives a note, in the autumn of 1961, from Ethel Kennedy, wife of the Attorney General, Robert Kennedy, and sister-in-law to the President. He had written to her explicitly objecting to the resumption of nuclear testing. "There is something very unsatisfactory, something not quite true about this whole moral question," he observes. "This idea that it is important to take a 'stand' as an individual. As if by mere gestures and statements one could satisfy conscience. And as if the satisfaction of one's conscience (emphasis on satisfaction) were the great thing. It can become a mere substitute for responsibility and for love."[3] Merton is acutely aware of how vain humankind is, how we pride ourselves on having a tender conscience, only to find that our moral consciousness vanishes like mist when put to the test.

A month later he notes, "I am perhaps at a turning point in my spiritual life: perhaps slowly coming to a point of maturation and the resolution of doubts—and the forgetting of fears."[4] As his resolve grows to work for the abolition of war and for nuclear disarmament, he is aware of how much it will cost him. "Walking into a known and definite battle . . . It appears that I am one of the few Catholic priests in the country who has come out unequivocally for a completely intransigent fight for the abolition of war, for the use of non-violent means to settle international conflicts."[5]

It is not just the inevitability of conflict over public issues that he is facing, it is the battle within himself, the *jihad* (in the truest sense of the word) against pride and self-satisfaction that he is steeling himself for. How to be selfless when the very abnegation of self can become a thing of pride? How to resist the image of oneself as a public icon? How to live transparently, to disappear, as Merton says, in spite of one's accomplishments?

Most of us will not have to face such temptations. As someone once said, some people are born to smallness, others have smallness thrust upon them. Yet so many are caught up in the effort to promote

---

3. Merton, *Turning Toward the World*, 158.
4. Merton, *Turning Toward the World*, 172.
5. Merton, *Turning Toward the World*, 172.

themselves that they seem like frantic little dogs chasing their tails, spinning endlessly, a retinue of publicists and media experts on hand to goose them from behind should they tire. You don't have to look far to find the pundits, paid by the word perhaps, who offer their paeans of praise to obvious and self-evident "truths." The best thing in these situations is to turn off the sound and watch the body language.

But I digress, if ever so slightly. There are several issues of moral conflict here. Merton points to one, the temptation to self-righteousness and pride in the midst of doing something that is righteous. Another is how to resist evil without becoming a tool of evil in the process. "By beholding we become changed," runs the text, and William Irwin Thompson, a social philosopher, adds, "We become the thing we hate." The epigram at the beginning of this piece points up another problem. Having arrived at last at a place where we feel confident and assured, we'll do anything to remain there—even flying in the face of changing circumstances and facts. Add all this up and it's enough to paralyze a person.

I remember a protest march held in Washington, DC, soon after we invaded Iraq for the second time. An exuberant group of students from Georgetown and George Washington Universities had gathered near the FBI building to join the march. It was meant to draw thousands to the Mall in order to register our complaint with the war and to speak our minds. I went down to it, arriving as the students were forming up the lines and trying out their cheers. It felt like I was at a football game with the drums, the marching bands, the banners and the self-conscious tribalism. I stood on the sidewalk, a bit lost and at loose ends. It wasn't that I supported the war; it seemed to me another horrific mistake with endless consequences. But on that bright, cool, and comfortable morning in our nation's capital the march suddenly seemed like a lark, something the whole family could enjoy, a revival service that left one feeling momentarily satisfied but came later to be a bitterness in the memory. It didn't feel like a sacrifice, a denial of anything precious, the giving up of which might have had some transformative power.

So I left, walking slowly back against the crowd to Union Station and a Metro ride back home. I will tell you what I was thinking. I was recalling a line in Merton's journal: "Non-violent action, not mere passivity."[6] That was years ago now, but the line is still with me. I think of it not in the

---

6. Merton, *Turning Toward the World*, 172.

imperative, "Do this! Don't do that," but in the indicative mood, "Look here . . . Consider this."

It's the journey of a thousand miles that begins with a single step.

25

Imagine That

For a humble man is not afraid of failure. In fact, he is not afraid of anything, even of himself... Humility is the surest sign of strength.[1]

Once when the king of Aram was at war with Israel, he took counsel with his officers. He said, "At such and such a place shall be my camp." But the man of God sent word to the king of Israel, "Take care not to pass this place, because the Arameans are going down there." The king of Israel sent word to the place of which the man of God spoke. More than once or twice he warned such a place so that it was on the alert.

The mind of the king of Aram was greatly perturbed because of this; he called his officers and said to them, "Now tell me who among us sides with the king of Israel?" Then one of his officers said, "No one, my lord king. It is Elisha, the prophet in Israel, who tells the king of Israel the words that you speak in your bedchamber." He said, "Go and find where he is; I will send and seize him." He was told, "He is in Dothan." So he sent horses and chariots there and a great army; they came by night and surrounded the city.

When a servant of the man of God rose early in the morning and went out, an army with horses and chariots was all around the city. His servant said, "Alas, master! What shall we do?" He replied, "Do not be afraid, for there are more with us

---

1. Merton, *Seeds*, 112.

than there are with them." Then Elisha prayed: "O Lord, please open his eyes that he may see." So the Lord opened the eyes of the servant, and he saw; the mountain was full of horses and chariots of fire all around Elisha.[2]

* * *

AND WHAT STOPS US in our tracks is not the cloak-and-dagger tension of military secrets revealed, and not the perfectly understandable reaction of the servant to besiegement, but the laconic way the man of God answers his servant's terrified cry. He may not have even looked up when the fellow burst in through the door as the first streaks of morning light shot across the threshold.

"They've come for you, you know!"

"Yes."

"What are we going to do?"

It was a matter of what one sees and what one understands. Was it a trick of the light, maybe a distortion in the retina that early in the morning? The eye sees dark shapes, maybe boulders . . . but then they move, and suddenly a vast army is revealed, and we cannot see it now as anything but rank upon rank of men and horses, standing silently, with a stamping of hooves occasionally, and a muttered command, and an awful dryness in the mouth as one's eye begins to twitch.

William James says we pay attention to what matters to us and yet we grasp so little. "One of the most extraordinary facts of our life is that, although we are besieged at every moment by impressions from our whole sensory surface, we notice so very small a part of them."[3]

Let us imagine the young man as one of us, a person who relies on the facts, sees for himself what is real, and runs everything he encounters through his field-tested, rigorized, and fully guaranteed BS filter. We are surrounded by insurgents in white Toyota Land Cruisers with turret-mounted 50-caliber machine guns and grenade launchers, and, farther back, armored trucks.

"Don't worry," says the master behind us. "There's more with us than are with them." And he prays, short and simple: "Lord, open his eyes that he might see."

---

2. 2 Kgs 6:8–17.
3. James, *Psychology*, 217.

We can see alright. We know what we see before us and what we see is a guarantee of a quick but excruciating death. If it were dark, we could still see with nightscopes, night-vision googles, all manner of devices to cut through the darkness and the fear. We see what can be touched. Our hope for survival is built on nothing less.

Thomas Merton says, "To know anything at all of God's will we have to participate, in some manner, in the vision of the prophets . . . who sometimes saw glimpses of that light where other men saw nothing but ordinary happenings."[4]

So, let us freeze this frame and ask ourselves what the old man sees that we are missing. What is out there that he is so sure exists that he doesn't even come to the window, doesn't even get up from the table nor close the book he is reading? What does he know that we don't?

* * *

In his *The Practice of Prophetic Imagination*, Walter Brueggemann asks what would happen if we imagined that the triune God was real. How would our perception of the world change? Brueggemann does not assume that such a claim is obvious, but rather that we must establish again and again the evidence for such words. "The key term in my thesis is 'imagine,' that is, to utter, entertain, describe, and construe a world other than the one that is manifest in front to us . . ."[5]

Against the evidence of our senses—and certainly against the prevailing common sense of this culture—the prophetic imagination invites us to see with the eyes of faith what the heart longs to experience.

We are witnessing two divergent narrative streams. The dominant narrative is rarely questioned, nor is its conceptual framework laid bare. Because its narrative arc sets our own expectations of life, we cannot stand away from it far enough to see it for what it is. Brueggemann calls it "military consumerism," the story of *self-invention* for *self-sufficiency*, a social construction whose origin we no longer recognize.

The alternate narrative is the story of YHWH, grounded in the prophets and reflected in the Gospels. In its simplicity and directness, it sets up a contest like Elijah's Mt. Carmel showdown between the gods and YHWH. Two construals of reality, one decision to be made.

---

4. Merton, *Seeds*, 124.
5. Brueggemann, *Practice of Prophetic Imagination*, loc. 178.

In our time, this story may flow through the preaching of those who are embedded in the alternative narrative of YHWH. It may also be ours if we can see with the eyes of humility. "Thus, the offer of prophetic imagination is one that contradicts the taken-for-granted world around us,"[6] writes Brueggemann.

In the Old Testament the expression of it is the Exodus story in which the "Lord brought us out of Egypt with a mighty hand and an outstretched arm . . . and gave us a land flowing with milk and honey."[7] In the New Testament Paul crisply summarizes the *kerygma* "that Christ died for our sins . . . that he was buried, and that he was raised on the third day in accordance with the scriptures."[8]

These are acts of the imagination; not that they are conjured up by us, but that we are asked to imagine ourselves living in *that* narrative stream instead of "in the old dispensation/With an alien people clutching their gods," in Eliot's memorable phrase.

* * *

So, Elisha prays that the young man will see through the surface appearance to the essence of the moment, a reality that shimmers just beyond the senses, a gift of magnification. Elisha's own seeing, seared into his memory when he saw his master, Elijah, caught up into the heavens, was enough to last a lifetime. He knows what is there without looking.

Today, we are that young man whose world is constricted to the obvious appearances. Against all odds and experience the Word comes to us as a gift.

Imagine that.

---

6. Brueggemann, *Practice of Prophetic Imagination*, loc. 182.
7. Deut 26:8–9.
8. 1 Cor 15:3–4.

26

The Grace of Simple Things

I believe in all that has never yet been spoken. I want to free what waits within me so that what no one has dared to wish for may for once spring clear without my contriving.[1]

THERE ARE TIMES IN our lives when the moment is so deep, so simple, as to be transparent and effortless. Within that moment we sense that the rush of events has subsided and we, quietly grateful, find ourselves turning in a gentle current to gaze, first here and then there, and to feel ourselves lifted and set upon our feet on a new morning at the edge of a far wilderness.

Those are moments that one treasures, storing them up for the times when the days turn to rust and the air sears as we sit in the stink of traffic waiting for the light to change. There are never enough of these moments, and in time they fade, although the mere desire for them can conjure up a train of images—some unrelated to the first experience—that gradually take on an iconic weight and bearing.

I've enjoyed enough of these that I can string them like pearls in my consciousness, holding them up to the light and seeing how they've changed over the years. There is curiosity in recalling which ones marked stages in my life. They are like ancient buried ships whose mounded

---

1. Rilke, *Rilke's Book of Hours*, 58.

boundaries we circumscribe unaware until we gain the heights and look back and down and gradually discern the outlines.

For me, these moments most usually come when I'm alone in the vicinity of strangers or near a lake or river or mountain or beach. I am booked up with a scripture (the Gospels, the Tao Te Ching, the Dhammapada, or the Bhagavad Gita), some poetry (Rilke, Blake, Eliot, or Stafford), and some philosophy (Epictetus, Seneca, Marcel, or Camus)—and a fine cup of strong, rich coffee. Setting off for these possible transcendences, there is anticipation of a good experience. We cannot plan for these moments, but we can be ready for them.

I had one such experience while on holiday visiting family in Banff, Alberta. Early on a Saturday morning, a time of special holiness for me, I moved through the streets alone in the cool dawn. In search of a quiet shop with coffee, I found one—Evelyn's Coffee Bar—on Banff Avenue. I was past the door when I noticed it, stopped, and backed up. The sign said "Saturday, 8 a.m. to 9 p.m.," but it was 7:45 and the door was open, so I went in, the first customer of the day.

The only other person was behind the bar, a polite and cheerful young man from the East End of London by the sound of it. With mug in hand I sat in the window that fronted the street and gazed in wonder at the mountain that rose thousands of feet in the near distance. There was morning light all around—I could see it filling in the space between the peaks—but the town was in that blue shade that only exists in the shadow of a mountain that is blocking the sun. Streams of light shot from its shoulders and I knew that in minutes I'd be in the full glare of the sun as it crested the peak.

I was reading *Rilke's Book of Hours*, in a translation I've come to revere, in a passage that carried all my longings to create:

> If this is arrogant, God, forgive me,
> but this is what I need to say.
> May what I do flow from me like a river,
> no forcing and no holding back,
> the way it is with children.[2]

By now one or two more early customers had come in. The English barista had been joined behind the bar by a young woman who spoke with a Scandinavian accent.

---

2. Rilke, *Rilke's Book of Hours*, 58.

"Wot time are we to open?" he asked, as they worked. I could not hear her murmured reply, but he responded, "Cos I wasn't sure if it was 7:30 or 8:00 so I opened at 7:30 just to be safe."

> Then in these swelling and ebbing currents,
> these deepening tides moving out, returning,
> I will sing you as no one ever has,
>
> streaming through widening channels
> into the open sea.[3]

And then the light burst over the peak and in one astonishing moment the street in front of me, the window, my books and cup—everything was shot through with white, pure light, warm to the touch but with hard-edged shadows.

> I want to know my own will
> and to move with it.
> And I want, in the hushed moments
> when the nameless draws near,
> to be among the wise ones—
> or alone.[4]

We move through this world in a sullen daze more often than not. We mind our own business, shuffling through the streets, not meeting the eyes of those around us, drifting like motes in the sun. But occasionally, if we dare to look up, if we glimpse—even in imagination or memory—the trembling, fiery annunciation of the morning, we might just be graced into joy.

> I want to unfold.
> Let no place in me hold itself closed,
> for where I am closed, I am false.
> I want to stay clear in your sight.[5]

---

3. Rilke, *Rilke's Book of Hours*, 58.
4. Rilke, *Rilke's Book of Hours*, 59.
5. Rilke, *Rilke's Book of Hours*, 59.

27

Resist and Love

Love is like a flame; it can never be still, and dies when it ceases to hope or fear.[1]

"Something there is that doesn't love a wall,"[2] says Frost, and thus rouses the silent kid in her ninth-grade English class who finds in the poet a resistance fighter. At the molecular level, within the genetic structure of the body politic, the germ of resistance can be isolated, understood as a trait that our American forebears had in abundance, and that we would do well to emulate.

We resist when we're young because we don't know what we're capable of; we resist because without something to push against we lose all feeling in our senses. To *be* someone we have to bump up against something, push something around, if only to find the edges of the universe we find ourselves floating within.

"The simplest idea of power," says James Hillman, "supposes that for work to be done, there must be something that resists."[3] If nothing else, resistance makes power possible, even something that can be measured.

But we measure ourselves by what we're not going to put up with anymore, by what rights we are owed, by the amount of pushback we get when we bend the world to our will.

1. La Rochefoucauld, *Maxims*, 10.
2. Frost, *Road Not Taken*, 112.
3. Hillman, *Kinds of Power*, 144.

We resist, therefore we are.

But this is tenuous, and we know it. We are living in times when identities are thrown like knives. "I am this!" "You are that!" "They are not this, not like us." "We would never do that, not like them!" We peer through our family and tribal filters that polarize the light around us by cutting out the interferences. There is precedent.

A man named Saul, a bona fide terrorist riding to Damascus with a license to apprehend and arrest Christians for their torture and death, is thrown from his horse, blinded, and pinned to the ground by a bolt of light and a voice from the heavens. The King James Version puts it best:

> And he said, Who art thou, Lord? And the Lord said, I am Jesus whom thou persecutest: it is hard for thee to kick against the pricks.[4]

Saul had been kicking against the pricks all his life and the pricks had returned the favor to the extent that Saul could easily have passed for one himself. Modern translations of the Bible have lost the latter phrase, but we can know that Saul was resisting with everything he had, kicking away all the faces of those he carried in his conscience day after day. "You have lost yourself," they whispered. "You must change your life."

And change he does. Resisting the dead weight of primitive prejudice, this Saul becomes a Paul, rebounds from his blindness to persuade his former victims that while he once was blind, now he sees. Now he's fighting not against flesh and blood, but against principalities and powers, unholy powers in high places who build their walls.

Years later this Paul is still resisting. He knows plenty about fighting the good fight, but he also knows a lot about love. Look, he says, now I only know part of the story, but someday I will know as fully as I am known. Faith, hope, and love, he says, these are the essentials, but the best part is love. You must change your life. We don't even know how to pray for change, but the Spirit prays within us, and in all things, there is something working out for good to those who believe that goodness still lives in the world.

We may call this Truth or God or Love; in the end they are quite the same.

---

4. Acts 9:5–6.

28

Devotional Doubt

There is no clean intellectual coherence, no abstract ultimate meaning to be found, and if this is not recognized, then the compulsion to find such certainty becomes its own punishment. This realization is not the end of theology, but the beginning of it: trust no theory, no religious history or creed, in which the author's personal faith is not actively at risk.[1]

I BELONG TO A small-group community at my church that has been meeting in one form or another for over forty years, as best we can determine. This version, with its present members, has been meeting together every week for well over two decades. Our name, Believers and Doubters, sometimes startles visitors until they realize that we are committed to keeping those two poles together in some kind of balance. The balance we achieve from week to week is a result of the respect and care we have for one another through all the vicissitudes of life.

One of the benefits of the group for each of us, something that we have belatedly come to consciously acknowledge, is our candor with each other about our struggles with faith. Within that circle that gathers each week we can look for honesty from each other. We can say what is on our hearts without fear of condemnation. We can also exercise the right to

---

1. Wiman, *My Bright Abyss*, 75.

speak from our experience in order to suggest to each other what we've found that helps us trust in God. We have seen our children grow up, we've weathered divorces and celebrated marriages, suffered through cancer treatments, operations, and loss of loved ones and jobs. Some of our number have passed on; our numbers fluctuate from week to week as one or another of us travel or serve in other capacities at this church and other churches. It is both a safe haven and a spiritual laboratory where we can experiment with ideas as we study, pray, and vigorously discuss together. And many Sabbaths we have bread, fresh from the oven of one of our members, and coffee, ground to perfection and brewed onsite by our resident expert and served in little porcelain cups.

Our method of study is to work our way through books that we select, spending as long as we wish on them. Since we rarely rush through a book, and since our discussions digress freely and cheerfully away from the main topic, we tell visitors that they don't need to have read the book to enter into the discussion—and we'll probably be on the same book when they return in a week or a month's time.

The possibility that we can be both believers and doubters simultaneously is liberating. We've recognized that as much as we doubt, we also believe, and that our belief is never wholly undermined by our doubt. We see doubt as the handmaiden of faith, and while we may not always conclude matters from week to week, we know that we have time. In the midst of doubt, we live in hope.

As a practical matter of faith, it matters how we regard our faith, and doubt is not a trivial matter when it comes to faith.

We regard doubt not as corrosive to faith but as a means of exploration on the way to faith. What do we gain in using doubt as a method in theology? The possibilities of imagination, the freedom to explore and inhabit Scripture, the *need* to expand our limits on how we think about God. To doubt our own platitudes, even to doubt our own unbelief and doubts, is a good thing. Some days we are not authentically doubtful; some days we are just tired, slow, and cranky.

We've discovered that there are two ways that groups can throttle hope and shut down enlivening discussion. One is through cynicism, the worm in the apple of a faith-filled community. All of us have had experiences in which the church let us down, perhaps even burned us, because like all institutions the church cannot live up to its own ideals. But cynicism, as someone has said, is dumping your toxic hopelessness into the lives of other people. Maya Angelou says somewhere that "A cynical young person is almost the saddest sight to see, because it means that he or she has gone from knowing nothing to believing nothing." Healthy doubting is something we take ownership of, freely admit, and don't let out of our sight.

The other way hope and imagination can be snuffed out is through dogmatism. If cynicism is the certainty that there is no meaning, then dogmatism is the certainty that meaning doesn't matter. Dogmatism, especially in theological matters, is a "might makes right" argument for religious authoritarianism. By reducing faith to uniformity of assent dogmatism closes off the possibility of new life, "present truth," and new understanding springing up.

The more we Believers and Doubters experience together our uncertainty, doubt, and contingency in spiritual faith, the more emotively real the connection seems between Jesus and ourselves. This is both puzzling and reassuring. Like Parker Palmer and Thomas Merton, two guides we have studied and walked with, our lives are lived in the belly of a paradox: the deeper we live into the resurrection of Christ, the lighter and clearer our faith becomes.

I imagine my faith to be stripped down to the core, as supple and as innocent as it can be despite my six decades of it being dragged through the mud, drenched in despair, desiccated in rationalism, and twisted and stretched between personal faith and corporate conformity. Now it is light enough for me to leap.

In the spirit of the epigram at the beginning of this essay, and in gratitude to the author, Christian Wiman, of the book we immersed ourselves in, *My Bright Abyss*, I will close with his quote:

> Honest doubt, what I would call devotional doubt, is marked, it seems to me, by three qualities: humility, which makes one's attitude impossible to celebrate; insufficiency, which makes it impossible to rest; and mystery, which continues to tug you upward—or at least outward—even in your lowest moments.[2]

---

2. Wiman, *My Bright Abyss*, 76.

29

Lane Walkers

Not till we are lost, in other words, not till we have lost the world, do we begin to find ourselves, and realize where we are and the infinite extent of our relations.[1]

How much of our life do we truly comprehend? We may feel like political observers at a rigged election: we can see what's going on but we lack the power to change it. Caught up in our routines, not daring to vary from them lest we lose a step, we see the surface changes of light and shadow, while we sense that tectonic shifts are taking place beneath us.

At a corner of an intersection frequented by panhandlers a man held a hand-lettered sign that proclaimed him to be God's anointed, a "prophetic, proud, American preacher." I held a dollar out to him while waiting for the light to change and listened while he spoke about his ministry. He was a handyman who had been touched by the Lord some years ago and sent on a mission to bring a message of hope, prosperity, happiness, and health to all who would listen. He gave me a flyer he had written up, complete with a website, and resources that, if ordered, would restore a sense of pride in America and gratitude to the Almighty. There was no irony for him in the fact that as the bearer of the message he was a walking refutation of its benefits. But that suspicion was answered by his earnest claim that it was his humility that marked him out for the divine dispensation.

1. Thoreau, *Walden*, 187.

His jaunty sanctity was touching. Far from being an object of pity, he thought of himself as a man with a mission. He wasn't begging, he was witnessing. The transactional nature of his work called for him to give as well as to receive. If I gave a dollar, he was happy to bless me and share with me the nature of his work. The dollar, a gesture of solidarity, was less a donation to an indigent than it was a validation of his calling. You've got to respect a man like that. As the light changed and the phalanx of cars pulled away, he proclaimed his willingness to work at anything—car repair, house painting, yard work, preaching.

I've wondered at the necessities and rules of panhandling. No doubt there are social norms that come with the occupation, perhaps even vocabularies and expectations that must be met. Does a median strip belong to those with seniority or is it "first come, first served"? Do you dress for the neighborhood or for the rigors of the job? On blazing hot days can the men go shirtless or is that a social *faux pas* that cannot be tolerated? Must the women always be mothers with four children and no rent money, or can they be young, single, and brave—with time on their hands? How does the body adapt to or resist the thrumming roar of traffic, the waves of heat radiating from exhausts, engines, and metal surfaces? Do you stay on the median or walk between the lanes? Smile and thank whoever pauses or keep the gestures to a minimum?

These are the lines of adaptation to which the organism conforms, the terrain that must be plowed, the rules of engagement for a public transaction of a moment. I've seen lithe, well-dressed young men, affable and surefooted in the traffic, whose only indication of need was the hand-lettered sign they carried. And I've seen men, perhaps veterans of our interminable wars, whose faces were roasted red from the heat, whose hair was bleached and lifeless from the exhaust and the wind, and whose clothes had lost all semblance of garments.

I have found myself asking, while waiting out the light, what slight movements of the spirit brought them to this place and this moment? What butterfly, blithely flitting from flower to bush in a garden on an island in Japan, set in motion the winds that blew these people upon our concrete beaches? Alone in a crowd, islands in a river of molded plastic and glass, do they wonder, as they pace their walkways, if there was an inexorable fate that brought them here? Were they singled out for punishment or just slower than the rest sprinting for the exits?

The consistency and persistence of these people is what lingers in the memory. Every day they are out there in all weathers, working the lanes, radiating a cheerful resilience, regulating their practice according to the elements they have found that work through necessity and chance.

Every one of them began as a child without guile. Most were loved, some no doubt carried the hopes of the family on their shoulders. There is no need to romanticize them or bill them as urban artists; they have too much dignity in themselves to be the object of our casual pity.

They live with the facts, the bare unadorned necessities of survival. They are not a tribe apart; they are the rest of us stripped down, without our pretense and assurances, without our facile privilege. There was a time when the Fates would have gotten the credit for having twisted up these lives in ways that could not easily be undone. Now those lives are proxies for the millions whose existence, when noted, is signaled merely by a downward tick on a graph in a Senate hearing.

"We know not where we are," says Thoreau near the end of Walden. "Beside, we are sound asleep nearly half our time. Yet we esteem ourselves wise, and have an established order on the surface."[2]

---

2. Thoreau, *Walden*, 360.

30

Three Degrees of Success

If the audience easily recognizes the three degrees of failure (birds, rocks, thorns), how would it interpret those three degrees of success (thirty, sixty, hundredfold)—even in the literal microcosm of sowing? Jesus's parable seems quite ready to expect and accept degrees of failure and of success.[1]

"Listen!" Jesus is saying, "a sower went out to sow." The people on the shore listening smile and nudge one another. The Master is on a roll, telling his stories. There are so many people gathered that he's in a boat a few feet off shore, speaking to the crowds by the lake in the late afternoon sun.

He speaks in parables, short stories whose meaning lies outside the literal elements of the story and points toward a moral or theological purpose, what New Testament scholar John Dominic Crossan defines as "a story that never happened but always does—or at least should."[2]

The Parable of the Sower in Mark's Gospel (4:1–20) assures us of God's pleasure at any degree of return on crops planted. In Mark's version of the parable, Jesus tells of the loss of seeds to the birds, to rocky soil, and to thorns that choke their growth. But for the seeds that land in good soil and survive there is an eventual harvest. Some patches have a return of 30 percent, some up to 60 percent, and others—perhaps optimistically—a

---

1. Crossan, *Power of Parable*, 25.
2. Crossan, *Power of Parable*, 4.

full 100 percent. The sower tends them through their growth cycle right up to the harvest and is glad for whatever they produce. Reading this, we never get the feeling there's anything less than delight and satisfaction for the 60s or even for the 30s. They've taken root, they've flourished, and they're ready for the harvest. Next year maybe there will be more.

Mark tells us that Jesus "began to teach them many things in parables," these pithy, sometimes enigmatic stories that puzzled and angered the religious authorities and seemed to trip up the disciples as well. This parable, by Mark's reckoning one of the most important in Jesus' teachings, shows us that God is realistic about our growth rate and unfazed by what we are now.

We grow and develop spiritually at different rates and in different ways. For some, the obstacles to trusting God can be formidable. If our trust has consistently been sabotaged by parents, friends, and others—those we can actually see—why would we trust an invisible God? For others, trust comes easier. They've had the good fortune to grow up with people who could be counted on to keep their promises and who usually chose to do their best for their children. Or maybe they just have the "religious knack," as religion scholar and author Karen Armstrong puts it.

After the crowds leave and Jesus is alone with his disciples, they press around him. Why does he speak in parables, they ask? Why doesn't he just tell the people straight out what they should and shouldn't do? It's easier, quicker, and there's less chance of being misunderstood. Don't you get it? he asks, surprised. "Do you not understand this parable? Then how will you understand all the parables?"[3] And he tells the parable again, annotating and explaining as he goes, filling in with more details the story he had told in brief to the crowds. He seems to think of this one as a template that in some way it holds the key to understanding how he uses any parable, which, in turn, is the way he most often communicates his good news about the kingdom of God. It may also keep him from being arrested.

Crossan puts forward the view in *The Power of Parable* that Jesus was using this common storytelling device in a new way as a challenge to the status quo. Parables operate as metaphors, a Greek term that means "'carrying something over' from one thing to another," writes Crossan, "and thereby 'seeing something as another' or 'speaking of something

---

3. Mark 4:13.

as another."⁴ The challenge in these metaphors, he continues, is this: "If tradition is changed, it *may* be destroyed. If tradition is not changed, it *will* be destroyed. That is the challenge of this and of all other challenge parables."⁵

It challenges those who place burdens of guilt cemented in tradition on the ones who seek the kingdom by telling them they are not worthy to come as they are. And it challenges we who are called—not because there isn't room for us in the kingdom, but because we do not stop to listen to the call. And if we *do* listen and respond, we may be fighting the idea that we have to be free from sin in order to apply and to qualify. But it's the Sower who sows, not us.

We are tempted to wait until our potential for spiritual growth comes naturally, without effort. We are tempted to measure ourselves by those we admire or against a list of virtues or the gifts of the Spirit. We succumb to these temptations because we compare ourselves to others and we become impatient when we don't see in our lives the virtues that take time to develop. As for gifts, we may be born with them or get them later in life, but in either case we don't generate them.

We are quick to judge others. If we keep our judgements of others to ourselves, it's all to the good. In time, we may even judge them less. When the ratio of judgement to empathy and understanding begins to change, we'll see them much differently. We will see ourselves differently too, perhaps as people who can forgive in spite of not yet forgetting. Patience, grasshopper.

We are quick to judge ourselves, a response that is hard-wired into most of us. Thankfully, we usually know when we've gone off the tracks. Thomas Merton has said that we don't need to create a conscience. "We are born with one, and no matter how much we may ignore it, we cannot silence its insistent demand that we do good and avoid evil."⁶ Still, a lot of us find ourselves rehashing the same arguments with others and with ourselves, over and over in our heads, attacking with our vorpal swords and blocking the parrying blows. And while passing judgment on ourselves is not quite the same as exercising our conscience, it often feels like it, enough that we may desire "the rotten luxury of self-pity," as Merton has said, and just leave it at that.

---

4. Crossan, *Power of Parable*, 8.
5. Crossan, *Power of Parable*, 47.
6. Merton, *No Man Is an Island*, 41–42.

But like the seed that the sower sowed, we grow as we go, for there is no practicing before we enter life, only a continual trial-by-error. Self-reflection—not the same as debilitating self-criticism—helps us see ourselves as we are. And, as someone has said, God loves us the way we are, but he doesn't want us to *stay* the way we are. So, we walk by faith, not by sight, as we are renewed from day to day.

Barbara Brown Taylor, in her collection of sermons, *The Seeds of Heaven,* gives us a way to read the Parable of the Sower that upends our expectations about the kind of ground we are supposed to be.

> The focus is not on us and our shortfalls but on the generosity of our maker, the prolific sower who does not obsess about the condition of the fields, who is not stingy with the seed but who casts it everywhere, on good soil and bad, who is not cautious or judgmental or even very practical, but who seems willing to keep reaching into his seed bag for all eternity, covering the whole creation with the fertile seed of his truth.[7]

As Jesus said, "Let anyone with ears to hear listen!"

---

7. Taylor, *Seeds of Heaven,* 26.

31

The Stories We Become

We do not discover ourselves in myth; we make ourselves through myth.[1]

ARE WE A PROJECT or a discovery? Do we make ourselves or are we disclosed to ourselves? The question has been for me a touchstone of sorts, something I return to with intensity in liminal moments—those thresholds we cross that change how we see the trajectory of our lives.

As a college student in the seventies I was drawn to existentialism, especially the kind that Albert Camus lived out. Somehow he brought together elements of Stoicism and romanticism into a resolute philosophy of life that emphasized commitment to principle along with a sensuous enjoyment of nature. Being brought up by English grandparents in California in the sixties, in a home that was religiously devout and loyal to the church, oddly enough, paralleled that outlook and even converged at some points.

My grandfather was English, from Yorkshire, average in height, stoic in his perseverance without complaint, and quietly consistent in his gentleness and understanding. His commitments to principle were unwavering, but his ability to forgive was just as strong. God was a presence he rarely named, but he lived in gratitude for how he had been led that expressed itself in moments between us, especially as we talked while

---

1. McAdams, *Stories We Live By*, 13.

wrestling boulders out of our volcanic soil under the heat of a California sun.

Camus, on the other hand, refused God, but never managed to turn his face away completely. Since his only perception of God was that portrayed by the Church, he was inevitably disappointed. It seemed to me that he lived as if he wished God were real. He saw life as a beautiful tragedy, something that appealed to my adolescent romanticism.

But above all, he believed that we made ourselves through our decisions and actions. Life required commitment, faith in each other, a willingness to sacrifice for principle. Dr. Rieux, in Camus' novel *The Plague*, daily faced death as he worked to relieve the suffering of his patients, simply because it was the right thing to do. That sense of duty to principle is where the Adventism of my grandparents and the humanism of Camus overlapped. There was a cross-pollination that has influenced me to this day.

Because of our strong heritage from one of the founders of our church, Ellen White, most of us of a certain vintage have grown up with phrases like being "as true to duty as the needle to the pole," and "Everything depends on the right action of the will." In effect, most of us were raised as Kantians, with a strong sense of duty, manifesting a kind of "disinterested benevolence," to use another of Ellen White's maxims. We were encouraged not to trust our emotions, since they could easily be swayed, but to trust in Scripture, our spirit of prophecy, and the moral precepts we derived from both.

The idea that we "make" ourselves can go in several directions. We could think of it as a byproduct of duty, not something to be sought after, but not something to be dismissed either. Or we could choose, like Aristotle advocated, to seek a higher end or *telos,* through cultivating the virtues, a choice that we make through reason.

Yet, as Adventists, we are conflicted about trying to become virtuous. It seems presumptuous to us to imagine that we could pursue such an end, even one directed to God. It seems to emphasize works over faith, as if we might work ourselves out of the need for a savior or somewhere along the way, slough off the Holy Spirit. We want to *be* virtuous, but we don't want to look like we're trying to be. There is also a virulent strain of perfectionism in current Adventism that is curiously hostile both to virtue ethics (because it relies on philosophy) and to grace (because it's not rigorous enough). So, an understanding of how we might be nourished and strengthened by practicing the fruits of the Spirit *and* the virtues, for instance, is timely and welcome.

There is another way that we make ourselves and that is through the stories we imagine for ourselves about who we are. Dan McAdams, in his groundbreaking book *The Stories We Live By,* calls them "personal myths," and defines them as "an act of imagination that is a patterned integration of our remembered past, perceived present, and anticipated future."[2] Over the course of years, from adolescence to middle adulthood, McAdams says our personal myths should reflect increasing coherence, openness, credibility, differentiation, reconciliation, and generative integration. These six "narrative standards" are the elements of a good story in human identity, one that reflects who we are and lures us onward to what we may become.[3]

As we become more differentiated in life, we face conflicts and paradoxes. Our personal stories become richer, more textured, as we learn to cope with suffering, disappointment, and conflicts. We seek reconciliation and harmony between the conflicting elements within ourselves and between ourselves and others. Reconciliation, says McAdams, "is one of the most challenging tasks in the making of personal myth," and psychologically we're not prepared to face it until in midlife.[4]

McAdams's research is original, but in some respects roughly parallels James Fowler's *Stages of Faith*. Fowler argued that faith was a universal in human existence, and that one did not have to be "religious" in order to have faith. We look for order and patterns in the universe, and we live by what we find. He identified "faith as relating" and "faith as knowing," and it is the latter that McAdams understands as contributing to our personal myths. McAdams sees the stories we construct for ourselves as developmental stages, "qualitatively different structures of religious belief and value."[5] He separates these into four positions, A through D.

Position A understands faith as specific rules about good behavior and has only vague notions about God, nature, human identity, and so forth. While it can be authentic, there is little reflection on meaning and even less on putting one's thoughts in order. Nevertheless, it's a beginning.

---

2. McAdams, *Stories We Live By*, 12.
3. McAdams, *Stories We Live By*, 110.
4. McAdams, *Stories We Live By*, 112.
5. McAdams, *Stories We Live By*, 179.

Position B, what Fowler calls "synthetic-conventional" faith, gathers up beliefs into a systematic creed or system, whether it be provided by the Church or the scientific enterprise. These are the positions, typically, of adolescents and young adults. There is structure within a system, but little questioning, either of beliefs or of the organizing principles.

With Position C the individual moves beyond the conventions and begins to fashion a more individual and personalized faith structure. There is a questioning of the conventions of the previous position and a good deal of soul-searching. We attempt to find something that is both authentic and truly expressive of who we think we are. And when we reflect on our faith and our conventions, we may ultimately reject some and accept others—but the ones we accept will no doubt be those we reason are most honestly ours. We try to reconcile inconsistencies between our beliefs and those of other people through reason and logic. We wish the world were as reasonable as we are.

Position D, however, understands that reason is not enough. "A very small number of people," says McAdams rather wryly, "beginning probably in mid-life, reorganize their beliefs and values in order to accommodate paradox and inconsistency in life."[6] In this phase we may gain a renewed appreciation for the simple stories of faith we grew up on, while at the same time recognizing that life is more complex and multilayered than it first appears. James Fowler calls this "conjunctive faith" because it allows a person to join together ideas and images that are usually kept separate. It makes room for paradox and irony, qualities that are needed to think about the mystery of evil or the redeeming characteristics of our enemies and the darkness of our heroes. It lives with ambiguity and paradox. Some of its most articulate expressions are found in Soren Kierkegaard, Thomas Merton, and Parker Palmer.

It's what I would call "innocent experience," the quality of perception that comes after we take a fall from innocence into despair and knowledge and are forgiven and raised to a point beyond our innocence. If we're fortunate enough to belong to a community, and humble enough to recognize our constant need for honesty, then we can live with paradox and uncertainty—and press ahead with faith.

If Position C—questioning and rejecting our conventional mores and theology—is the prodigal leaving home, Position D is the prodigal returning: wiser, humbler, and armed with a no-nonsense BS detector.

---

6. McAdams, *Stories We Live By*, 183.

The prodigal leaves home innocently arrogant, crosses over into weary cynicism, and returns with the gifts of openness and empathy.

***

In the summer of 2015, after our church held its worldwide organizational gathering in San Antonio, Texas, and managed—yet again—to deny women pastors the right to be ordained, I posted the following observation on my Facebook page:

> It may be that in the post-San Antonio era, with another five years under Ted Wilson [the current President of the Seventh-day Adventist Church], many who have been Adventists all their lives, and many who may never have questioned church policy, procedures, and prejudices, will quietly realize how little they need to look to the church structure for their spiritual strength. They may see their friends, their pastors, those they have met online, their non-Adventist and non-Christian friends, as their spiritual community. They may understand that it's possible to be *in* the church, but not *of* the church, that we don't have to be hindered by unjust practices and blatant mismanagement to the extent that it blinds us to who Jesus is for us today. If we want, we can carry the invisible church within us every day. It will be exciting to see how we may grow and learn through adversity. We need to hold our fellow travelers close on this journey.

We can write a new story of faith that can make us what we are.

> Cease to dwell on days gone by
> and to brood over past history.
> Here and now I will do a new thing;
> this moment it will break from the bud.
> Can you not perceive it?[7]

---

7. Isa 43:18–19.

32

Sing, and Keep Walking

For we have not an high priest which cannot be touched with the feeling of our infirmities; but was in all points tempted like as we are, yet without sin. Let us therefore come boldly unto the throne of grace, that we may obtain mercy, and find grace to help in time of need.[1]

ONE OF THE MEMORIES that ties Protestants of a certain vintage and social class together is the revival meeting. In my religious neighborhood this was visited upon us longsuffering teenagers during our annual Week of Prayer. At our parochial elementary school or high school, a speaker, usually known as a "youth pastor" for his position in guiding the youth, would take up residence in our midst for a week to bring us to the Lord. This meant that we had chapel every day of the week, instead of our usual assembly once a week. Invariably, the last day of the week would be given over for—we were tensed for it—a call, in which the speaker would appeal to us to give our hearts to Jesus.

The organ or piano would play, the speaker would stand astride the platform, an immovable object through whom we would have to pass in order to see the sky, the light, the earth again. Our ticket, our passport to freedom, was to admit our sins and to publicly stand for Jesus, proclaiming by our verticality that we had cast aside our old life and had given ourselves over to a new attempt at sanctification. I was usually tolerant

1. Heb 4:15–16, AV.

of this, sometimes moved by it, but on one occasion I hardened my heart toward the speaker and his wiles.

For wiles they were, and he wielded them with the skill of a trained propagandist. There were the glittering generalities, the card stacking (only certain facts allowed), the plain folks approach (I'm just like you; I sin too), the testimonials (I turned my life over to Jesus and you can too), and—as the numbers of those standing inched upward—the bandwagon effect (won't you join us?). But the twin screws of fear and guilt were usually enough to break the most recalcitrant. It was *our* sins that had nailed Jesus to the cross and that kept him there—never mind the resurrection and the promise of eternal life. The sight of squirming fourteen-year-olds trying to come up with sins toxic enough to kill Christ was disheartening.

There was a point in this emotional fire-hosing when we realized that we'd left a real encounter with Christ behind and that now the speaker was running up the score, carving notches on his belt, and counting scalps. That's when I hardened my heart and prayed for release. Not wanting to offend or cause another to stumble, I was struggling to stay in my seat, and yet I knew I should not be false to my own relation to Christ. I had a tentative, but sincere, connection with God; if there remained anything standing between me and a commitment to Jesus, it would not be bulldozed aside just to give the speaker the satisfaction. So, I remained sitting, to the consternation of my teachers and some of my friends, since I occasionally assisted as a student leader in religious activities.

Fear and guilt, endemic as they are to humans, are not the best roads to paradise. I think guilt has a place in waking us up to our situation—the move is called repentance, *metanoia* in the Greek, and it means "to turn around"—but no one ever built a lasting and healthy communion with another based on fear and guilt alone.

Moreover, such tactics in the hands of a skilled and unscrupulous religious leader too easily result in counting for numbers, herding impressionable people toward a decision they barely comprehend and cannot articulate. It is enough that we see how futile our efforts to walk on water really are and that we reach out to God in Christ.

Richard Rohr has said that "Salvation is not sin perfectly avoided, as the ego would prefer; but in fact, *salvation is sin turned on its head and used in our favor* [emphasis the author's]."[2] It is in that context that we can ask what it means to say that Jesus was tempted as we are.

---

2. Rohr, *Falling Upward*, 60.

However, we derail ourselves if we insist on a detailed catalogue of the temptations that a first-century Jesus couldn't have been subjected to. How would Jesus have handled the easy access to online pornography, the money to be made in drugs, plagiarism by students in term papers, or vaping?

If we broaden the scope beyond personal temptation to include ethical dilemmas made unavoidable through advanced technology, it illustrates the fact that as a society our achievements are double-edged: they are gifts that change our environment and our values even as they benefit us. What about genetic screening for inherited diseases, surrogate pregnancies, assisted suicide and DNRs, biological and neurological enhancement, and the use of placebos in clinical testing? Science and technology in our era often outrun ethics; this is the world that we have made. So, presenting God with a list of exemptions based on our technology isn't going to help us, nor does claiming that he couldn't possibly understand what we are going through. As the Buddha said about discussions on the afterlife: "This does not lead to edification."

We are opened to a new perspective with Richmond Lattimore's translation of Hebrews 4:15–16 as he writes: "*For the high priest we have is not one who cannot sympathize with our weaknesses, since he has suffered all the trials we have, except that he did not sin.*"[3] The solidarity Jesus extends to us comes not from specific temptations faced, but from suffering the weaknesses of being human.

To be human is to live in paradox. We are made of earth but aspire to the heavens. We wish to be infinite but are bounded on all sides. We want to please those whom we love, placate those whom we fear, be admired by those we admire. We want to be the masters of our destiny, but on some days we fall and we can't get up.

> We work our jobs
> Collect our pay
> Believe we're gliding down the highway
> When in fact we're slip slidin' away[4]

We can stand apart from the path we are on in the present and ask ourselves what the trajectory of our lives points toward and where we might arrive at if we continue. No other creature can do that, and it is

---

3. Lattimore, *Acts and Letters*, 224.
4. Simon, "Slip Slidin' Away."

both the blessing and the curse of our condition that we can perceive—if only in hindsight—our misdirections, wrong turns, willful diversions from the way, and lost opportunities.

We are flesh and spirit; we are blind, but we can *see* that we are blind. We give in to the power of sin and yet we resist. "The fact that we accuse ourselves," said Paul Tillich, "proves that we still have an awareness of what we truly are, and therefore ought to be. And the fact that we excuse ourselves shows that we cannot acknowledge our estrangement from our true nature. The fact that we are ashamed shows that we still know what we ought to be."[5]

God may not snatch us out of temptation or even necessarily lessen our suffering. We may ask, then, how God is present to us in our time of trial. Christ's credentials here are not a smug "been there, done that" throwaway line. Nor does he peddle cheap grace like some ham-fisted TV evangelist. Christ lives with us in our temptations, suffers with us in our temptations, and does not abandon us when we are tempted.

Christian Wiman says in *My Bright Abyss* that "Herein lies the great difference between divine weakness and human weakness, the wounds of Christ and the wounds of man. Two human weaknesses only intensify each other. But human weakness plus Christ's weakness equals a supernatural strength."[6] And, we might add, "Let us therefore come boldly unto the throne of grace, that we may obtain mercy, and find grace to help in time of need."[7]

"Let us sing alleluia," says Augustine in a sermon from 418 CE. God doesn't say he will keep us from temptation, but "with the testing he will also provide the way out, so that you may be able to endure it."[8]

I wish I'd understood that when I chose to remain seated during that call to stand. The way it was presented to me, I was either in or out: sunk in sin and at war with Jesus or cleansed and on the right side. Somehow, instinctively, I knew that it wasn't that cut and dried. My heart's cry and my intention were to live in Christ; the reality was that this would take some time.

What I later came to realize is that Christ takes the intention of our hearts as what we really are. Living up to that intention is living within

---

5. Tillich, *Eternal Now*, 54.
6. Wiman, *My Bright Abyss*, 25.
7. Heb 4:16, AV.
8. 1 Cor 10:13.

the new being, the new reality, one day at a time. "So now, my dear brothers and sisters," concludes Augustine in his sermon, "let us sing, not to delight our leisure, but to ease our toil . . . Sing, and keep on walking. Don't stray off the road, don't go back, don't stay where you are."[9]

Sing, and keep on walking.

---

9. Augustine, *Essential Sermons*, 313.

33

Wisdom for the Contingent World

The truth is, that Jesus remains too disturbing a figure ever to be left to himself. Christianity in all its multifarious manifestations, Orthodox and heterodox, has been a repeated attempt to make sense of him, to cut him down to size . . . How oblique and how terrifying a figure he actually was in history. Terrifying, because he really does undermine everything.[1]

IT IS A REMARKABLE fact, given Christianity's two thousand years of history, that Jesus was not a Christian, nor is it at all certain that if he could walk among us in the flesh he would know what to make of what we have made of him. Like a child's bendable toy, Jesus can be made to assume almost any posture that we choose. And it has been pointed out innumerable times that what we make of Jesus says more about us than it does about him.

When we try to measure his effectiveness as a reformer in terms of how closely his followers adhere to his ideals, we have to admit that Plato, Aristotle, St. Augustine, St. Paul, Mohammed, and Darwin, Marx, and Freud have had a far greater direct influence on the human race.[2] Even so, for a figure in history whose story has nevertheless touched billions of people, it is sobering to realize how little we know of him as a man.

1. Wilson, *Jesus*, 252.
2. Wilson, *Jesus*, 253.

Millions invoke his name as a prayer or an oath and of his image there is no lack in art, music, drama, poetry, and scholarship. Bumper stickers proclaim him, from the testy "Do you follow Jesus this close?" to the smug "Jesus Christ is the answer" to the cloying "Jesus is not a Republican or a Democrat. His party is the Kingdom of God."

A. N. Wilson's book *Jesus: A Life,* quoted above, attempts to grapple with the powerful story of Jesus (Wilson calls it a "myth"), a story that cannot be fully contained by the factuality of history, but spills over in narrative and imagination. Wilson, who read history at Oxford as an undergraduate, cannot shake off his fascination with Jesus and Christianity, despite his skepticism about the divinity of Christ. He sees Jesus as ultimately a tragic figure whose attraction for us is unparalleled, and who was a Jew who only longed for faithfulness in following God. Our encounter with his story, says Wilson, arises from a careful reading of the Gospels, while knowing that they are not biographies nor are they historical accounts as we understand them.

Jesus did not fit neatly into the various strands of Jewish life and thought of his time. He was raised in Galilee, traditionally a hotbed of revolutionary activity, and included among his friends Simon the Zealot (read terrorist), a tax collector, professional fishermen, several women, and various members of the priestly ruling class. Swirling around him during that time were Pharisees, Sadducees, Samaritans, followers of John the Baptist, zealots, and the thousands of simple, often desperate common folk. He was accused of loving his food and wine too much and of flouting the rules about Sabbath. All of this made him suspect in the eyes of the religious authorities. Yet, in the last week of his life he has dinner at the home of a prominent Pharisee and another one, Nicodemus, comes to him at night to speak with him directly.

To be a Jew in his time was not to belong to a religion set apart from political life, but to be suspended in a web of religious, historical, and cultural threads that composed a whole life. Jesus cuts across all these threads in his own way, and yet somehow appeals to people of all classes.

Greg Riley, in *One Jesus, Many Christs,* says, "People, apparently, did not follow Jesus for his words. For all the attention given in the modern era to the sayings of the historical Jesus, his precise words seem hardly to have mattered at all."[3] Yet for us, the Gospels are stories *about* Jesus with claims to be the teachings *of* Jesus. Each Gospel writer has reshaped

---

3. Riley, *One Jesus, Many Christs,* 17.

the oral traditions of Jesus' sayings and each one views Jesus from a particular perspective. Their time lines of events in Jesus' life differ—for different reasons—and they transpose his sayings into contexts that vary considerably.

But there are enough details here and there that could not be anything but authentic because they are too specific, too unusual, too unique to be a literary fiction. The Gospel writers were not writing history, but neither were they writing fiction.

"A culture tells its members stories that embody its ideals and reinforce social norms and goals," says Riley. "We in the modern world tell ourselves consciously or unconsciously a story of success, the Horatio Alger story, that no matter what our circumstances, if we work hard and try our honest best, we will eventually climb the social ladder to wealth and status."[4]

There could hardly be a more definitive contrast to the lives people lived in the Greco-Roman world of the first Christians. Most people's lives were short, subject to sudden reversals of fortune, prone to disease, and frozen in social structures that defied mobility or change. They looked to heroes, people whose physical attributes of beauty and strength and their exploits in war to win glory and honor blurred the lines between the gods and humans. For us, Jesus was neither a conventional success nor was he close to being a hero, save in the bravery he exhibited in going to the cross. Nevertheless, for many in the first century after Christ there were cultural templates in place to regard him as just such a hero type.

Flannery O'Connor's novel *Wise Blood* gives us Hazel Motes, the God-haunted preacher who "saw Jesus move from tree to tree in the back of his mind, a wild ragged figure motioning him to turn around and come off into the dark . . ."[5] I find myself drawn to that figure too, the enigmatic Jesus who rejoices because God has hidden "these things from the wise and the intelligent and have revealed them to infants."[6]

So, who is Jesus for us? Who do *we* say Jesus is?

---

4. Riley, *One Jesus, Many Christs*, 15.
5. O'Connor, *Wise Blood*, 2.
6. Luke 10:21.

***

Jesus' presence in my mind is like a low murmur rising at times to unspoken prayer, and then slipping back into images, questions, and memories. Every now and then I take out a book of art about Jesus, images of him in painting, sculpture, and drawing. There are Black Christs, Korean Christs, Native American, Spanish, Russian, Samoan, and Filipino Christs—and many more besides. It is a visual conversation, a congress of voices that raise in praise of Christ as the embodiment of us all, God incarnate.

I grew up with Harry Anderson's paintings, which adorned pamphlets, churches, and memory verse cards. Jesus is invariably depicted as a tall White man in robes, standing amongst a rainbow of little children, a kindly expression on his face. Later, in the sixties, as Jesus was seen as part of the counterculture, other artists depicted him as a healthy and vigorous young man, hair tousled and face sweaty, more a rock star than a man of sorrows.

Through graduate school, Jesus was an object to be studied from all angles, a being whose main effect was to stimulate several centuries of scholarship, but whose inner light and expression receded behind waves of theories and contending ideas. I didn't lose sight of him in those days, but there was distance between us.

Jürgen Moltmann's *The Crucified God*, Gustavo Gutierrez's *A Theology of Liberation,* and Segundo Galilea's *Following Jesus* swept away my unconscious assumptions of a middle-class and respectable Jesus. Their combined shockwave cleared my horizon about how and why he died and spun me around to face systemic evil and suffering.

Then, as I began teaching *Jesus and the Gospels* to first-year students, their questions forced a pause. How could Jesus help with school loans? Did he ever have an older brother who suffered through addictions? What if he had brought home a girlfriend his parents didn't like? What if Pilate had set him free? Would he still have had to die? Gradually, we began to realize the obvious: that Jesus spoke in story rather than in precept and that the exercise of our imaginations is what would best open those stories to us.

Without question, there was much we could learn about his times from archeology and history, and there was a wealth of information about the formation of the Gospels. We could reason our way through competing theories about the worldview of the Gospel writers, but we could not see how radical Jesus was unless we let him lead us back to the root, the *radix* of God's searing justice and love. "If you've seen me, you've seen the Father," Jesus said. Together, we tried to imagine how that would change our lives.

If we are reading the Gospels to understand *and* to feel, we will sense how terrifying Jesus is, how disruptive to those who would attempt to contain him in a system. "Neither do I tell you by what authority I do these things." As A. N. Wilson says with only slight exaggeration, "A patient and conscientious reading of the Gospels will always destroy any explanation we devise. If it makes sense it is wrong."[7]

Life is uncertain, a truth that may seem to some perplexing, if not heretical. What makes Christianity real for me right now is the humanity of God in Jesus, the total commitment to seeing the contingency of this world from the ground level. The pain, the weariness, the flashes of anger as well as the quick compassion, all of that is there in Jesus. His constant deflection ("Why do you call me good? Only God is good."), his humor, irony, and hyperbole ("If you have faith the size of a mustard seed, you will say to this mountain, 'Move!'"), and his sense of proportion ("The Sabbath was made for man, not man for the Sabbath.")— these things speak of God's deep plunge into his creation.

In Jesus' very helplessness we see our own pain and fear writ large: *"My God, my God, why hast thou forsaken me?"* In Jesus' last words from the cross, *"Father, into your hands I commend my spirit,"* we need not hear desolation and resignation. Through imagination and faith, they may become our daily thanksgiving for God's sustaining love. Such is the wisdom of the infants.

---

7. Wilson, *Jesus*, 252.

34

In Wildness the World Preserved

I am the lover of uncontained and immortal beauty. In the wilderness, I find something more dear and connate than in streets or villages. In the tranquil landscape, and especially in the distant line of the horizon, man beholds somewhat as beautiful as his own nature.[1]

WE CAN DIVIDE THE world and everything in it into two great piles: that which was created or evolved—it doesn't really matter which at this point—and that which was engineered. The two are threaded together in innumerable ways and cannot be extricated except by the imagination. Yet when we look at the world, we see the "natural" and the human constructs. Concrete, oil, broken glass glinting in the sun, heat radiating off the pavement, a guard rail twisted, two parallel prints where tires bit deeply and then abruptly lifted off—elements we glimpse as we churn by at sixty miles per hour. All this is happening on the skin of the earth as it suffers our constant abrasions.

I sometimes try to imagine what these forests and low hills of Maryland must have looked like two hundred, five hundred, one thousand years ago. We are not far from one of the oldest ranges of mountains in North America, the Appalachians, worn down through the millennia to a gentle slope, lying patient as a cat in the sun, and dropping roughly northeast to northwest through the Mid-Atlantic states. Even traversing

---

1. Emerson, *Selected Essays*, 39.

the landscape atop six inches of tarmac, aggregate, sand, and bedrock, one can sense the vast body of the earth, breathing quietly, flexing now and then, the deep silence of its presence there beneath the furious assault of midday traffic.

By some counts we are losing a species every twenty minutes of every day of every year, year in and year out. But how would we know, encased within our tin boxes on wheels, speaker systems thumping with the imprecations of the latest urban prophet of conspicuous consumption?

These particles of information arrive quietly through the research of scientists who pick their way through the Amazon, scour the Outback, jounce over dusty trails in the Southwest, and hover over the Great Barrier Reef. Occasionally, the tip of a message surfaces in the media tide pools to the effect that scientists speculate we have, at best, a decade or slightly more to turn the effects of global warming around. And then the local anchor will chirp brightly, "So, Candy, what kind of weather have you got for us today?" Candy, just back from the ritual hazing of new weatherpersons during hurricane season, assures us that tomorrow we'll be done with all this awful rain and that she's doing her best to gift us with sunshine. But these days scientists must pitch their findings in six words or less, the bulk of their work submerged under the surface of our collective skittishness.

I used to think that if people could just put their stuff down, stop their twitching and gyrating, and just stand silently in the midst of a forest for a few minutes, they'd be blessed into awe and wonder. But for many nature is an acquired taste and one that they have little patience to savor. We get our minimum daily adult requirement of ecology from advertising these days, corporations having learned the value of "going green" to increase the net return on investment.

As a teenager, growing up in the foothills above the Napa Valley in Northern California, I roamed the woods with my friends on the weekends. We came across a simple tragedy one winter Saturday, as we jumped from rock to rock across a foaming creek. A doe had broken a leg as she tried to cross and had apparently drowned in a pool near the base of a waterfall. We approached cautiously, thinking she might be alive and not wanting to alarm her. But the body was cold, the eyes blank. We hauled her beyond the rocks to an open space under the dripping trees, and it was then that we discovered she was swollen with pregnancy. We could see the outlines of the fawn in her belly. We decided to open her up. With a hunting knife, we carefully slit her from sternum to hindquarters, and there it was: a tiny fawn, perfectly preserved, hooves white and soft like almonds, its long lashes plastered wetly, its fur dappled with patches of white. We gazed at it in silence, feeling perhaps, amidst the thunder of the creek waters and the fog between the trees, that mysteries were there for the seeing.

There was little sentimentality about it; we buried the doe in a shallow grave and covered the spot with branches. We carried the fawn through the woods, clambered up the cliffs above the creek, and eventually found our way to our high school biology teacher's house. He came out at our knock and listened patiently as we excitedly told him the story. Then together we found a box, placed the stiff little body in it, and dug a grave in his backyard. The man never blinked. I think he felt that what we'd learned that afternoon was deeper than anything he might have said in the classroom.

When I look back on it now two things stand out in reflection. One is the utter physicality of the moment: the weight and denseness of the doe's body, the graceful arch of the fawn's neck, those tiny hooves not yet hardened and black. There was the story of a life on our sweet, old earth, a moment's wavering on a slippery rock, a crack of pain and a brief struggle alone in the forest. The fragility of our existence, any existence, magnified through the lens of adolescent wonder.

And the other thing, as fresh now as it was then, is the steady realization that this other world, the one that pulses just out of sight, is, for now, our true home.

35

Abundance in the Midst of Plenty

I am come that they might have life, and that they might have it more abundantly.[1]

I confess that I do not know what this means, but it has been a text that I have read with a mixture of hope and skepticism. The skepticism arises from living in a material world that consistently promises more than it can deliver; in fact, more than it contains. The hope arises because, whatever it means, it's a pretty good bet that it has little, if anything, to do with material things.

In the Greek text of John's Gospel, the word for "abundantly" is *perissos,* from *peri,* which means "above" or "beyond." It has about it the connotations of excessive, extraordinary, remarkable, extravagant. Perhaps today we would say "over the top."

But the intriguing thing about this text is how our interest rises upon reading it—and then how we sprawl, puzzled and rubbing our heads where we bumped them on the low ceiling of our expectations. In a culture as resolutely acquisitive as ours, where everything has an instrumental worth in the pursuit of happiness, a quick default reading of this for a lot of us will no doubt mean that abundant life means abundant wealth.

The operating manual for life in an upwardly mobile society has been written by advertising and marketing firms. We are trained from an

1. John 10:10, KJV.

early age to see a direct line from desires to goods to possessions to happiness. Many thousands of people bend the resources of their minds and energies to create the shortest possible distance for us between desire and happiness. But it's the stuff in the middle—goods and possessions—that derails the end product of happiness.

The very idea that happiness is the expected *product* of desire fulfilled has been a philosophical question for as long as people cared to reflect on their inner lives. Aristotle devoted most of the *Nicomachean Ethics* to it, to what he called *eudaimonia,* usually translated "happiness" but more closely thought of as "flourishing." A life of virtue resulting from seeking and practicing that which would fulfill one's calling to be fully human was Aristotle's aim. The Epicureans, wholly misunderstood as hedonistic party animals, taught that a simple life of tilling one's garden in the country and living minimally was the best route to satisfaction. Epictetus and the Stoics thought that our attitude toward the rough-and-tumble of life determined our happiness. There has been no shortage of advice, devices, and methods for achieving happiness, through wealth or other means.

But this is not what Jesus is talking about with his above-and-beyond abundance of life.

This short text is embedded in a longer passage about sheep, gates, sheepfolds, thieves, predators, bad shepherds, and a good shepherd.[2] There is no mention of money or wealth. There is plenty of talk about true voices and the laying down of a person's life.

The passage begins with a warning: everyone who climbs over the wall into the sheepfold is a thief and a bandit. Only the shepherd goes in through the gate. Once in, he calls out the sheep and they follow him because they know his voice. They don't know the voices of strangers and they won't follow a voice they don't know.

Jesus tries out this parable on some Pharisees nearby, but they don't get it. Barbara Brown Taylor has observed that Jesus' parables are less like explanations and more like dreams or poems. They are derived from ordinary things, small moments, "illustrations of some truth that seems clear . . . one moment and hidden the next."[3] Their meanings are elastic, expanding to fit the time and culture in which they are read and heard. In her collection of sermons from the Gospel of Matthew, *The Seeds of Heaven,* Taylor says, "By speaking in parables, Jesus could get his message

---

2. John 10:1–18.
3. Taylor, *Seeds of Heaven*, 24.

across without saying it directly, so that his followers nodded and smiled while his critics scratched their bewildered heads."[4]

So, he tries again, this time making it personal and explicit. "I am the gate for the sheep," he says. Everyone else who tries to get into the sheepfold without going through the gate is a thief and a bandit, and the sheep won't listen to them. Just in case they still didn't get it, Jesus repeats himself: "I am the gate," he says, unequivocally. Me, right here in front of you. "Whoever enters by me will be saved and will come in and go out and find pasture."

There are many people who would like access to all those sheep. They come dressed in shepherd's clothes; they might even carry a staff. They wouldn't bother to pick off one or two here or there: they would want the whole flock. They want the whole flock, because the bigger the flock, the greater their status.

The first thing this parable teaches us, then, is that if you want to lead the sheep you've got to go through Jesus to get to them. No climbing over the wall or tunneling under or breaking in or removing the gate. Those who do so are thieves, bandits, and predators who come to break and destroy. They are not shepherds.

This may include those who came to the sheepfold with the best of intentions, but who found entering by the gate to be an obstacle and an impediment. They are impatient to play the shepherd, to lead a large flock, to call the sheep and watch them come running. They talk at length about their sacrifices, shed tears about the cost of upkeep, proclaim themselves humbled by how awesome they are, and congratulate the sheep on having a shepherd who truly, deeply, cares. Then they go around the back and try to climb over the wall.

If you're a hired hand—one who came in through the gate and not over the wall— it's going to take some time for the sheep to get to know your voice. Hired hands are usually there for the season and then gone; it takes time to build trust, even with sheep. Hirelings must have been known for their unreliability or the mention of one would not have evoked knowing nods and grins. If the hireling does not have the trust of the sheep, he must harass and coerce them into moving where he wants them to go. They are listening for the voice of the master. If they do not hear it, they will not be compliant.

---

4. Taylor, *Seeds of Heaven*, 24.

The sheep in this story are not easily fooled. They know the master's voice and they will not follow just anybody. Here is definitive proof that in this regard sheep are smarter than people. But if the sheep know and love and trust the shepherd, they'll move because they want to be with the shepherd. Love and trust over fear and coercion.

When *we* see Jesus holding a lamb in his arms in countless stained-glass windows, there's a Teflon factor working on us. We register the image: Jesus, tall and stately, a lamb nestling in his arms, safety at hand—it's a smooth and impervious surface, rather sweet and sentimental, truth be told, and ultimately forgettable. What we don't see on the surface, but what Jesus' listeners would have understood instinctively, is how the shepherd is a leader, someone with authority as well as interest, with power as well as love.

In a dry and lean land, with scarce resources and danger afoot, the analogy of a shepherd protecting the sheep is common sense, part of the fabric of one's life. A shepherd, a *good* shepherd, stays and fights for the sheep, even at risk to his life. The Good Shepherd not only has an interest in protecting his investment, but far more consequentially, he loves the sheep and they love him. The Good Shepherd is good not because he leads the sheep—even the hireling is expected to do that—but because he'll lay down his life for the sheep.

We are so far removed from sheep and shepherds that what was common and core to everyday life back then is for us a quaint and awkward symbol. We don't think of ourselves as sheep, passively following someone over hill and dale. We are moral agents in charge of our own destinies. Moreover, if we *did* belong to a particular sheepfold it's because we chose to and we could just as easily unchoose. We might even remove ourselves to another sheepfold or just go off over the hills.

We do not see that this is about life and death.

In an atomized society such as ours, with our comparative wealth and ease, we may not find the comparison to sheep persuasive. It might even be offensive. It certainly offended the Pharisees. This is an encounter in which Jesus makes claims that are bold even for him.

"I know my sheep," he says, "and they know me, just like I know the Father and the Father knows me." Could there be a stronger bond? And then he ups the ante. "I have other sheep that do not belong to this field. I must bring them also, and they will listen to my voice. So there will be one flock, one shepherd."

And here is where the light sweeping across a verdant field darkens and those who hear his voice pause with caught breath as he says, "I lay down my life in order to take it up again. No one takes it from me, but I lay it down of my own accord. I have power to lay it down, and I have power to take it up again." It is a taunt against the powers that be, the ones that break in and steal and destroy, the ones who will strangle the breath out of the voice that calls to the sheep.

If there is life it is because of the Shepherd, and if we have abundant life—extravagant, pressed-down-and-running-over life, life that cannot be crushed by death—it will be so because we heard the voice and followed the one we love.

36

Outrage and Longing

The desire to surpass our limits is as essential to the structure of the human as the recognition that we cannot.[1]

TO LIVE WITH INTEGRITY these days is to live inside the conflict between outrage and longing. But, if we become practiced in the art of paradoxical living, we will see that dancing on the high wire between these two towers may be our best chance for grace-filled living.

"If we were God," says philosopher Susan Neiman, "we could change moral principles into sovereign law. Were God Himself to enact such a law, moral principles would lose all connection with freedom."[2]

And there's the rub. Being made "a little lower than the angels," in the quaint phrasing of the King James Bible, means we are beings who desire wholeness; the state of *being made* means that we will never experience that. We live within the limitations—and the grandeur—of moral freedom in which the desire for the reign of goodness sometimes overrides the understanding that goodness flourishes only where it is wanted, gifted, and received. As Neiman points out, magically changing moral principles into law, even if done by God, would jinx the whole thing because freedom means there is a genuine choice to be made. Making those choices every day is the burden of freedom and the brightness of being

---

1. Neiman, *Evil in Modern Thought*, 80.
2. Neiman, *Evil in Modern Thought*, 79.

human in the image of God. Moral freedom is a form of creativity, available to all of us.

Rollo May, one of the pioneers of existential psychotherapy, quotes Rainer Rilke on withdrawing from psychotherapy: "If my devils are to leave me, I am afraid my angels will take flight as well."[3]

Rilke knew that creativity for the artist surges up from the depths, a necessary fire in the mind and heart. Rollo May puts creativity and evil in the same room. Creativity, he muses, comes from the rage within us against death and destruction.

If we are made in the image of God and that image in us is the power to create, then how could evil threaten creativity? God, as creator, never creates for destruction because all God's work is created for life. When *we* create—and we do—our sense of direction is not inerrant. We create in all directions, some of them winding off to evil and all of them subject to losing their way.

But creative power, moral or artistic, is no guarantee against a certain perversity. Put up a sign for "Wet Paint" and see how long it takes for fingerprints to appear. What would happen, we think, if we did this, this thing we've been warned never to do? Let's try it—just to see what would happen. If it's awful, we'll know, and we'll never do it again. And off we go. And we find that this evil, now loosed in the world, arrives without a warning label, with no expiration date, and without operating instructions. The terrible truth about creative work is that it can be turned to destruction and that there are always some who will do that just for the hell of it.

One of the ways our outrage can lead our moral creativity astray is to imagine that God resents our natural powers and is suspicious of our freedom. Thomas Merton calls this "Promethean theology" and comments in *The New Man* that "This means that man must either save his soul by a Promethean *tour de force,* without God's help, or else that man must turn his freedom inside out, stew up all his natural gifts into a beautiful guilt-complex, and crawl towards God on his stomach to offer Him the results in propitiation."[4] But this is to deeply misjudge God's love and the grace that is ours.

We are not worms. Our moral and spiritual freedom before God raises us to our feet, lifts our sights, and erases the false image of God we

---

3. May, *Love and Will*, 121.
4. Merton, *New Man*, 41.

conjure up. "Grace," says Merton, "is given us for the precise purpose of enabling us to discover and actualize our deepest and truest self."[5]

"The fantasy of replacing God is the test by which morality itself is decided," says Neiman.[6] To imagine, with longing, a better world is the flip side of outrage at the present one. It's the outrage that compels us to imagine a newer world; it's the longing that endures when we admit that our best efforts will probably not outlast us. But the visioning of such a world, even with all our limitations out at the edges of our sightlines, gives us the energy of hope.

Neiman opens the windows and runs up the shades: "Integrity requires affirming the dissonance and conflict at the heart of experience," she writes. "It means recognizing that we are never, metaphysically, at home in the world. This affirmation requires us to live with the mixture of longing and outrage that few will want to bear."[7]

Reaching beyond our expectations is part of our human destiny; falling short is our fate. We are threading our way between hubris and humiliation. There is another way, but it's much more difficult. This is where faith rides the rails to keep us safe. We need the reach to go beyond, but patience, humility, and good humor helps in knowing that we can do so without trying to usurp God or having to crawl before him.

Another take on this is from Reinhold Niebuhr's *Beyond Tragedy* when he writes, "The church is that place in human society where men are disturbed by the word of the eternal God, which stands as a judgment upon human aspirations. But it is also the place where the word of mercy, reconciliation and consolation is heard: 'Thou dost well that it was in thine heart.' Here human incompleteness is transcended though not abolished. Here human sin is overcome by the divine mercy, though man remains a sinner."[8]

Outrage and longing is not about winners and losers; it's about "Those who endure to the end . . ." *We're* not required to win; we're invited to travel with "that great cloud" of large-souled ones who have borne their witness before us in all times and all places. If hope means anything and if love lives up to its reputation, a time will come when justice and mercy will be the way in the great day of the Lord.

---

5. Merton, *New Man*, 43.
6. Neiman, *Evil in Modern Thought*, 79.
7. Neiman, *Evil in Modern Thought*, 80.
8. Niebuhr, *Beyond Tragedy*, 62.

It makes no sense to set a date and expect the arc of justice to touch down in that precise moment. We don't set the clocks or even wind them up. They were running before we got here and will continue after we're dead. But it does matter to regard our time and how we spend the little of it that we have.

Our outrage alone will not save this sorry, stubborn, strange, and beautiful world; according to our primal myth that has been done in hope already. So, there's no need for us to presume that we are the hinge of history the universe didn't know it was looking for. Nor will longing alone be enough. We need them both: the push of outrage to change our world, the pull of longing to heal our restless souls.

Yet, we each have a part to play—perhaps several parts. That much is clear. *How* we play it is the question, and for that we need patience for ourselves and each other.

If we have a conscience and compassion our outrage can propel us beyond our reticence. If we also live with longing our limits will be no barrier to God's healing and sustaining grace.

37

The Mystery of Iniquity

Recognizing reality and demanding to change it are fundamentally different activities. Both wisdom and virtue depend on keeping them separate, but all our hopes are directed to joining them.[1]

IN A RELATIVISTIC WORLD, a murder mystery in the hands of a master writer can be a sword, rightly dividing hypocrisy from truth. The mystery writer is also a problem-solver and a moral arbiter; the pleasure for the reader is in the careful twining of many threads to make a coat of justice.

James Lee Burke, author of thirty novels and two collections of short stories, is a master of the genre—indeed, he was named a Grandmaster by the Mystery Writers of America in 2009 and has twice won their Crime Novel of the Year.

Dave Robicheaux, former cop for the New Orleans Police Department, a dry alcoholic and a police detective in Iberia Parish, is one of Burke's most compelling literary creations. Robicheaux, a Vietnam War vet and a lifelong resident of coastal Louisiana, has no qualms about calling out the evil ones in our midst.

In Robicheaux's cultural hierarchy the small-time hoods and grifters make up the lowest level. They are the bottom-feeders, those desperate enough to attach themselves to powerful and twisted people whose need for distance and deniability make them almost invulnerable. Robicheaux

---

1. Neiman, *Evil in Modern Thought*, 61.

is not without sympathy for these figures whose lives are steeped in violence and despair. It's a measure of Burke's vision and compassion that he gives them a solid dignity in the midst of every trigger pulled or fist cocked. As for the rich, morally bent, and self-righteous, Robicheaux finds them, binds them to the case, and pulls the threads together.

Reading Burke at his best is like swallowing nails dipped in chocolate. On the one hand, he's a word painter who can put you in a late-summer electrical storm along the bayou in a flash. In the next moment, violence erupts as inevitably as lightning. Robicheaux believes in evil because he has seen it in the eyes of the wealthiest, the most powerful, and often the most revered in his society. What truly distinguishes these people from their small-time counterparts is the level of self-deception they are capable of maintaining. While they believe themselves to be virtuous, natural-born citizens of the elite, educated, and genteel, their feral nature is only a few insults from the surface. In those moments Burke's prose reveals the skull beneath the skin. It's like walking in a thoughtful daze through a gallery of impressionist paintings and rounding a corner to find George Bellow's paintings of bare-knuckled and bloodied fighters surrounded by dissolute ghouls.

But Robicheaux—and Burke—live in a universe that is tragically evil; that is, those who are marked as evil may have chosen their actions but were acting on compulsions beyond their control. Through a long apprenticeship in deceit and denial, they now look back in anger to see how far from their innocence they have come. There was no moment in which they stepped across a threshold into evil, but they are undeniably in that far country now.

Perhaps the one thing, besides shock and grief, that unites us in the face of an unspeakable tragedy, like the shooting of concertgoers in Las Vegas, is that we search for a reason Why? We look for trace elements of aggression in the killer's childhood, we mine the memories of his neighbors, we sift the impressions of doctors, teachers, relatives—anyone who might be able to put the mark of Cain on his forehead with some degree of certainty. Psychologists and pundits stack up the similarities in the profiles of mass murderers and we all look for patterns. This is natural and commendable, as difficult as it is for determining cause. But if society does not care enough to search for answers in the face of such tragedies, then we are truly at a moral tipping point. Outrage is a sign of conscience: the lack of it may be the first symptom of moral paralysis.

The moral philosophers of the Enlightenment separated natural evil from moral evil. Tsunamis, wildfires, hurricanes, avalanches had all been thought to issue from the hand of God as punishment for sin. But Rousseau took the evil out of natural evil by thinking of them as simply nature following the laws of God. What mattered more was the "evil that men do," and especially so since we are beings endowed with reason. Why do we do evil, then? It makes no sense from a rational standpoint, so we have to seek an explanation elsewhere. Broadly speaking, Rousseau located the cause of evil in the subversion of the individual by society. Kant saw moral evil arising from our denial of our autonomy and our moral duty.

Rousseau thought the key to moral improvement was education. He spent much of his time trying to work out a social contract between the individual and society. Most problems, he thought, could be negotiated by reasonable people working together. One result of this was the decreasing role of God in human affairs. In her rewriting of the history of philosophy in *Evil in Modern Thought*, Susan Neiman says, "The more responsibility for evil accrues to the human, the less belongs to the divine."[2]

This resistance of nature that we see and experience, says Neiman, is not the work of angry gods "but simply part of the arbitrary stuff of the universe."[3] They are part of living with limits. Finitude isn't a punishment, it's simply part of our structural framework. As Neiman so succinctly puts it, "We have purposes; the world does not."[4]

So, the problem of evil became irresolvable. The way Kant figured it, the problem of evil was that we are dissatisfied with the difference between the way things are and the way they should be. The first is the realm of nature, the second of reason. "Happiness depends on events in the natural world,"[5] comments Neiman, and virtue depends on us exercising our reason. We can't control much in nature—and that includes our happiness—but we may have more control in the realm of virtue driven by reason. "The one [reason] is a matter of what ought to be; the other [nature] is a matter of what is."[6] For Kant, what was most important was distinguishing between the two. "Recognizing reality and demanding to change it are fundamentally different activities. Both wisdom and virtue

---

2. Neiman, *Evil in Modern Thought*, 57.
3. Neiman, *Evil in Modern Thought*, 60.
4. Neiman, *Evil in Modern Thought*, 60.
5. Neiman, *Evil in Modern Thought*, 60–61.
6. Neiman, *Evil in Modern Thought*, 61.

depend on keeping them separate, but all our hopes are directed to joining them."[7]

Or as the Rolling Stones said, "You can't always get what you want, but if you try sometimes, you get what you need."

Kant would agree. The gap between the is—the way things are—and the ought—the way things should be—will never be entirely bridged. But we've got to try: our dignity as humans and our hopes for this world demand it.

Such tragedies as the San Bernardino shooting, the Charleston killings, and the massacres at Las Vegas and Sutherland Springs demand a rational explanation. We struggle to find one and if we can't find a common pattern or a series of movements we despair, because above all else we want to live in a rational universe. We shudder to think—and we dare not say—that there may not be a rational explanation for these people running amok. If that is true, then we are faced with the fact that without a clear cause these events cannot be predicted nor can they be prevented. And the tragic result of that is a fortress mentality and officially sponsored societal paranoia.

Social psychologists and psychiatrists hope to find a cause someday that will explain—as fully and as clearly as possible—why these killings occur. They will continue to gather evidence, try out theories, hope to understand. But we must also realize, as Kant so brilliantly works it out and as most scriptures testify, that we humans are limited, finite, broken, and fractured. This is not a cause for despair, said Kant, but rather simply the way things are. We can do better, and we should try, even while realizing that all our efforts will fall short of perfection. For Christians, this means we live under sin while sustained by grace. Resistance to evil, says Scripture, is not futile.

And the worth of our striving can be measured by the degree to which we act with compassion toward those who are suffering and wisdom toward those who bring the suffering.

---

7. Neiman, *Evil in Modern Thought*, 61.

38

Consider the Lilies

Freedom comes from understanding the limits of our own power and the natural limits set in place by divine providence.[1]

"Consider the lilies," says Jesus.

Is it a demand, like "Go and learn what this means, 'I desire mercy, not sacrifice'"? Or is it an invitation like that extended to Matthew, who, as a taxman, was sitting in his booth collecting the blood money from his people to be handed over to the occupying Roman force?

Jesus is walking along, says the scripture, and he sees Matthew in his little booth, like those photo booths you'd see in parking lots of grocery stores, not even as big as a restroom at a Sunoco station, and he just says, "Follow me," and "he got up and followed him," says the Gospel according to Matthew (no relation).

This invitation comes to Matthew as something of a command, for how else to explain leaving a job in which the money is made so easily (the size of the booth notwithstanding), just a matter of slipping an extra 10 percent on the standard tax so the empire gets its money, you get your slice (in addition to your paltry salary), and everyone is happy—well, everyone with the exception of your people, who await with dread and resentment the next shakedown at your command. If you didn't mind being a pariah and knowing that every face turned toward you was either

---

1. Epictetus, *Art of Living*, 20.

coldly indifferent or seething, then the job had its advantages. A pariah you might be, but a rich pariah you were, and that almost made up for being alone.

The lilies, then.

"They toil not, neither do they spin."

***

Our work, what we do for most of the life we have, how do we see it? Is it a command or an invitation? Were we sitting in the little booths of our adolescence, bored and avaricious, waiting for a summons that only we would know when we heard it? Did we think the summons would be dispersed in general to everyone like us around us or that it would single us out—we alone—lifted up out of the ordinary on the strength of a talent long buried like a bone in the garden, a talent perhaps, that we had ourselves buried for shame for even imagining it was our talent?

Or did we back into the spot, the one available at the time, that would become our place for so long that the weeds would grow up around the tires and the seasons wear down the frame as it settled?

Our self-image, like a Polaroid snapshot, emerges gradually from black to gray to color as we phase through our work life.

We imagine ourselves to be vaulting over all obstacles, achieving that which others have despaired of reaching, or bending down kindly to raise up those behind us who are slipping on the rungs of achievement. Suddenly there is no one ahead of us, the field is clear, we have been called to lead! We turn with an encouraging shout, only to find that the others, leaders and followers, have calmly dropped back. They regard us from a distance with pitying looks. We are alone.

We do not recognize the person we are until we see ourselves at work in the vocation we believe ourselves to be called to. Then we wonder if the gap between perception and vision can be bridged. We give ourselves to the work, glancing to the side at colleagues and up ahead at those who beckon—they make it look so effortless. We feel like imposters. It is in those moments that a fundamental truth is revealed to us: we have entered a conversation that precedes us by thousands of years and will continue after we cease to speak. It is possible that by listening we may learn and by speaking we may remember what we have learned. In speaking our own minds, we may find that we have also spoken what others have thought but could not say. With Emerson, we may be like the one who is "happy enough if he can satisfy himself alone that this day he has seen something truly."[2]

***

Matthew followed Jesus, seemingly without hesitation. Was it a relief to shuck off the taxman's cloak? He gave up routine, the comforting groove of repetition, for day-to-day dislocation and the tingle of the unknown. In a moment he jackknifed himself from solitude into a band of brothers, discarding ambition like a fraying belt and making no plans beyond the setting of the sun. What his former life had been was the mention of some nudges and terse comments at first, but then that arc of his life evaporated and was gone. Filled with a strange elation, he fell into the rhythm of the days, feeling his stride lengthen and his horizons widen. What was he now? The first time someone asked, "Where is your master?" he almost laughed before he realized that he had become a disciple, a follower.

"The loneliest people above all contribute most to commonality," said Rilke. "The individual who could hear the entire melody would be at once the loneliest and the most common."[3]

Strangely, what Jesus offered was a hallowedness that made every action seem both familiar and sacral. There was an inwardness about him that lingered even when he smiled. Matthew found it compelling, a sense that even as Jesus was among them, sharing meals and stories and the hard ground under the stars, he was yet just beyond their reach.

His intensity was infectious, if exhausting. "I came to bring fire to the earth, and how I wish it were already kindled!" he cried out. He acted like a man whose life was converging with a future that was accelerating toward him at the speed of light.

The next day they were moving through a springtime field awash with flowers, heading north following the line of hills to the west. "Consider the lilies," he said, trailing a hand through the blossoms as they walked. "They neither toil nor spin." They didn't *need* to toil to justify their short time on this earth. They simply were: they were their own reason for existing. As brief as their lives were, he said, God took care of

---

2. Emerson, *Essential Writings*, 53.
3. Rilke, *Letters on Life*, 84.

them. Wouldn't he do the same and more for you? God knows what you need.

That night he said to them, "Strive first for the kingdom of God and his righteousness. Don't worry about tomorrow." He looked round at them, quizzical faces turned up in the firelight. "Tomorrow will bring worries of its own. Today's trouble is enough for today."

And now Matthew *is* considering the lilies, even as he turns over all that Jesus has said. He thinks about those for whom life is one hardscrabble decision after another, those who could never imagine that the story provides an excuse for blithe idleness. For them, subsistence is necessity and tomorrow is never guaranteed. For them, faith is all the guarantee they will get—and all they will need.

He decides it is an invitation: "Consider the lilies!"

39

Rooted Sideways

Strictly speaking it is incorrect to say that the single individual thinks. Rather it is more correct to insist that he participates in thinking further what other men have thought before him.[1]

ONE CAN LOOK AT this in both positive and negative lights. Negatively, we'll never have an original thought. Everything we think and wrestle with is contingent and formed from time immemorial before us. We may rearrange the words, and thus arrive at some new shadings or nuances, but essentially everything has been thought of before. More ominously, these patterns that we inherit may be racist and sexist, prejudiced to the core, modes of thinking and acting that appear normal unless they are countered by different patterns.

Positively, we are connected with our past and with everything that has been expressed before. And that means, in like manner, we may continue to have an influence on those who come after us, who read what we write and think about what we have said. This is an argument for choosing our formative societies wisely or, more realistically, for experiencing, with eyes wide open, a variety of societies.

Karl Mannheim (1893–1947) was a Hungarian-born sociologist who was one of the cofounders of the sociology of knowledge. His best-known book, *Ideology and Utopia*, argued that our ideas and ideologies

---

1. Mannheim, *Ideology and Utopia*, 3.

are products of our times and of the social status of those who hold them. Knowing that this could lead to a harmful relativism, Mannheim proposed instead "relationism," in which we understand that our ideas are limited and that we must trace them back to their roots in our history to see how they have influenced how we relate to society. He broadened the concept of ideology beyond its political roots to include how we arrive at ideas and how those ideas mirror our life and times.

This idea can be fruitful for religious groups who take the time to recognize that their conceptions about God, religion, social and religious behavior, and culture are rooted in history. In my view, as an Adventist Christian, it calls me to recognize that my beliefs are born in history and can be traced back to their sources. It both gives me a link to the past and helps me to recognize that my group and I don't hold the key to all the secrets of life. It builds in epistemological humility without sacrificing awareness of what we owe to our forebears.

Mannheim says we think in patterns that are established by our societies. Which patterns become the dominant patterns? How do they change? He says that groups of people, scattered along the social strata, will not change unless there is tremendous upheaval to their way of life. Only when there is a conflict of ideas can change be possible—and even then, the ideas must somehow impinge on us or push us into radically new ways of thinking and seeing.

Mannheim again: "As long as the same meanings of words, the same ways of deducing ideas, are inculcated from childhood on into every member of the group, divergent thought-processes cannot exist in that society."[2]

I think it's questionable if we each are imprinted with the template to this extent or if *every* person in our group falls as easily into these patterns. Most of us can remember some who stood out—often the quiet ones—in our school or college years because they would not follow the stream. I found them interesting, even admirable, and later came to think of them as remarkable for their independence of spirit against the pressures to conform.

Nevertheless, Mannheim is right, I believe, that for the most part we fall into a comfortable sharing of rituals, symbols, references, and habits that mark us as belonging to the same tribe. The question is, how do

---

2. Mannheim, *Ideology and Utopia*, 6.

we think and act in new ways? Perhaps more to the point: What would prompt us to question that which we are?

Recently, I went to a reunion at the college I had attended in England back in the seventies. Aside from the delight of seeing people I had met almost fifty years ago, there was also the more sobering effect of hearing the stories of their journeys of faith in all that time. Illnesses, deaths of loved ones, divorces, reversals of fortune—none of us had escaped these molders and shapers of experience. Tentatively, at first, and then more confidently, we began to open up to each other about our faith and our doubts. Many of us had worked for our church's educational, medical, and religious organizations for decades and now we were verging on retirement or had already ventured into it.

The stories emerged, blinking in the sunlight, over the weekend. Consistently, as I listened I found myself thinking of the (somewhat) innocent youths that we were all those years ago compared to the (somewhat) more experienced persons we are today. The people that we were and are presently serve as bookends to the volumes of years in between; over the weekend we found we could distinguish between the bookends and the books.

Some of these friends had worked in many different cultures and countries around the world, moving in and out of places as disparate as Rwanda, London, Iceland, and Michigan. All of this while raising children, finding homes to live in, establishing gardens, and getting the car fixed. Others had remained teaching or pastoring—or both—in one country, while seeing their societies evolving, changing, growing ever more diverse and sometimes more polarized.

Over the weekend you could see clusters of people together laughing, leaning in to listen, pausing to remember something and then going on with a chuckle, knowing that what they were trying to retrieve would return to memory after the conversation was over. In any given group of four or five people there could be a combined total of over two-hundred years of work and service. And now these people were sensing gaps between what they had done and experienced and what they had hoped their church might become. They had diverged from the theological and social boundary markers they had been raised to guard because those positions were stationary, and life moves on.

It was not that those beliefs were now invalid, but more that from day to day, in living and working with people, the larger concerns of compassion, patience, and humility had edged those beliefs to the periphery.

Now they were wondering if they were alone in this or if there were others who also felt these gaps. They were like people who set down their burdens to travel lightly with the essential provisions.

"I believe in absolute truth and absolute contingency, at the same time," says Christian Wiman in *My Bright Abyss*. On this side of the bookends, and at this stage in our life journeys, we *are* down to the essentials. They are essentials because they have been proven through experience to be useful for making one's way through life faithfully and with care for others. "And I believe that Christ is the seam soldering together these wholes," continues Wiman, "that our half vision—and our entire clock-bound, logic-locked way of life—shapes as polarities."[3]

At times we change our minds and our lives, decisively and consciously; at the same time we are *being* changed passively and incrementally over time. When we pause to look back, it is then that we realize how different our outlook presently is from the other end of the bookshelf where we began.

Mannheim says we only break out of the conventional ways we were raised to think in through horizontal or vertical mobility. Horizontal mobility is where we change locations or even countries without changing our social status and, in this way, we come to realize how differently people think and live. Vertical mobility is where our social status ascends or descends rapidly, and this, says Mannheim, "is the decisive factor in making persons uncertain and skeptical of their traditional view of the world."[4]

In conversation about this with a friend, she remarked that those of us who find ourselves in these gaps have not radically stepped away from our Adventist roots and from our social context as she has. Viewed from her perspective on the outside, our unease is merely trifling, our "gap-mindedness" arising from being too close to the trees to see the forest. Yet, there are many in this position who have paid dearly for their honest doubts and who are viewed with deep suspicion and distrust by those who hold power inside the Adventist religious organization. Depending on one's vantage point, we have moved an inch or a thousand miles. In practical terms, this means that some in power in our church may already regard us as "outside the camp" with no possibility of being accepted back in. By contrast, some of those I spoke with at the reunion thought of

---

3. Wiman, *My Bright Abyss*, 164.
4. Mannheim, *Ideology and Utopia*, 7.

themselves as at the boundary—but still within the circle. Most striking was the feeling that no one in authority should define us out of the church by drawing the circle tighter and thus excluding us. Being woke means being responsible for one's actions.

Mannheim asks, "how it is possible that identical human thought-processes concerned with the same world produce divergent conceptions of that world . . . May it not be found, when one has examined all the possibilities of human thought, that there are numerous alternative paths which can be followed?"[5]

One of the central metaphors of the New Testament is the idea of a spiritual communion with enough room for many different kinds and ways of serving and living. It is an expansive view rather than a constricted and exclusive position.

"There are varieties of gifts," says Paul, "but the same Spirit. There are varieties of service, but the same Lord. There are many forms of work, but all of them, in all (people), are the work of the same God. In each of us the Spirit is manifested in one particular way, for some useful purpose."[6]

There were some I spoke with who had found spiritual succor in other faith communities. They talked of being accepted, of simple caring and friendship, of the delight in finding shared spiritual communion. While they were not about to abandon their Adventist roots, it was invigorating to realize that spiritual sustenance could be found outside the camp.

Gary Gunderson notes in his *Deeply Woven Roots* that trees send their roots sideways, searching for other organisms, sharing light and food even among different species. Instead of sending our roots down deep, like we've always been told, Gunderson says, we should be sending them sideways, reaching out to others in communities different from our own. Recalling a day in which he lay on his back in a redwood grove in Northern California thinking about faith and human relationships, he says, "I realized that it is nonsense to describe one redwood tree. Not only are they tangled together at the top, they are inseparable at the bottom, where their roots are deeply woven together."[7]

---

5. Mannheim, *Ideology and Utopia*, 9.
6. 1 Cor 12:4–7.
7. Gunderson, *Deeply Woven Roots*, loc. 371.

40

Can a Leper Change His Spots?

There is so much more meaning in reality than the soul can take in . . . This, then, is an insight we gain in acts of wonder: not to measure meaning in terms of our own mind, but to sense a meaning infinitely greater than ourselves[1]

I'VE BEEN THINKING LATELY about the ten lepers that Jesus healed, and the one that returned to thank him. The story is in Luke 17:11–19, and at first glance it seems oddly out of place in the narrative of that chapter. It is one of those *pericopes,* the nuggets of stories that make up so much of the weight and heft of the Gospels. They are like pearls on a necklace: cut the string and they scatter in every direction, losing value as they bounce away. But scoop them up and place them next to one another and they gain a certain nobility of place.

Jesus and the disciples are heading south to Jerusalem, coming through the region between Samaria and Galilee. As they enter a village, ten lepers, keeping the prescribed distance, call out to him in desperation, "Jesus, Master, have mercy on us!" Jesus sees them and answers, "Go show yourselves to the priests." And Luke adds laconically, "And as they went, they were made clean."

Where do we find ourselves in this story? Who do we identify with and why? One of my professors in graduate school told us that in reading

1. Heschel, *God in Search of Man*, 107.

the parables, for example, we should stand in the audience that Jesus was addressing instead of standing next to him, basking in our self-righteousness and our proximity to the Master.

If we stood in the audience hearing Luke's Gospel read out loud in gatherings, we would instantly and instinctively react to the prejudice behind this story. Jews and Samaritans did not get along; they hated each other with a religious passion that ran deep, generation after generation, like Irish Catholics and Protestants used to. Luke places the event at the border of Samaria and Galilee, a flashpoint of possible conflict or perhaps a neutral zone where peace could break out. The roving band of lepers, cast out with curses from their villages, find a bond of mutual misery together. Jesus is their last, best hope.

Perhaps his notoriety had proceeded him. Perhaps a sympathetic relative tipped them off that Jesus and his disciples were on the road. In any case, the exchange between Jesus and the lepers is brief, decisive, and effective. They ask, he responds, and they are healed when they move.

Nine of them are Jews. We know this because they immediately set out for Jerusalem to be certified as clean by the priests—a journey of several days. So . . . no time to lose.

The verse doesn't mention how long it took for them to realize they were healed. But one of them saw the new flesh, pink with life. He spun around, praising God loudly (loudly enough for the other nine to hear?), and ran back and threw himself down at Jesus' feet, thanking him. The one who returned was a Samaritan. Luke points it out in a way that cannot be mistaken, and Jesus rather caustically asks, "Were not ten made clean? But the other nine, where are they? Was none of them found to return and give praise to God except this foreigner?"

Jesus' sense of irony rings through this. Here are his own, his people, off down the road without a backward glance, while a traditional enemy, one not deserving of respect by tribal measures, comes back to praise God and thank God's servant. It's enough to make a person erase the lines in the sand.

Luke raises the contrast between those getting on with their lives and those who, unexpectedly, in one glorious moment, see God like a fountain springing up from within the eyes of this man. The nine were no less healed in their haste but, having received much, they had perceived so little.

New Testament scholars tell us that Luke's Gospel was intended to show how Jesus' message of the kingdom of God was open to everyone, strangers and foreigners as well as Israel. That would include us, readers searching the stories for points of contact, people of an era that desperately claws at the slope down which it is plummeting headlong. If there is a "still, small voice" of God to be heard we will have to remove our earbuds first.

Here we are, over two thousand years later, picking up a Gideon's Bible in a Motel 6, flipping it open to a random place and finding this story. What could make us pause, finger tracing the words, long enough to turn from the window and sit on the edge of the bed? Northrop Frye says in *Words with Power* that "Experience is of the particular and the unique, and takes place in time; knowledge is of the universal and the assimilated, and contains an element withdrawn from time."[2] Both are needed: the expected flow is from experience to knowledge. Could it be reversed? Could knowledge of an event long ago on a dusty road create an experience that blooms within us? Isn't that implicit in every story written down and sent into the world?

Abraham Heschel writes in *God in Search of Man,* "The soul is endowed with a sense of indebtedness, and wonder, awe, and fear unlock that sense of indebtedness."[3] Look both ways and hold hands when you cross the street together, say please and thank you, clean up after yourself, be good to each other, and don't tell lies. These are some of the universals, and as we mature we realize how much we owe to others; the indebtedness that has not only kept us on the way, but has made the way even possible. "Oh, the debt I owe," sings James Taylor in "*Watchin' Over Me.*" "I said oh the damage done / How'm I gonna pay that debt I owe."[4]

Jesus looks at the man at his feet: "Get up and go on your way," he says, "your faith has made you well." What was freely given was freely received. All of the ten asked, all were healed. One came back to thank the Master. What does this act reveal?

An indebtedness acknowledged to an enemy of one's people renders that enmity chained. And in turning back the Samaritan not only offers thanks, but sees in the man before him the God of *all* people, lepers and Samaritans included. Like the others, this man's body was restored and his social curse lifted; unlike the rest, his faith opened his eyes to the wonder of a meaning he now carried that was greater than himself.

2. Frye, *Words with Power*, 74.
3. Heschel, *God in Search of Man*, 112.
4. Taylor, "Watchin' Over Me."

And we may respond, also, to a story with a life beyond its telling. Abraham Heschel writes, "We cannot survive unless we know what is asked of us. But to whom does man in his priceless and unbridled freedom owe anything? Where does the asking come from? To whom is he accountable?"[5]

Our leprosies may be the means for seeing how great is the height and depth and breadth of the love that sets us free.

"We journey through a narrative," writes Northrop Frye, "and then we stop and confront what we have read as though it were objective. It is not objective, because it is already a part of ourselves. There is a further stage of response, however, where something like a journeying movement is resumed, a movement that may well take us far beyond the world's end, and yet is still no journey."[6]

---

5. Heschel, *God in Search of Man*, 113.
6. Frye, *Words with Power*, 96.

41

Our Infinite Choice

The religious life or practice that I become part of must not only be my choice, but it must speak to me, it must make sense in terms of my spiritual development as I understand this.[1]

ONE OF THE EXTRAORDINARY features of religion, as one studies it, is the infinite variety of its expressions. The moment we step out of the holy place wherein we worship, and into the crowd swirling past outside, we are enveloped in a multitude of faiths, each one with a history, symbols, myths, art, language, casualties, diagnoses, and prescriptions. They pour past us as we stand transfixed in the midst of the stream.

Some might picture themselves as a rock, immovable and stalwart, dividing the waters that flow past, resisting the current, sure in their grounding in the streambed. Others, less sure than curious, join the flow to ask those at their elbows and around them where they're going, what set them on their path, or why they continue. Still others will do their best to divert the stream into side channels, away from the swiftly flowing current into quieter, shallower rivulets, and eventually to pools of standing water.

We will step lightly up on the riverbank now, away from the analogy, carrying with us the twin observations of the variety of religious expressions and our attitude toward them.

1. Taylor, *Secular Age*, 486.

The sheer number of religions sparks in us wonder that God could be filtered through so many veils and still be perceived in coherent form. At the very least the history, traditions, and practices cause us to view our own thin wedge of religious history as one among many.

Ask yourself this: If you joined your religion as an adult, what was the deciding factor? If you were born into your religion, why do you continue in it?

Joiners or borners? The questions stand open.

Is a religion a vehicle to deliver us to a destination, at which point, our quest fulfilled, we will enter into a sacral bliss? Is a religion a chrysalis within which we are transformed into another creature, a new creation? Perhaps we are pilgrims traveling through a barren land, seeking a city not made with human hands. If we become disciples of Jesus, we will have no place to lay our heads, even if foxes have their dens and the birds of the air their nests.

"Transcendence is the test of religious truth," says Abraham Heschel. "A genuine insight rends the enclosure of the heart and bestows on man the power to rise above himself."[2] Religion, despite its flaws and obsessions, and depending on its light source, can be both a mirror and a window to transcendence.

Metaphors matter, because they both reflect and shape our experience and behavior.

Machiavelli regarded religion as a paltry crutch for an individual, but he saw the value in it for creating conformity and confining the masses. Durkheim regarded it as the social glue that created community and provided fellowship between people—*solidarité*.

When we bow in epistemological humility before our need for evidence that will undergird our faith, it is bracing to recall the debate between W. K. Clifford and William James.

Clifford, a British mathematician and a psychologist like James, was a friend of his, but also someone with whom he was delighted to debate. Clifford's assertion in his *The Ethics of Belief* begins with the idea that our hypotheses ought never to be accepted until we have solid evidence for them. We find easy comfort in that which pleases us and soothes our doubts, says Clifford. We need to resolutely turn our backs on these superficial comforts and take the manly road of ethical integrity to face the universe as it really is. As it is in science, so it ought to be in all matters

---

2. Heschel, *God in Search of Man*, 162.

of life, including religion. As James quotes Clifford: "Belief is desecrated when given to unproved and unquestioned statements, for the solace and private pleasure of the believer . . . *It is wrong always, and everywhere, and for anyone, to believe anything upon insufficient evidence" (emphasis added)."*[3]

James answered Clifford in a closely reasoned essay entitled *The Will to Believe*, a title that James came to regret because so many erroneously took it to mean "believe what you will." In fact, it is about both the right *and* the will to believe.

There are two ways of dealing with received opinion, says James: "Believe truth! Shun error! . . . by choosing between them we may end by coloring differently our whole intellectual life."[4] Clifford, asserts James, would have us choose the latter, to remain in suspense forever as we wait for conclusive evidence in order to avoid the risk of believing lies. In the thousand ways each day that we believe and act on the thinnest of evidence, says James, even Clifford fails his own stringency. But in withholding our trust until all—how would we even *know* if it was "all"—the evidence is clocked, tallied, and catalogued, James says we have already made our decision. Not to decide is to decide—a forced option.

Where do we get the spark of trust in order to light the fuse of faith? Augustine writes of the faith that precedes faith in God—and intimates that God gives us that faith as well.

No trust is without risk, as anyone who has ever fallen in love knows. We *think* that the currency of trust is backed by the gold standard of the degree of risk involved. In our calculus great risk should equate to great reward. But when it comes to trusting God, we often find that a step taken in clenched fear, with a breath of hope, turns out to be merely a passing shadow in the waves of joy and relief after the act.

The debate between W. K. Clifford and William James in *The Will to Believe* is an example of calcified certainty (Clifford) versus the right to believe (James). We cannot wait for all the evidence to be in before we make decisions; James chooses to believe with *both* reason and passion.

For those of us born into our religion, we must choose at some point to make it our own or search elsewhere for transcendence. What goes into choice? Circumstance, inclination, temperament, and tradition. But also reason, coherence with our reality, conviction, and passion.

---

3. James, *Will to Believe*, 8.
4. James, *Will to Believe*, 18.

"But the spiritual life can be lived in as many ways as there are people," says Henri Nouwen in *Making All Things New*. "What is new is that we have moved from the many things to the kingdom of God. What is new is that we are set free from the compulsions of our world and have set our hearts on the only necessary thing. What is new is that we no longer experience the many things, people, and events as endless causes for worry, but begin to experience them as the rich variety of ways in which God makes his presence known to us."[5]

---

5. Nouwen, *Spiritual Life*, 19–20.

42

Hear the Pennies Dropping

He looked up and saw rich people putting their gifts into the treasury; he also saw a poor widow put in two small copper coins. He said, "Truly I tell you, this poor widow has put in more than all of them; for all of them have contributed out of their abundance, but she out of her poverty has put in all she had to live on."[1]

THERE ARE FEW THINGS that get us Christians rearing up on our hind legs and clawing at the air as talking about Jesus and money. Talking about Jesus' love is no problem, just as talking about money is easy. Money and its value is the *lingua franca* of our world, the language that all of us are taught to speak from an early age. But when we put Jesus and money together it's a whole different story.

For one thing, he didn't have any. The Gospels record him as sleeping rough while on the road. Even animals, he noted wryly, lived better than he did. At least foxes had their dens to retreat to at the end of the day, and the birds had their nests. Having left his home, his mother, and his siblings for a life as an itinerant teacher and healer, Jesus had nowhere to lay his head.

Not that he was complaining. We never get the sense that Jesus resented the path he was walking, although the burdens he carried just being himself were heavy enough. Nor did he chafe at thwarted ambition

---

1. Luke 21:1–4.

or linger wistfully at the edge of the crowd as the rich and powerful swept by. "I coulda been a contender" never passed his lips.

On the other hand, their relative poverty was a sore spot with some of the disciples. "We here have left everything" was a common refrain among them. Mark shows us two of the disciples, James and John, asking Jesus to commit to giving them whatever they want. "What do you want me to do for you?" he asks. Without hesitation they answer, "We want to sit on either side of you when you set up your kingdom."[2] Incredulous, Jesus responds, "You don't know what you're asking." Later, in Matthew's version of the story, which he picked up from Mark, he has the mother of James and John ask the favor. Maybe it was just too embarrassing for the early church community to believe these two would try to muscle their way into positions of privilege, but a mother . . . well, that was to be expected.

Jesus talks about wealth and poverty more than almost anything else, including all the usual subjects one would expect, like heaven and hell, the law, sexual morality, and violence. Jim Wallis, cofounder of the Sojourners Community, says in *The Call to Conversion* that "One out of every ten verses in the Synoptic Gospels is about the rich and the poor; in Luke, the ratio is one out of seven."[3] Some of Jesus' most scathing remarks are directed against the wealthy for their callousness and their foolishness in putting all their attention and their trust in what they pile up. The disparity between the wealthy few and the many poor was evident—and evidently on Jesus' mind a great deal.

"But woe to you who are rich," he warns, "for you will go hungry." It will be impossible for the rich to enter heaven, he says bluntly. You might as well try to jam a camel through a needle's eye. The disciples are duly staggered. Then who can be saved? they want to know. Jesus looks hard at them and says, "With man this is impossible." He pauses, and as they gasp, he finishes, "But with God all things are possible."[4] Only God can save the rich.

Jesus is teaching daily in the temple in these passages, and he is sitting with his disciples one day, watching as people drop their offerings into the temple box. The rich come up with their long robes and their

---

2. Mark 10:37–38.
3. Wallis, *Call to Conversion*, 58.
4. Matt 19:23–26.

bags of money and make a show of pouring the coins in for maximum effect.

Then, as Jesus and the others watch, a widow slips up quietly and drops in two coins so small and light they barely make a sound. She does not raise her head nor look around, but simply disappears into the crowd. Jesus watches thoughtfully, two fingers tapping his lips, then shakes his head.

"She out of her poverty has put in all she had to live on," he says.[5] The verses immediately preceding this in Luke's Gospel are warnings by Jesus about position and power. "In the hearing of all the people Jesus said to his disciples: 'Beware of the lawyers who love to walk up and down in long robes, and have a great liking for respectful greetings in the street, the chief seats in our synagogues, and places of honor at feasts. These are the men who eat up the property of widows, while they say long prayers for appearance' sake; and they will receive the severest sentence.'"[6]

This is a difficult story. Our sympathies are with the widow in her plight, and our admiration even more so for her unshakable faith. This woman and her pennies stand before us like a moral stop sign for her willingness to contribute everything she had to an institution she believed in because of the God she believed in. The rich believed in God too, but they believed more in the power of position and social influence.

She may well have been one of the victims of the lawyers who snatched up homes and displaced their owners. In any case, a widow, especially one without grown children to support her, had a hard road to walk, as it has ever been.

Jim Wallis gives us another insight to the significance of her act when he writes: "The gospel story of the widow's mite (Mark 12:41–44) makes a related point . . . It had to do with her relationship to God, which had transformed the economics of her life. . . . How much is given is less important than how much is left over after giving."[7]

Jesus says in another context, "Take no thought for tomorrow, for tomorrow has troubles of its own."[8] But we do take thought; we take thought so much that it can tie our brains and our stomachs in knots. As I write, close to a million federal workers are out of work and without pay,

---

5. Luke 21:4.
6. Luke 20:45–47.
7. Wallis, *Call to Conversion*, 70.
8. Matt 6:34.

as the government shutdown grinds on. That doesn't include the small businesses that are dependent on providing services to a functioning government. For millions of people, the norm is living two paychecks away from homelessness.

Perhaps the meaning here is best conveyed by another translation which says, "So do not be *anxious* about tomorrow; tomorrow will look after itself. Each day has troubles enough of its own."[9] We cannot help thinking hard about such things. But we *can* learn to live by faith without anxiety.

Jesus says without a trace of irony that everyone who lives in the kingdom that is here and still to come *could* live without anxiety, "For it is the Gentiles who strive for all these things; and indeed, your heavenly Father knows that you need all these things."[10]

And so, our widow, bless her heart, lives from hour to hour, supported by the gossamer threads of her own unpretentious faith, and slips out of the temple, unaware that her silent act, remarkable in its unassuming nature, becomes a witness remembered for as long as Jesus' words are treasured.

And Jesus? After teaching all day in the temple, "at night he would go out and spend the night on the Mount of Olives, as it was called. And all the people would get up early in the morning to listen to him in the temple."[11]

---

9. Matt 6:34, REB.
10. Matt 6:32.
11. Luke 21:38.

43

The Hope in Shame

We have lost a sense of moral clarity that would give rise to the fear that certain actions—whether we privately feel guilty about them or not—could lead to disgrace. For they don't. If enough, and enough well-placed people do them, the only disgrace you need fear is the failure to get away with it.[1]

IN 1994 QUENTIN TARANTINO's *Pulp Fiction* was released and immediately bent the needle of the outrage meter. No matter. It went on to win an Oscar and solidified Tarantino's bad-boy status. Critics said it glorified violence, but they were not quite right. It didn't glorify violence so much as trivialize the pain behind the violence.

After the outcry died down, I went to see it, lured like anyone else by the promise of sex and violence. In one scene, John Travolta turns on a guy in the back seat of his car and threatens him with a gun. But the gun accidentally goes off, splattering the guy's brains all over the back window. Travolta's reaction provoked an instant response in the theater: almost everyone laughed. Nervously at first, and then in embarrassment, but laughing nonetheless.

I felt three reactions in rapid succession: shock with revulsion, spasmodic hilarity, followed by shame and embarrassment. It was the shame

---

1. Neiman, *Moral Clarity*, 369.

that stayed with me long after the plot line had faded. I was trying to understand why I and so many others had reacted that way.

It's not hard to figure that we cover our embarrassment with laughter, but *why* are we embarrassed? It's not as if we need to apologize to the character, a fictional being after all. Would we have laughed watching it by ourselves? It occurred to me that one reason for our shame and embarrassment was that we didn't want others to think we were heartless, stone-cold bastards. On reflection, I came to think that these were the appropriate responses. It means that there's still something in us that can't bear to watch someone's humiliation at their most vulnerable moment.

"Guilt," says philosopher Susan Neiman, "is the internal sense that you've done something wrong, even if no one ever discovers it. Shame records your consciousness of wrong before a community whose values you honor."[2]

There it is: our moral behavior has a powerful social kick behind it. We *want* to do right, to be in favor with God and man. Like it or not, we carry the community with us and we measure ourselves up against its approval; "approbation" is what philosopher Adam Smith called it in his *Theory of Moral Sentiments*.

Smith thought that we were basically good people, but he saw the approval or contempt of society as a means for keeping our conduct in line with social norms. It was in our interest to do right and receive the praise of others just as the implied threat of community anger at our actions would fill us with shame. That depends, of course, on whether we cared at all what others thought of us. Smith was pretty sure most people did care, leaving out the insane and the psychopaths. And just as his "invisible hand" guided the spirit and function of capitalism, so his "moral sentiments" appealed to our self-interests as well as the interests of a stable society. Balance and order were kept because most of us had both the need and capacity to love and be loved as well as the need to avoid the disapproval of our community.

Neiman makes a persuasive case that shamelessness is pervasive in our culture and our lack of shame is what made such violations of human rights as Abu Ghraib possible. "If the ideal of human rights is destroyed by the violations that were said to be needed to realize it, our children will

---

2. Neiman, *Moral Clarity*, 369.

pay the price. Many of them are already paying, for they believe in next to nothing."[3]

It's easy to lose sight of the presence of human decency when we face into the perfect storm of perversity in the media every day. I'm not ranting about particular TV shows, films, fashions, musicians, Wall Street shysters, TV evangelists, or politicians. What I'm trying to get at is the underlying tone of mockery at the human plight that runs through so much of media culture. You can't avoid it at movie previews where upcoming films, all PG-13 at least, are reduced to slapstick or thunderous exhibitions of firepower. It was there in the photos of grinning soldiers posing with heaps of humiliated and terrified Iraqi prisoners at Abu Ghraib. It is there when Lance Armstrong, a symbol of courage and endurance to millions, bullies his way through years of doping, lying, and degrading the sport. And it is there whenever we read another derisive tweet from the president of the United States.

Neiman believes that the only way to reverse the erosion of shame is to "return to the language of good and evil."[4] In a culture such as ours, in which a helpless relativism reduces moral dialogue to diatribes or a pouty solipsism, this is strong stuff. The word "evil" is overused and abused, trivialized and rendered almost meaningless when it is applied where it does not belong. But even more threatening to our own sense of human dignity is when we refuse to apply it to our own actions—we frail, bumbling, confused, and pitifully arrogant human beings.

Kant thought the foundational principle of right action was this: act so that you never treat other people as a means to an end, but always as ends in themselves. That means that we treat ourselves with respect and treat everyone else, even our enemies, with respect also. To demean and demonize them means first of all that we could wish for such a world in which everyone did just that.

We have the means but not the wisdom nor the right to call anyone evil. But recognizing our limitations in that regard does not mean we should give up on trying to understand why we—and others—may do evil actions. We are so easily drawn into situations in which evil actions are the consequence of fear and ignorance; we need a reverence toward words and language such that we could choose to speak of good and evil again.

---

3. Neiman, *Moral Clarity*, 368.
4. Neiman, *Moral Clarity*, 369.

The degradation of our humanity sometimes pulls us down through enormous events such as genocide or systemic rape and exploitation of women. But if we regain, as a society, the capacity to be ashamed of our evil actions, there is hope. We can retrace our steps, make amends, learn humility, and receive grace.

If evil is not in our nature, but in our actions, there is hope. We *do* have choices, tragic though they might be at times. But if we wish to remain human, we cannot be passive. Our humanity erodes, slips away, sifts through our fingers when we look only to our own self-interest. This freedom to shape our responses in situations both mundane and extreme is what separates us from lentils and aphids. It truly is the image of God in us.

44

Our Moment at Jabbok

When you are through with your tradition, it must be different from what you found or else you have failed. It is your responsibility to make your religious tradition, whatever it may be, Christian or otherwise, more truly religious by the time you are through with it. That's the great challenge we face.[1]

IN STORY AND IN myth, crossing rivers signals a shift of identity, the overcoming of not only a natural force but of a personal barrier to a new experience. In Greek mythology, the River Styx is the boundary between life and death. In Norse mythology, the Ifing River separates Asgard, the land of the gods, from Jotunheim, the land of the giants. It runs so swiftly that ice can never form on it, and thus it is an effective barrier for any giant who wants to take on the gods. The Jabbok River, a tributary of the Jordan River, is the place where Jacob wrestles with God before he meets his estranged brother for the first time in years.

Jacob sent his family, his household, and all his possessions over the river before the sun went down, but now in the darkness he is alone. Scripture can be so stringently laconic at times: the text in Genesis 32 simply says, "Jacob was left alone; and a man wrestled with him until daybreak."

1. Steindl-Rast, *Meeting the Shadow*, 133.

Spiritually, Jacob is at a crossroads in his life. Even within the womb he struggled to gain an advantage, but Esau emerged first. Esau had the brawn; Jacob had the guile. What he couldn't get through honest effort he gained through deception. But he had his comeuppances too. The blessing he had stolen from his brother as he deceived his father curdled in his heart: his beautiful bride, Rachel, was found instead—on his wedding night, no less—to be her stolid and morose sister, Leah. His servitude to his father-in-law, Laban, a man renowned for his chicanery, stretched on year after year. Jacob survived through cleverness, bordering on fraud.

He had his moments of light though. Making his way through the desert, he lay one night under the stars and dreamed he saw a ladder stretching to the heavens, alive and glowing with angels, stunning in their beauty and haughtiness. When he awoke, gasping and disoriented, all he could whisper across the sands was, "Surely the Lord is in this place—and I did not know it! How awesome is this place! This is the house of God and this is the gate of heaven." And so he called it Beth El.

But this night he is alone with his anxieties, a man approaching middle age who carries responsibility for an extended family, slaves, and herds. Jewish philosopher Martin Buber saw in Jacob the existential man, wrestling with life's questions until he wins through to some spiritual release.

Psychologically speaking, we can see Jacob struggling with his shadow, the part of himself that he could not acknowledge, that constantly raised its head to confront him with his weakness, his suspicion, his fear, and the ache in his heart that pounded into him with every breath that he would never be good enough for his father.

In Carl Jung's development of the shadow it appears in our dreams as a figure of the same sex as ourselves whom we fear or dislike or regard as inferior. In trying to live up to the standards of conduct set for us by parents, church, and society, we identify with those ego ideals and reject the qualities that contradict them. "But the rejected qualities do not cease to exist," says John Sanford in *Evil: The Shadow Side of Reality*, "simply because they have been denied direct expression. Instead they live on within us and form the secondary personality that psychology calls the Shadow."[2]

Unless we recognize them and integrate them into our consciousness, they will only cause us pain and confound our psychological and

---

2. Sanford, *Evil*, 50.

spiritual growth. But the shadow personality can also be a positive force for us if we can relate to it in the correct way. If we have always repressed anger in an attempt to be kind and "Christian," it becomes part of our shadow. But if we can integrate part of that capacity for anger it can help us become stronger, more resolute people, who are able to respond in a healthier way to intolerable circumstances and especially to injustice. Sanford offers the example of Jesus' anger in driving out the money changers who were profaning the temple of God. "Obviously, Jesus' capacity for controlled anger gave his personality a strength that he would not have had had he lacked the capacity for such a response," notes Sanford.[3]

People in whom the shadow is repressed often lack a sense of humor. They are not able to see themselves as anything but striving for perfection—and humor is often a release for all the tension that comes from falling short—and from falling. If we can have humility without humiliation, then we can laugh at ourselves in those awkward situations. The shadow helps us forgive ourselves and others too.

Jacob at Jabbok is one of those stories that stays with one throughout a lifetime. It is about a man being reborn through struggle and suffering, who wins through failing, and who limps off into the sunrise a hero. He had been passive-aggressive all his life, looking for an advantage where he could not prevail through strength or credibility. Now, as he struggles through the night, he puts his whole heart into it, assertive, not violent— so alive for the first time that the superior strength of his opponent is his joyous challenge. Even as the Stranger strikes his hip, throwing it out of joint, Jacob will not let him go without a blessing.

The audacity of one who sees his spiritual liberation within his grasp is stunning. And in that moment his name, Jacob, "The Supplanter," is flung away, and a new name, Israel, "The God-Striver," pours down on him like oil. As the first light strikes the mountain tops in the distance, the Stranger slips out of Jacob's sobbing grasp, lowering him to the ground.

When he rolls over and looks around, he is alone again. Once, he had seen the angels; now, with a thrill of awe, he struggles to his feet: "I have seen God face to face and lived!"

***

The ability to admit one is wrong and to change one's ways and direction is part of the toolkit for any Christian. Lord knows we get enough

---

3. Sanford, *Evil*, 52.

practice at it to be experts, but it's a lesson we apparently must learn and relearn. As individuals, we may stop in our tracks, look back, see where we diverged, and change course. As institutions? Not so much.

It takes humility to admit that we are wrong; it takes perception to see it. To perceive is to see our situation with new eyes: that we may be right in our results but wrong in how we got them; that we may have magnified the incidentals and overlooked the essentials; that we may have gotten some of it right—but there's so much more to discover.

Jacob struggling at the River Jabbok is a metaphor. Facing his greatest crisis, he bares his soul like an offering. The struggle is not about winning, but about dying and being reborn. Jacob struggles against himself that his true self might emerge. He bears in his flesh the wound that never heals, every step the ache of Love's weight. From now on, Jacob's empathy for those frozen in their pride draws them to him; he becomes a warming, healing presence to those whose self-righteousness wedges them apart from others.

**

Every church has its Jabbok moment. As we confront our hubris and our guile, we may finally acknowledge our shadow. "True justice must resolve a conflict in a way that leaves the community whole," writes Paul Woodruff in *The Ajax Dilemma*. "It's not merely what you decide that matters, but how you decide it, and how you communicate the decision."[4] We have thought of ourselves as templates for perfection, nothing short of a model for the world. But we are human, fretful in our weaknesses, and yet bright with promise. If, as a church, we struggle now for a rebirth, we will hear God's breath close to us. "I never asked for perfection," God will say, "only that you become complete. And I will take care of that."

Our changes are painful, extended in time, bending our form to the breaking point. That is how change is made in this dimension of time and space. On this plane our changes usually cause friction and disturb the peace. There is a time coming when we shall all be changed, in a moment, in the twinkling of an eye, as we are transformed from the perishable to the imperishable.

---

4. Woodruff, *Ajax Dilemma*, 8.

45

On the Boundary

The man who stands on many boundaries experiences the unrest, insecurity, and inner limitation of existence in many forms.[1]

WHEN PEOPLE OF FAITH look at the world, they see multiple images. There is the *natural* world that is given, not produced by us. There is the *cultural* world, the objects and ideas of which are imagined, thought, built, and produced by us. And there is the *supernatural* world of powers, spirits, angels, and God. If we are honest with ourselves, the first two image sets are more recognizably real to us than is the last.

The challenge is to understand what the world is for us, we who belong to many different communities as well as our own communities of faith. We can think of it through two phrases that are thick with possibilities for understanding: the first is "to be *in* the world, but not *of* the world," and the second phrase is "to live on the boundary."

A phrase like "in the world, but not of the world" is a paradox rather than clever nonsense. This phrase is familiar to us, although it doesn't appear in Scripture as such. We must address both sides of it.

We are in the world in more than just a geographical sense: we are inextricably embedded in this world right down to the molecular level. We share air, water, and space with other creatures and life forms, and our continued existence on this earth is interdependent with theirs. Much

---

1. Tillich, *On the Boundary*, 97.

of our DNA we share in common with other species. This world is our home.

Yet, we are not entirely at home in this world. That is the paradox in which we live. Christians—people who see themselves as pilgrims passing through—are also citizens, parents, homeowners, students, patients, leaders, farmers, manufacturers, and politicians. Like everyone else, Christians are invested in this world. It is hard to anticipate the end to the world when you are trying to build a hospital or take out a loan for graduate school. How do you live with one foot on the throttle and the other on the brake?

"You are the salt of the earth," says Jesus. The remark is placed by the writer of Matthew just after the Beatitudes, which are themselves reversals of common sense in any well-ordered society. "Blessed are the meek," he says, "for they will inherit the earth." We glance up; surely, he is not serious. "You are the salt of the earth. If the salt has lost its savor, it is thrown out and cast underfoot."

It is not so much a warning (don't become obsolete!) as it is a pronouncement: you bring flavor to the world. And a little goes a long way; you may be few in number (just a pinch will do!), but you make the plain fare of life worth tasting.

"You are the light of the world," says Jesus. No hint of sarcasm, but more than a touch of irony. Look what we can do with a few good lights! These people of poverty, these people of the shadows, these persecuted pursuers of peace, they are lighting up the world and they will *not* be hidden. Do your good work in the world where it can be seen—that's how people will know God exists.

If we do not love this world then we do not love its Creator, for God so loved the world that he gave his own Son for it.

To love the world, despite its sinfulness and despair, is to love like God—with patience, long-suffering, and commitment.

Like Jesus himself, we are to be faithful to this world and to the possibility of its ultimate transformation.

We must also speak to the other side of the phrase: "not of the world." To say this is to "re-cognize," that is, to "know again," that we have been called out of the dead ends of this world into a new life in Christ.

To be in the world is to be constantly confronted with choices. It can become exhausting. Why couldn't God have made us so that choosing the good was automatic? Instead, God seems to have set it up so that we need freedom to make our way in the world. Our freedom to choose means we can work in the world without fear—fear of the world and fear of failure. Because we are covered with God's grace, we can take chances, try new things, and step out in faith. In that sense, the big picture becomes rather simple. In fact, the tagline for Christians might be: "We've fallen, and we can't get up. By the grace of God, shall we try it again?"

We may be overwhelmed by the cruelty and the suffering of people in the world. We may be tempted to abandon the world to itself. But this is our world, the place where we find our calling. Playwright Christopher Fry writes, "In our plain defects we already know the brotherhood of man."[2] There is much to dare and to try while we are here.

There are times when we are called to stand up, stand out, and give light to the world. During times of despair and fear, we must be visible, calling out injustices where they occur, and offering an alternative to hopelessness.

The other phrase about us is "on the boundary." We are boundary people, we Christians, because we are both in the world, but not entirely of the world. We are a living Venn diagram of the kingdom here and yet to come. We see and respect the difference. We identify both with the suffering in the world and with the Christ who suffers for the world. On our best days we live and serve in the world *and* in the church. Straddling that boundary can be hard and uncomfortable. It may stretch our imagination and patience until they begin to fray.

Between theory and practice, between what we are taught and what we practice together in the world, there is a tension. If we lean too far toward the theory, that is, toward our beliefs and customs, we run the risk of losing touch with the world. If we lean too far in the other direction, toward our practice, we begin to lose our memory of the community and its history. Both are important.

We are on the boundary also with church and society. It is a question once again of translating our experience with God into language that is both prophetic and imaginative. Can we speak a word of truth to a society that deliberately lies? Can we work to understand those whom we'd just as soon see struck down with fire? Do we have the humility to examine the ways we humiliate those even within our church? Perhaps most importantly, can we listen before we speak?

Finally, we are on the boundary between religion and politics. A religion that cannot speak a prophetic word to the political structure will

---

2. Fry, *Dark Is Light Enough*, 21.

soon lose its voice. But a religion that seeks first the power of the political structure will eventually lose its soul.

The questions we might ask today do not begin with "Whose side are you on?" but rather with "How may we help?" In order to be in the world, but not of the world, we must remain on the boundary.

46

This Is Only a Test

Man is always being challenged; a question is always being asked of him.[1]

WHEN I WALKED OUT of my comprehensive exams at graduate school, it was a beautiful Southern California day and I thought, "That's it, I'm done. No more exams!" Of course, I was wrong, which is concrete evidence of how much I still didn't know. Life is a series of tests, none of which we can cram for and many of which we will not see the results of until long after we've forgotten what we were tested on.

It's not that I hated exams; I rather enjoyed the opportunity to explain, describe, and analyze complex issues. It was the build-up to the exams that brought anxiety, the persistent feeling that no matter how thorough your preparation there would always be some question designed not to show what you knew but to punish you for what you didn't know.

When I started teaching, I kept in mind how I felt about exams. I steered clear of minutiae and tried to design questions that gave students an opportunity to take a long view. I made it clear I expected accuracy in portraying the positions of others, honesty in expressing one's own position, and clarity in writing. Nobody was getting paid by the word; brevity and conciseness were virtues. On questions of ethical practice as distinguished from analysis of ethical theory, I blessed responses that

---

1. Heschel, *Moral Grandeur and Spiritual Audacity*, 251.

were exploratory and forward looking. I encouraged students in philosophy and ethics to use their imaginations as well as their reasoning and analytical powers. Above all, I asked them to see themselves as both teachers and learners.

How would they describe and explain what they knew to someone who was deeply interested in what they had to say, but lacked their foundational knowledge on the subject? Could such a person pick up their written responses and understand them? Could those responses be the starting point for a deep and exciting conversation? Could they lead others to see what they had learned? And could connections be made in all directions from the subject they were studying? What had they learned in their American history class that their ethics might address? Could their ethical theories apply to their health practices, their economics courses, and their intercultural communication?

"There is only one subject-matter for education," said A. N. Whitehead in *The Aims of Education*, "and that is Life in all its manifestations."[2]

***

There are two kinds of exams in education: one tests what we *have* learned (summative assessment) and the other tests what we need in *order* to learn (formative assessment). Generally speaking, the life of a spiritual wanderer, someone seeking the water of life, is a process of formative assessment. If life is for learning, then we can look to every day as experimental research into that which helps us learn of God, of ourselves, and of others.

"Speculation does not precede faith," says Abraham Heschel in *God in Search of Man*. "The antecedents of faith are the premise of wonder and the premise of praise. Worship of God precedes affirmation of His realness. We *praise* before we *prove*. We respond before we question."[3]

For those who have been on this path all their lives, and who find themselves no nearer knowing God than when they began, this may almost sound like mockery. How can a person in their fifth or sixth decade of life on this planet regain this wonder? "Can one enter a second time into the mother's womb and be born?" asks Nicodemus.[4] We get

---

2. Whitehead, *Aims of Education*, 6–7.
3. Heschel, *God in Search of Man*, 120.
4. John 3:4.

worn down by life; our capacity for wonder ebbs and our willingness to suspend our disbelief diminishes in inverse proportion to our need to appear objective and aloof. All the evidence that the world is indifferent to our struggle swarms before our eyes and we shake our heads in exasperation. Experience cannot be reverse-engineered back to innocence.

Heschel invites us to look again: "It is not from experience but *from our inability to experience* what is given to our mind that certainty of the realness of God is derived."[5] Our very lack of what we seek takes on the outlines of a God-shaped vacuum in our lives, the *via negativa* of the medieval mystics and contemplatives.

But we are twenty-first-century people who respond more readily to the merest factoid, rather than venturing beyond our skepticism. The trust that is the DNA of faith does not come easily, despite the brave face of certainty that we profess when pressed. Instinctively, we believe that a testimony given must be anchored, not understanding that a profession of belief without the trust of commitment can sometimes be a grappling hook thrown heavenward to draw us up.

Doing can result in being, a genuine form of faith.

But there are some caveats to the formative assessment of our education in faith. "Knowledge is not the same as awareness," notes Heschel, "and expression is not the same as experience. By proceeding from awareness to knowledge we gain in clarity and lose in immediacy. What we gain in distinctness by going from experience to expression we lose in genuineness."[6]

It's a risk worth taking. Heschel assures us that "To the prophets wonder is *a form of thinking,*" a way forward when faced with the numinous, with the burning bushes, and with the whispers of God within the hurricane. "Our certainty," says Heschel, "is the result of wonder and radical amazement, of awe before the mystery and meaning of the totality of life beyond our rational discerning. Faith is *the response* to the mystery, shot through with meaning; the response to a challenge which no one can forever ignore."[7]

For Christian existentialists, of whom I am one, authentic faith is a leap beyond what can be wholly certified through reason. "Keep some room in your heart for the unimaginable," suggests poet Mary Oliver.

---

5. Heschel, *God in Search of Man*, 117.
6. Heschel, *God in Search of Man*, 116.
7. Heschel, *God in Search of Man*, 117.

That challenge comes in the form of questions put to us by God, corporately and personally. Some of them are formative: they shape us going forward. Others give us a needed pause on this journey, a timeout to catch our breath and look around us. They are summative of what we have learned through our experience.

***

These are some of the questions I am seeking to be shaped by and to answer to:

"Where are you?" – Gen 3:10

"What does the Lord require of you?" – Mic 6:8

"And can any of you by worrying add a single hour to your span of life?" – Matt 6:27

"You of little faith, why did you doubt?" – Matt 14:31

And the most important question of all . . .

"Who do you say that I am?" – Mark 8:29

We are questions to ourselves. Life itself throws us demands that we may field as questions. The ones that draw us in, turn us inside out, and lift us higher come to us from the Spirit "who searches everything, even the depths of God."[8]

---

8. 1 Cor 2:10

47

The Acts of the Disciples

The spirit of the Lord is upon me,
because he has anointed me
to bring good news to the poor.
He has sent me to proclaim release to
the captives
and recovery of sight to the blind,
to let the oppressed go free,
to proclaim the year of the Lord's
favor.[1]

AND LUKE'S GOSPEL SAYS that Jesus "rolled up the scroll, gave it back to the attendant, and sat down. The eyes of all in the synagogue were upon him."

Let us sit with them for a moment, in that holy silence. Jesus carefully, reverently rolls up the scroll. He does not hurry. He holds the knurled ends of the scroll in his hands, feels the polished wood turning against his palms, as the papyrus curls back to its resting position. The attendant reaches to take the scroll as Jesus sits down. No one stirs. It is the silence of expectancy, not of inattention and boredom.

What were they expecting, and why would they be transfixed, holding their breath for the next moment? Perhaps it was the way Jesus read the passage, ascending the hills of the text to each crest, hitting the "me"

---

1. Luke 4:18–19.

of each one with emphasis, descending to the plains in between, and then scaling the highest one to summit in triumph on "the year of the Lord's favor."

If you have always been told that a day was coming when everything that breaks you every day would vanish, and you would be able to take a full breath, and you could lift your head and you could stand up and you could smile and even laugh—then you will know what each person knew when Jesus said, "You've just heard Scripture make history. It came true just now in this place."

The people in that meeting place that Sabbath turned to one another excitedly and remarked at how well Jesus spoke. They were not talking about his elocutionary style, but about the thrill of hope that jolted through them in that moment. The words from Isaiah 61, so familiar and so tantalizing, rang in their ears.

But then there were doubts. Wouldn't the Day of the Lord come with trumpets, thunder, signs in the heavens? And wouldn't it be announced by the Messiah, the awesome figure of power and glory of whom the prophets spoke? Instead, we get a local boy, smart but shiftless, who left his mother and travels the countryside. "Isn't this Joseph's son?" they asked. "We've known him since he was a little kid. Is he saying that he's the One? He's getting way above himself."

And then Jesus went off script. You'll probably tell me to heal myself, he said. You want me to do tricks, like what you think I did up in Capernaum. If I don't do the same thing here, you won't believe me. Well, let me tell you something. No prophet is ever welcomed in his own country. There were a lot of widows in Israel during the famine, but our own prophet, Elijah, was sent to a widow in Sidon instead of them. And there were a lot of lepers in our country, but Elisha was sent to heal Naaman, the Syrian. Not one of ours was healed.

As they say, the optics weren't good. Excitement and admiration turned to doubt, and doubt to hostility and rage. More than just grilling the preacher's sermon over Sabbath lunch, they were infuriated. Leaping to their feet, the whole congregation—families, men, women, and children—dragged him to the cliff on which the town was built to fling him bodily out and down.

Imagine the scene: people so angry, so completely consumed by rage, that they seem demon possessed. Neighbors he has known all his life, shoving and kicking him, his arms stretched out in their grasp, and him falling and stumbling back up, his eyes riveted ahead to where the ground drops away for hundreds of feet.

This is a video that will go viral, but before it does, let us freeze the frame with Jesus at the lip of the cliff—and since this is imagination, we can do this—and ask ourselves what they are thinking.

If you saw them on the street you would have no idea they were capable of killing. They look like ordinary people. But seeing them now, ranged behind the figure twisting in their grasp, we see the leers, the harsh laughter, the sweat. A woman's face is framed behind his shoulder. She is jeering, the veins in her forehead distended and throbbing. She feels forgotten, neglected; the hopes that were stirred by the promises of the prophets have vanished, and all that fills her mind is the thought of foreigners receiving the healing that is rightfully hers. Next thing they'll be pouring across the border, Syrians, Caananites, Samaritans, lepers! It is a betrayal of everything she stands for, made worse by one of her own, a traitor in their midst like a devil among them.

Luke places this story near the beginning of Jesus' mission, while Mark and Matthew record it as further down the time line. Commentators suggest that Luke's purpose is to show us that this is how Jesus' mission is going to play out. The rejection he endures by his own people is triggered by his hints that God's Spirit will be poured out on *all* who need it, those in other nations as well as in Israel. The nationalist fervor that roils this crowd into a murderous rage fulfills the prophecy that Jesus speaks.

We know how the incident ends, although we don't know how it is done. Jesus teeters on the cliff's edge, and then suddenly he is striding back through the crowd, parting them before him as if a force field surrounds him. Luke gives it one line, ending with "he went on his way." What matters most is that the kingdom has been announced, the Spirit is present, and Jesus is on his way into the world. Evil is no longer safe.

Jesus *announced* the kingdom in that dusty town on that Sabbath. He also *denounced* the fear that gripped the congregation in a snake's coils. Annunciation and denunciation, two sides of a coin that has been carried by prophets and preachers and ages of sages. Wherever there is denunciation by the prophets, annunciation can be found in the neighborhood. And where the announcement falls upon deaf ears, denunciation of their callous disregard soon follows. The denunciation clears away the thickets, allowing the annunciation to spring forth.

But we must add something else to this prophetic witness between these two movements: the *renunciation* of our sins. Denunciation of the power structures in church and society, the uncovering of that which is intentionally hidden, is a necessary step toward the freedom of justice. But for the Christian, and any person of good faith, there follows in response another step, equally important—that of renunciation.

Jesus began with the annunciation because he is the one who brings in the kingdom. In our time it is up to us as people of faith to begin with the denunciation of systems and structures that oppress and break the spirit of people. It would then be the most natural thing in the world to leap to the annunciation. Problem and solution; it's how the world works.

But we are called to walk humbly as we act for justice. It is with the gospel in trust that we are invited to renounce our sins. The public renouncing of the sins of our discrimination opens the way to announce the good news of the gospel. And the gospel lived out is what reconciles us to God and to each other.

These are the acts of disciples who follow Jesus: they denounce, renounce, and announce. A movement begun by One is carried on through the Spirit by those who are willing to follow.

***

Twenty centuries after Jesus announced the kingdom, we tell ourselves, "The arc of the moral universe is long, but it bends towards justice." Fifty years after Martin Luther King Jr. famously uttered that phrase, we look up to see that arc crossing overhead, but with no discernible point on the horizon where it could touch down. That is, unless we prepare the way by renouncing our sins of injustice, as a nation, as a church, and as individuals.

Unity without equality for everyone is conformity to injustice for all.

Mark Oakley, in *The Splash of Words,* invokes a Franciscan blessing: "May God bless us with discomfort at easy answers, half-truths, and superficial relationships. May God bless us with anger at injustice, oppression and exploitation. May God bless us with enough foolishness to believe that we can make a difference in this world, doing in his name what others claim cannot be done."[2]

---

2. Oakley, *Splash of Words*, 40.

48

My Bibles, My Life

The Bible, more than most books, forms part of one's life once it is absorbed into the system. It does not remain static, any more than you remain ever the same. Your perspective of it will change with the years.[1]

I CANNOT REMEMBER A time in my reading life when a Bible was not within my reach, both literally and figuratively. In the home I grew up in, Scripture was the primary source of one's instruction and inspiration. It was read aloud morning and evening, discussed at church, memorized as Bible verses, emblazoned on bulletin boards at school, and called upon in times of celebration and grief. Its phrases came naturally to the lips, its stories became the video of our imaginations long before there were pixels, the grand highway of its narrative from Genesis to Revelation (pitted with potholes in the Pentateuch) provided both a spiritual history of humankind and a kind of eschatological weather report ("Look for a cloud on the horizon the size of a man's hand!"). Later, through the ministrations of our well-meaning elders, its revelations came to us like birthday gifts from distant uncles who still thought of us as five-year-olds. It was unavoidable and indispensable.

But I find I can trace out the course of my life by looking at the Bibles on my bookshelves, each one having played a role in my life that was both episodic and cumulative.

1. Wilson, *Book of the People*, 3.

***

In high school my Bibles of choice were The *Living Bible* and *Good News for Modern Man: The New Testament in Today's English.*[2] The *Living Bible* was a paperback brick, lovingly slipped into a doeskin cover that my grandfather had gotten for me in Canada, with a painting of an Indian brave on the front. Inside the end pages I wrote notes of favorite verses, quotes from religious authors, and lines of poetry. T*LB* was fresh, a bit cheeky, conversational without falling into cultural jargon. The *Good News* New Testament was plain, small enough to carry in one hand, and modest in its literary aspirations. Its line drawings were simple, evocative, and good-humored. I was also reading a lot of C. S. Lewis at the time, along with *Lord of the Rings, The Hobbit,* Byron, Shelley, Yeats, and Matthew Arnold. It was a heady mix.

My first year in college, working on a double major in religion and journalism, I used a standard-issue King James in my religion classes. I'd had it since my baptism at age twelve and I knew my way around its paths by sight. These were the phrases and verses I had heard all my life. They seeped into my consciousness and became the language of my operating system, an eloquent counterpoint to the informality of the modern versions.

***

In the summer of 1971 I left California for England to work with friends in Coventry in starting and running a Christian folk club and then to spend the school year at Newbold College. Away from home for the first time, I spent the year in a constant state of wonder and discovery. That summer I bought my first *New English Bible,* a paperback Penguin version of the New Testament whose language and verses seemed like poetry to me. I found a tanner's shop in Leamington Spa and made a book cover for it from suede leather, stitching a peace symbol with a cross in the center on the front. The cover art on the Penguin version was a reproduction of Georges Rouault's *Head of Christ,* thus beginning a lifelong admiration for his art. In the fall, as a student at Newbold, I hitchhiked down to Reading and bought J. B. Phillip's *New Testament in Modern English*. I also started a year-long course in *Koine* Greek. I was terrible at

---

2. This is the first, New Testament-only edition of the Good News Translation, formerly known as Today's English Version.

it, but I scraped by with enough margin to be given a copy of the British and Foreign Bible Society's *Greek New Testament* with critical apparatus. Burrowing into the permutations of Greek verbs and nouns reinforced my life-long fascination with word origins and their meanings.

That year I always carried in my backpack at least one Bible, usually two. As I hitchhiked to Scotland or down to Wales or up to London, these Bibles became my traveling companions, provoking comment and conversation from the generous people who gave me rides. Comparing these translations and paraphrases jolted my imagination and gave me different lines of sight to their meaning. And always I carried a small Authorized Version whose cover could be zipped closed. I left it behind in a train station in Milan one December; two years later it showed up in my mailbox at home in California, having made the journey through the kindness of strangers on the strength of my college address at Newbold.

***

All through graduate studies at Andrews University in Michigan and Claremont Graduate University in Southern California, my familiars were the *New English Bible* I had bought in Wales in 1974 when I worked in evangelism there, and *the Jerusalem Bible,* another chunk of a Bible whose lyrical Psalms were refreshing and whose Job was high tragedy. Later, teaching Jesus and the Gospels, Hebrew Prophets, and Paul and His Letters at Columbia Union College, in Maryland, I entered into a professional relationship with *the New International Version.* Those who knew their biblical languages assured me it was the latest and most accurate rendering, but its starched and anemic language gave me no joy. Time and again I went back to my NEB, by now so annotated and stuffed with typed-out quotes and photos of friends that when the spine finally collapsed my wife made me a book cover for it from the jeans I wore out hitchhiking through the UK.

***

In these later years I have come back to the *New Revised Standard Version,* not to be confused with the *Revised English Bible,* a second take on the *NEB*. As I write there is one just behind my shoulder on the bookshelf, another one next to my comfy chair across the loft, and a third one, barely marked, on another bookshelf. Recently, having finished teaching my courses for the semester at Trinity Washington University, I stopped into the Saint John Paul II National Shrine, right across the street from Catholic University, and indulged myself in a beautifully leather-bound Catholic edition of the *Revised Standard Version* with the Apocrypha.

***

I've entered the Bible as into a vast and varied library—*ta biblia*, the books. Not a single, coherent narrative, but stories of wonder, beginning in a garden of light and ending in a city with a river running through it. To try to understand the people within the stories is to read with a dual vision: that, in certain irreducible ways, they and we come from the same stock and harbor the same emotions and motivations; and in other ways, bound by time, culture, language, and technology, we arrive at our final home having traveled such disparate paths. I am grateful to the archeologists, linguists, anthropologists, and theologians who have peeled back the layers of the Bible for us and interpreted its structures.

The Bible has meant different things to me through many different stages of life. It has both revealed and hidden God, and it has held a mirror up to myself. The Jesus I have found there is no less enigmatically divine than when I first began with the Gospels, but now even more touchingly human. The Bible, I've found, is large enough that it can play many roles in a person's life. Like the earth itself, it presents a different but constant face to the observer hovering in orbit above it. It is guide, wisdom, puzzle, danger, mystery, and light. It is still the literary foundation for many of us.

The Bible is an alternate world that runs parallel to our own. It is like holding two magnets in tension so that you feel the pull of one to the other. Let one go and the tension is gone, the case closed, the story resolved, the horizon suddenly walled up. Unless we see both the fragments of light it illumines around us and the Light itself—and the distinction makes all the difference—the Bible remains just another revered bestseller.

49

The Worlds We Make

We can have words without a world but no world without words or other symbols.[1]

THE FIRST LINE OF the *Dhammapada*, a collection of the Buddha's sayings, is, "All that we are is the result of what we have thought." With that, the Buddha signals that thought precedes action and mind shapes character. This is in common with the words of another sage from Proverbs: "As a man thinketh, so is he," a maxim that suggests in its context to beware of the stingy who insincerely invite one to share a meal. They are not to be trusted, for the hidden thought will be exposed in the interplay between the two.

So, I am here quoting those who once lived upon this earth, people we know only through their words. The gulf that lies between the utterance of those words in time and where we stand today is not just about the millennia that have passed between us, but about the worlds those words brought into being and the worlds that arise when we read them today. Are they the same worlds?

We create worlds through our words, says Nelson Goodman in *Ways of Worldmaking*. In a few pages of closely reasoned arguments, Goodman shows that the frames of reference we construct to describe what we experience are *systems* of description; they are not that which is

---

1. Goodman, *Ways of Worldmaking*, 6.

being described. We never truly apprehend the object of our experience, only the description we construct to talk about it.

An example: If we say, "The sun always moves" and "The sun never moves," both statements are equally true and equally at odds with one another. Goodman asks if these statements describe different worlds—whether there are "as many different worlds as there are such mutually exclusive truths?" No, rather we make accommodation by saying that under this frame of reference this statement is true and with another frame of reference the other statement is true. "Our universe, so to speak," says Goodman, "consists of these ways rather than of a world or of worlds."[2]

I find this invigorating and disconcerting. Goodman is playing games—language games—to make a point: there is no irrefutable foundation for all truth, only descriptions that are more or less right for their context. The fact that we construct these descriptions out of what we find in anthropology, physics, psychology, literature, philosophy, theology, and other disciplines means that we are constantly remaking our worlds of thought. "Worldmaking as we know it," says Goodman, "always starts from worlds already on hand; the making is a remaking."[3]

***

Here are some materials at hand that we can make a story out of, a description of something and someone that matters a great deal to us.

Jesus is crucified about 33 CE and the first Gospel, generally thought to be Mark's Gospel, is written about 70 CE. That is a gap of about forty years—a whole generation—without any written sources of Jesus' life. The people who gathered each week in small groups to remember the Lord were those who had had firsthand knowledge of Jesus. The boy who gave over the loaves and fishes that Jesus fed five thousand people with would have been a man with children and grandchildren of his own. Lazarus, raised from the tomb and given a second life, would have passed on by this time. The disciples, men with families when Jesus chose them, would have grown old and scattered, some to Rome, others staying in Jerusalem, Thomas (as legend has it) making his way to India to establish a Christian community, and Philip probably down in Ethiopia. All of these people lived and died on the stories that were told and retold about Jesus,

---

2. Goodman, *Ways of Worldmaking*, 3.
3. Goodman, *Ways of Worldmaking*, 6.

as they met together in upper rooms, sometimes in a wealthy person's home, sometimes on the run, often over a meal with song and celebration. They were people, quite literally, of the word, the Word that came and lived amongst them.

Think of the stories they told, the anecdotes tenderly passed down through the family chain like pearls of great value. From the sayings of Jesus to the signs he performed to the parables he told, these narratives sustained these groups through their days and eventually formed the web of Mark's Gospel.

In his breathless and rustic style, the author of Mark's Gospel creates a narrative—a world!—that Matthew and Luke break down to use in the remaking of their individual worlds. Later, around 90–100 CE, comes John's Gospel, a parallel universe to the previous gospels, converging at points, but drawing its own course through its orbit. It closes with these tantalizing words:

"But there are also many other things that Jesus did; if every one of them were written down, I suppose that the world itself could not contain the books that would be written."[4]

These Gospels are the gospel, the good news about Jesus who came into the world and "the world came into being through him; yet the world did not know him."[5]

***

We read these words today, millennia away from their creation, in the awareness that the bone and sinew, words and meaning of their author and the person of which he wrote come down to language and symbols, marks on paper or pixels on a screen. Despite the billions of words devoted to this Jesus, the stories that could be told have no end because these words, having been written, continue to produce new stories in the strength that "The light shines in the darkness, and the darkness did not overcome it."[6]

Instead, we may become accustomed to these stories to the extent that we no longer take in their meaning. Our eyes pass over the letters; we register the shape of the words as we would the silhouette of objects

---

4. John 21:25.
5. John 1:10.
6. John 1:5.

whose outlines against the light are familiar only because of the form of their darkness.

"This world, indeed," notes Goodman, "is the one most often taken as real; for reality in a world, like realism in a picture, is largely a matter of habit."[7]

"Language can create faith but can't sustain it," says Christian Wiman in *Ambition and Survival*.[8] I'm not so sure. When I read of the Buddha holding up a flower before his gathered disciples and one of them—only one—smiles, and Buddha says the equivalent of "He gets it!" something in me thrills to that imagined scene. When Jesus begins with "The kingdom of heaven is like . . . ," it's "Once upon a time . . ." all over again. We are hardwired for stories: good, bad, mediocre, we pick them up, and turn them over and over in our hands until we find the seam that opens them. From these we fashion a world that we can live in.

"To have faith in a religion, any religion," continues Wiman, "is to accept at some primary level that its particular language of words and symbols says something true about reality."[9] That I can agree with.

He goes on: "This doesn't mean that the words and symbols *are* reality (that's fundamentalism), nor that you will ever master those words and symbols well enough to regard reality as some fixed thing. What it does mean, though, . . . is that the only way to deepen your knowledge and experience of ultimate divinity is to deepen your knowledge of the all-too-temporal symbols and language of a particular religion."[10]

Separated as we are by thousands of years and the innumerable worlds of language and imagination between us and Jesus, these slender figures on our pages are the portals between our worlds. The path to the divine remains, astonishingly, through the darkness and light that is our world.

---

7. Goodman, *Ways of Worldmaking*, 20.
8. Wiman, *Ambition and Survival*, 160.
9. Wiman, *Ambition and Survival*, 161.
10. Wiman, *Ambition and Survival*, 161.

50

The Eyes of Your Heart

> *. . . so that, with the eyes of your heart enlightened, you may know what is the hope to which he has called you, what are the riches of his glorious inheritance among the saints, and what is the immeasurable greatness of his power for us who believe, according to the working of his great power.*[1]

ONCE WE UNDERSTAND THERE are many ways to enlighten our hearts, the horizon of possibilities before us widens. This is especially true when we seek beauty and truth—distinguishable and thus equally indispensable. When we find these sources, whether they be bathed in the center of God's glory or reflecting God's light from their centrifugal swings around the Son, they open to us new channels for perception.

Poetry penetrates deep to the heart, but indirectly so. If you're willing to look you can find the poets who somehow hear the music that beats in your bloodstream, and when you read them you understand yourself in ways you couldn't have arrived at on your own. "When you encounter this splash of words," writes priest and poet Mark Oakley, "you understand that ultimately poetry is not about factual information but human formation. Like water, language goes stagnant if it doesn't move."[2]

---

1. Eph 1:18–19.
2. Oakley, *Splash of Words*, xv.

When I first read Rainer Maria Rilke, this poet of the great silences, the man who was christened with a girl's name for the sister who was lost, it was as if he had read my heart's way and was speaking my longings in words that were almost holy. When I began with his *Sonnets to Orpheus,* I could only manage a page or two and then I'd have to put it aside and do something else for a while, something that didn't lay me open to the bone. If we can bear it, this is an opening to wonder and mystery.

Or maybe it's music—Faure's *Requiem,* or Bach's *St. Matthew Passion,* or U2's *"I Still Haven't Found What I'm Looking For,"* or the tears that flow from Eric Clapton's guitar through *"While My Guitar Gently Weeps"* during the "Concert for George." That's what Carlos Santana calls "Holy Ghost music," something that happens between musicians and audience that goes beyond artistry and technique to a communion of fire and spirit.

These moments, these strands of bright beauty, are all around us, and if we choose, we can weave them together in our memories for a coat of many colors to wear on our dull and darker days. Their beauty, though ephemeral, is real in the moment: we can *see* them and feel them as they pass through us. But their greater power is that they remind us of something we've known and lost or once had but did not fully appreciate. They are signs of the ineffable, signals received from a source whose coordinates seem strangely familiar. As such, they give us practice in the exercise of faith.

***

"It is within man's power to seek Him," writes Rabbi Abraham Heschel in *God in Search of Man,* "it is not within his power to find Him. All Abraham had was wonder, and all he could achieve on his own was readiness to perceive. The answer was disclosed to him; it was not found by him."[3]

Heschel turns to Maimonides, who did not offer proof for the existence of God but said that the source of our knowledge of God is the "inner heart," the medieval name for intuition. We don't apprehend God through a syllogism, but through an insight, a spiritual discernment.

It's not that reason can't play a role in spiritual things; reasoning often brings us into the neighborhood of faith and removes barriers to our

---

3. Heschel, *God in Search of Man,* 147.

willingness to listen. It provides a way to organize our categories: faith, evidence, rationality, miracles, finitude and infinity, eternity and time-boundedness, perfection and inexactitude, the sacred and the mundane. It helps us bracket our prejudices and recognize our standpoint. And it can reveal our inconsistencies and lapses in judgement. This is the stuff of the philosophy of religion, all of it intriguing, fascinating, compelling. But it can also keep God at a distance, an object to be argued about, not a being who enthralls us. For that we need the eyes of the heart. "Faith terminates not in a statement, not in a formula of words, but *in God,*" writes Thomas Merton in *New Seeds of Contemplation*.[4]

Heschel continues: "But the initiative, we believe, is with man. The great insight is not given unless we are ready to receive."[5] Faith commences, God completes.

So here now is Paul, writing to his friends in Ephesus, rejoicing with them that their sins are forgiven, that God has chosen them to be filled with love, and that when the right time arrives the whole universe—heaven touching earth—will be brought into joyful harmony in Christ. *That time is now,* Paul insists. The "eyes of your heart" will perceive it through faith.

Here is the audaciousness that characterizes the apostolic community and that still— perhaps even more now—takes our breath away. In the midst of wearying journeys, dissensions and disputes, divisions that cut to the heart of who Paul and his friends thought they were because of Christ, he gathers up the threads of their faith in action and promises that this is indeed the first light of the new day of God's kingdom.

Two millennia later this promise almost seems like mockery. Far from being a community without divisions, the Church seems to model the political world with all its coercion, bad faith, and posturing. We see the same underhandedness and false hope in the Church that plays out in a daily livestream from any number of our politicians and corporate leaders. The Church as a body sometimes does not even reach the standard of respect and equality for people that our society continues to struggle toward. We Christians have a lot to answer for. Are we wandering in the wilderness?

Paul's message to Jew and Gentile was that God was in Christ reconciling the world to himself. What had been promised for centuries,

---

4. Merton, *New Seeds of Contemplation*, 132.
5. Heschel, *God in Search of Man*, 147.

though covenants made were broken and straight places fell into crookedness, had now, in the fullness of time, come to pass. Quite beyond any power they might have exercised to move the cosmic forces into alignment, the promise was made good in spite of their weakness. Nothing they did could bring it into being, nor could they prevent what God had planned from the foundation of the world. It was a gift open to all who could see it, a world reborn.

Paul has heard of the faith of these Ephesians and their "love toward all the saints," and he prays that God may give them "a spirit of wisdom and revelation." To his friends at Ephesus —and to us—he says, "you are no longer strangers and aliens, but you are citizens . . . of the household of God."[6]

To Paul, every little community of believers that formed *was* the household of God, a wavering light that would bloom brighter as their faith was seen in action.

The question was whether they could see this potential for themselves, if the bonds of friendship and community they had begun could strengthen and flourish. Could they perceive God in the whirl and flux of this world? The eyes of their hearts would see the hope to which God had called them, the richness of belonging to this great cloud of witnesses, and the greatness of God's power to sustain them.

Faith commences, God completes. Believing is seeing.

---

6. Eph 2:19.

51

No Guarantees

Communication as a bridge always means an abyss is somewhere near.[1]

ACCORDING TO THE GOSPEL of Matthew, Herod slaughtered every child of the age of two and under in Bethlehem and its surroundings, because he was trying to kill the king of the Jews whom the *magi* from the East had come to worship.

To put the Bethlehem massacre by Herod in its full horrific context, the writer of the Gospel reaches back to the prophet Jeremiah's lament for the slaughter of children in Ramah, an Ephraimite village eight miles north of Jerusalem, before those who remained were deported to Babylon. He needs a historical parallel of sufficient magnitude.

> Then was fulfilled what had been spoken through the prophet Jeremiah:
> "A voice was heard in Ramah,
> wailing and loud lamentation,
> Rachel weeping for her children;
> she refused to be consoled, because
> they are no more."[2]

---

1. Peters, *Speaking into the Air*, 16.
2. Matt 2:18.

Thus, the good news (for that is what *euanggelion,* the "gospel," means) of the coming of the Christ child, the promised one, the Son of God and the savior of the world, unfolds in haste and secrecy in the midst of a bloodbath. But it has ever been so, as powerful and corrupt rulers are threatened by women and children.

The family escapes to Egypt, being warned in a dream, and they remain there—we don't know how long—until news comes that Herod is dead. They make plans to return to Bethlehem, but Joseph is again warned off in a dream. Instead, they find their way north to Nazareth, a village in Galilee so insignificant that there is no mention of it in historical records outside of the New Testament. Their caution is well founded, for Herod's son, King Archelaus, rules for only two years before the Roman emperor, Augustus, removes and banishes him for brutality. If Herod could kill a generation of Judean children with impunity, what must Archelaus have done to incur the wrath of the emperor? Or perhaps it was a pragmatic decision on the emperor's part, knowing that even the poorest, weakest, and most oppressed will eventually rise up.

Advent is a season when Christians celebrate the coming of the Christ-child, the earthly beginning to Emmanuel, God with Us, and the short, intense journey that brings that child, now a man, to an abrupt end on the cross. But then there is Easter and resurrection; the unexpected turn of a tragedy become comedy, the ultimate trick on the trickster, and a silent nod offstage to where Job stands alone in the wings, with an amused shake of his head and a smile. There are innumerable crucifixions without a resurrection, but in this story there is no resurrection without a crucifixion.

When lies become the norm we cherish the truth even more, and for us in this century, truth is found in facts. We want the gospels to be history, a medium we think we understand as a story that corresponds to the facts. But behind the facts lie assumptions, and assumptions are most often invisible to those who hold them and inaccessible to those who don't. What is *not* mentioned in the Gospels about Jesus may not have been known by the Gospel writers, or was known, but thought so obvious that their concise narratives did not include it, or was known, but considered insignificant to the core of the story. Their assumptions are not our assumptions; the stories that result are strange to us and sometimes even inexplicable.

Albert Schweitzer devoted years to a search for the historical Jesus and finally concluded that "Each successive epoch found its own thoughts in Jesus," because one typically "created him in accordance with one's own character." "There is," Schweitzer said, "no historical task which so reveals someone's true self as the writing of a *Life of Jesus.*"[3]

Thus, there are multiple versions of Jesus in all ages, as Jaroslav Pelikan so lucidly illustrates in his *Jesus Through the Centuries*, a cultural history. "For each age," he comments, "the life and teachings of Jesus represented an answer (or, more often, the answer) to the most fundamental questions of human existence and of human destiny, and it was to the figure of Jesus as set forth in the Gospels that those questions were addressed."[4] And we could add that people of faith, as well as those who profess no faith, nevertheless carry refracted images of Jesus in their minds that are often at odds with each other. We see Jesus as through a kaleidoscope rather than through a microscope. The Gospels give us a collage, not a portrait.

The fragmentary glimpses we get of Jesus are not the result of inattention on the part of the eyewitnesses, nor are they lapses in the discipline of the story. Rather, they are the best that people could do to reveal a figure so mysteriously complex and yet so transparently good that no one close to him could ever say they knew him through and through.

Jesus was not an open book to those who knew him. The disciples were often confused and distraught by his words, drawing him aside to ask for the meaning of a parable or to clarify for them his differences with the religious authorities. Jesus rejoices that God has hidden his truths from the sophisticated and has opened them to those who learn best from actions and images.

We simplify the story of the nativity down to what we can carry without dropping all the other things that fill up our lives. In a creche, the animals form the background, their benign expressions of placid acceptance mirroring our own. Joseph stands to one side, proud but peripheral. The wise men, kneeling or standing, present their gifts with reverence. Mary and Jesus are front and center, the focal point of everything and the period to the exclamation mark of the star that stands above the stable. There is something so achingly touching about this, a child's toys arranged just so to mimic the world she imagines. Add to this the innumerable Christmas plays in schools and churches acted out in front

---

3. In Pelikan, *Jesus Through the Centuries*, 2.
4. Pelikan, *Jesus Through the Centuries*, 2.

of proud but anxious parents, each play another means to build a bridge from an ancient culture to our own.

The question for Christians and other people of faith is how to tell this story, this coming-to-earth story of divine *kenosis*, of an emptying out and pouring in of God become human. As the epigram suggests, a bridge implies an abyss, otherwise what is its purpose? In communication with one another, in telling the story yet again, we recognize the abyss to be the fact that we cannot clearly and completely express the truths we comprehend, nor can we be assured that our comprehension is correct. We are the "speaking animals" whose verbal options are almost limitless, but by that very fact we must often grope for the words to match the images we have in our heads.

From within our comfort zone, the Advent story is theologically safe, hermetically sealed, predictable in its results. It's a ritual we cannot do without, yet it often bypasses the heart.

We need to recapture the otherness, the very alien nature of this story of God become a human, a story that rings through history with tones both dark and bright. There are other gods who have appeared in human form, but none of them as a baby and none who stayed around to be murdered—and then rose again.

The thing that we must never forget, that if understood will disrupt our lives and break our complacency, is that *nothing* in the events of this story can be taken for granted. Joseph could have laughed off his dreams, Mary could have said no, the baby could have died before the age of five from diseases that take the lives of fifteen thousand newborns per day in this world. The family seeking asylum in Egypt could have been turned away at the border, held for questioning, or simply murdered on the way.

People made choices without much to go on, save what they held in faith. As strange as those times and that culture may be to us, the common factor we may share if we wish is that God was in Christ reconciling the world to himself and that from the foundation of the earth this has been a work of love.

52

The Light Coming into the World

The true light that enlightens every man was coming into the world. He was in the world, and the world was made through him, yet the world knew him not.[1]

God's entry into the world in the Gospel of John begins with two powerful metaphors: the Word and light. The author plays with these metaphors, turning them this way and that, like a craftsman looking to join two pieces of wood with mortise and tenon rather than nails and glue.

Words, the building blocks of meaning, stack up behind us in the long histories we come from, and we pull them down to make anything out of something, a trick we've perfected over eons. But the original magician of words is he who creates something out of nothing with the Word alone, who morphs an idea into action and the ineffable into flesh.

The Word, according to John, becomes flesh and lives among us. The Word lives among us in grace and truth; we see his glory, the glory of God reflected somehow through the lens of a human being, a human being in whom all the fullness of God dwells. This is a mystery too deep for us, a treasure we leave buried in our field for a later time.

As Lewis Carroll wrote in *Through the Looking Glass*, "When I use a word," Humpty Dumpty said, in rather a scornful tone, "it means just

---

1. John 1:9–10.

what I choose it to mean—neither more nor less." "The question is," said Alice, "whether you can make words mean so many different things." "The question is," said Humpty Dumpty, "which is to be master—that's all."[2]

Does the Word mean what we want it (him) to mean? Is it a screen upon which we project whatever image fits our mood? Or is this metaphor one so rich in variant meanings that it becomes—in the way Paul characterized himself—"all things to all people"?

We read these verses of John's Gospel, especially within this Christmas hour, as we might read the letter of a relative who, long ago, writes to a friend about her love for another. We are witness to this love through her words. We ask ourselves if "glory" could be a form of love. The letter falls into its remembered folds; we follow in a reverie as the traffic of our lives passes blindly before our eyes, but we see only what we are longing for. We see it wordlessly, the incarnation of Emmanuel, God with us, the Word, *Logos,* become flesh.

In some readings, the *Logos* is that energy of life which pours through the universe and is expressed within every molecule and sinew. The resonance of *that* expression—glory compressed into vulnerability—creates a new reality of *kenosis,* an emptying out and a pouring in of God to birth.

That the Word is life and can call forth life is deeply embedded in the Christian tradition. From the creation of the world to the healing of a leper to the awakening of faith in a person, the Word, in the form of Jesus and in the words of Jesus, has been the content of character for those who have awakened through the Spirit.

***

For many people, Christmas is a memory formed of light. In the deepest, darkest, engulfing days of the year we raise our lights and are drawn to them. In our churches, our cathedrals, in our windows, and even around our public squares, the lights go up as in no other time of the year. At Christmas we are drawn into these overlapping circles of light that show us a way forward, like stepping-stones across a river of light. We are drawn out of our darkness to them because from within our darkness we cannot not see them.

---

2. Carroll, *Through the Looking Glass*, 178.

But it remains a question whether the light defines the darkness as all that is not light or if the darkness actively resists the light. Therein lies the mystery of evil and suffering.

"The people who were sitting in darkness saw a great light," Matthew says, paraphrasing Isaiah. "They were sitting in the land of the shadow of death, and the light dawned on them."[3] Isaiah's wording, by contrast, is that the people were "walking in darkness," stumbling their way toward the light of dawn. Matthew's people are no longer even walking; they've given up. They're huddled in darkness in a country that lies under the shadow of death.

We may feel this way too. The darkness comes for us in different guises, but it comes for us all. It may come in a diagnosis of cancer, or the death of a loved one at the hands of a drunk driver, or the pitiless drip of poverty and the daily gusts of discrimination and racism. At Christmas, for those who are alone, the darkness can seem impenetrable and its weight all the heavier for all the brightness seen in other people's windows.

God can be found, suggests W. H. Auden in his famous poem "For the Time Being," in the Land of Unlikeness, in the Kingdom of Anxiety, and even in the World of the Flesh. Roger Housden muses that in the midst of the glitter and gifts of a commercial Chrsistmas, it may be difficult to perceive the redemption of the incarnation, but in the "confusing and uncertain world we live in from day to day . . . in the drab period of the year that follows" Christmas, we find the light we need.[4]

Can we sing the Lord's song in the dark times as well as the light? We may not have the words, but the incarnation means we can sing, even if only about the dark times.

But the dawn comes! It comes whether we are walking toward it or whether we can no longer walk or even remember what the dawn looks like. Christmas, with all its lights, reminds us that the dawn comes with power that is beyond our imagination. It is a gift from the Father of Lights, the one in whom we may trust, against all odds.

A birth in the midst of death and dark forces is a tragic commonplace in our world, but in this wildly improbable tale, this Christmas story of God the Word becoming light and life in a manger, there is a touchstone for millions. Yet, the Gospel storyteller reminds us that he

---

3. Matt 4:16, Lattimore trans.,
4. Housden, *For Lovers of God Everywhere*, 41.

who is Light shines on in the darkness and the darkness will never eclipse it—a message for all of us who find ourselves in a country shadowed by death.

53

Seeing Things

And so as Christmas comes again, think about this extraordinary truth: that God can make himself known only with our consent and co-operation.[1]

IN THIS ADVENT SEASON we await the coming of the Christ-child. Our sources for this are Matthew and Luke. Mark begins his Gospel breathlessly with Jesus as a man, coming up out of the waters of baptism, the skies splitting open above him. John's Gospel begins even farther back, among star trails of light in the cosmos, the Word materializing out of the blackness of the space between the stars, to arrive uncloaked as the very being and presence of God across the universe. It's Matthew who gives us the credentials first, the genealogy of the Savior, beginning with Abraham and running neatly through three sets of fourteen generations each until we arrive at "Joseph the husband of Mary, of whom Jesus was born, who is called the Messiah."

And it's Matthew who calls up astrologers from Babylon who, in their glad and awe-struck homage, ply the family with precious gifts of gold, frankincense, and myrrh, and then, after being warned of Herod's baleful intentions in a dream, take another road back home. No sooner had they gone, and the family settled down for fitful sleep, when Joseph yields to a dream (a language he was learning still) to take his wife and newborn child and slip through Herod's slaughter of the innocents. So,

1. Mayne, *Responding to the Light*, 27.

with the gold he buys his neighbor's horse in whispered haste at 3 a.m., shuts up the house, and off they go, under the stars, across the rock-strewn miles of desert to seek asylum in Egypt.

With Luke we get the bells and whistles—no wise men this time, but more dreams and angels and shepherds and cousins and songs of humility and unalloyed triumph; an older woman with child who thought herself barren; and a mere girl-child trembling before the sudden, glittering form of a being who stoops to enter her room, and toward whom she bows her head and shields her eyes because, against the evidence, she is certain she is seeing things.

We look at our own infants and imagine who they might become, what they might do, even (God forbid) the harm that might come to them and the resolve we feel to protect them from anything like that. We wonder how the world will change in the time that passes as they grow into adulthood.

In time, we realize that they are not clones of ourselves, but persons in their own right, with personalities and temperaments that may reflect our influence, yet with their own perspectives and motivations. They are not us; they have their own path to travel.

The being whom Luke names as Gabriel greets Mary in a way that is deeply troubling to her. "Greetings, most favored one! The Lord is with you." The angel hastens to add, "Do not be afraid, Mary, for God has been gracious to you; you shall conceive and bear a son, and you shall give him the name Jesus."

The singular event that transforms human history has begun. It begins, as Luke tells us, with a girl, one among thousands, who is filled with awe and confusion at being singled out, placed at the head of the line, in the spotlight, up on the stage.

Every woman and girl could wonder in quiet moments if she might be the one to bear the Messiah. More than one watched with secret joy at the sweetness of her child, only to have her hopes dashed when he turned out far less messianic than even the most generous grandparent could vouch for.

Luke's Gabriel is hitting all the keys with full chords now. "He will be great," the being sings out, "and will be called the Son of the Most High, and the Lord God will give to him the throne of his ancestor David. He will reign over the house of Jacob forever, and of his kingdom there will be no end."

There is silence. The being looks at Mary expectantly. "How can this be," she says deadpan, "since I am a virgin?" She may have only been fourteen or fifteen, but she knows how babies are made. The being sighs; this is going to be tougher than he thought.

"The Holy Spirit will come upon you," he says, and glances sidelong at her. "And the power of the Most High will overshadow you; therefore the child to be born will be holy; he will be called the Son of God." A simply deductive syllogism, he thinks. Two premises followed by a conclusion—a conclusion that must be true if the premises are true. And, of course, they are. There is silence. Mary's head is down, but the being can see that her gaze is fixed and unmoving. She does not blink. He looks more closely; yes, she is still breathing.

He tries again: "And now, your relative Elizabeth in her old age has also conceived a son; and this is the sixth month for her who was said to be barren." He pauses. "For nothing is impossible with God," he finishes up with a flourish. Mary's shoulders shudder and she lifts her head. Her cheeks are wet with tears, but now she is smiling as she presses her palms into her eyes. She looks up, this girl who has been lifted and spun, whose heart is ablaze with ancient titles, prophetic proclamations, words spoken that were always like objects of wonder heard but not touched, words so overwhelming that they overshadowed the sky and made tense the present.

"Here am I," she says in a whisper, "the servant of the Lord; let it be with me according to your word." And Luke recounts laconically, "Then the angel departed from her."

Let us not diminish the utter awesomeness of this scene. The word "awesome" has been debased in our time, liberally applied as easily to ice cream as to lending someone a stapler. I want to reserve it for the *numinous*, that which raises the hair on the back of your neck, that which is awe-full. "The Lord is in this place," breathes Jacob, looking around in the velvet desert darkness as his eyes adjust to the explosion of light as ten thousand angels ascend and descend on a stairway to heaven. That's awesome.

No matter how many times we may read of angels appearing to people in the Scriptures, we mustn't forget that it was at least as strange to them as it would be to us. The difference between them and their time and us is that we've built in defenses against this kind of thing, so that the *numinous* cannot be part of any algorithms we might use to calculate what we agree is reality.

She could have said no, Mary could. That is just one of a thousand decision points that could have diverted or ended the stream of this story. Without that yes, that heart-stopping yes, none of our own yeses would have been possible.

The threshold at which we can linger and then stumble through into Mary's room after the being is gone is in the thought of the perilous journey ahead for this promised child. In a matter of moments, Mary has gone from a girl with a predictable life ahead of her to the promised portal through which the Son of God enters the world undetected. This is a joy so deep it can only be expressed with tears. There is a holy terror that rockets her up above the world, giddy at that height and breathless as she yields to the heat that courses through her body.

It is a glorious madness that she has opened herself to. If we are brave enough, we will not turn our eyes away as the arrow arcs into the sky to pierce her heart with the certainty that darkness impenetrable also lies ahead. Joy and terror; this is how her "Yes!" thrills through her body.

From our distance, looking back, we are both the girl-child that says yes to the being and the guardians of the child still to come. Our hearts are full for that child in his early peril. In the Advent season we await his coming into a world both cruelly cold and wondrously beautiful.

54

A Scandal We Can Live For

He was in the form of God, but did not think to seize on the right to be equal to God . . . being born in the likeness of a human being; and being found in the guise of a human being, he humiliated himself and was obedient to the death, death on the cross.[1]

EVERY LIFE THAT BEGINS points forward to a death, a truth we mortals carry like a stone in our shoe.

Does every father grasped in the clenching fear and joyous awe of the birthing hour cast his mind forward to the death of his son? Perhaps Joseph did, caught up in a mystery whose dimensions seemed to waver in and out of focus with his young wife's hoarse cries. There is no mention of a midwife in the Gospel nativity stories. Does Joseph deliver the child himself?

Questions like these are how we fumble our way to the heart of the nativity story. We ask them because we want to time-travel back, to be there in that moment to try to grasp how—no, why—an infinite God plunges deep into our world in order to surface as an infant, an infant for whom the mere rumor of existence is enough to trigger a massacre.

From a reasonable perspective it would be hard to find a less auspicious beginning for a clandestine King of kings and Lord of lords: a baby born into poverty under one of the most corrupt governments of

1. Phil 2:7–8, Lattimore trans.

an empire notable not only for its reach but also for its cruelty. From a revolutionary standpoint, chances for success in overthrowing the empire hover around zero. I don't think we can exaggerate how awful the odds are here.

Imagine the story line pitched by the producers of a film company to the head of a major studio:

"What kind of film is this?"

"It's kind of an action-adventure, but with a strong underdog angle."

"Let's hear it."

"Okay, a baby is born under mysterious circumstances to a poverty-stricken couple who have to flee to another country to avoid a massacre of all children under two by a corrupt and paranoid tyrant."

"I see."

"And the kid survives and grows up to form a roving band of—"

"Guerrilla fighters?"

"No. They go around this country healing people and teaching them about loving their enemies and turning the other cheek."

(silence)

"And finally, he's captured, all his friends desert him, and he's killed."

"Wait. He's got no superpowers?"

"No."

"No last-minute rescue mission?"

"No."

"Too depressing. What's the point?"

"Well, he comes back to life."

"Like what, a zombie? That could work—"

"No, no zombies. He comes back to life and then after a while he disappears."

"And that's it? Are you kidding me?"

"Well, he returns later and sorts everything out."

"When?"

"When what?"

"When does he return?"

"Nobody knows, it's just that—"

"Get outta my office."

We have an advantage over Joseph—we know that the end of his son's story is the beginning of an even greater story. We know the end of our story too, the one we share with our human community. What we cannot fathom is the *beginning* of this baby's story.

The nativity scenes we witness in paintings are as peaceful and placid a scene as one could imagine. The baby Jesus coos and waves his little fists. Mary is dressed in robes of cerulean and white and gazes benignly on her infant son. The *magi* are there, having arrived not a moment too soon, but months after they set out from their city. In some of the paintings there are shepherds kneeling by the manger. They've already seen angels that night, a heavenly host of them, their burning towering forms lighting up the hills for miles around. Naturally, the shepherds are terrified, but it's a terror that becomes raw energy; they race down off the hills and into the town. (How do they know where to go?) But they find the place and slip inside, some to kneel, some to stand in the shadows, panting and glancing at one another with wondering eyes.

***

God must now think from behind the eyes of a human being. Those considerable limitations are what remains to work with. No superpowers here, just the steady consistency of vulnerability and love. Will that be enough?

If this really was the *kairos,* the right time for this intervention in earth history, we wouldn't have seen it had we been there. Even if we had been in Jesus' roving band of disciples, we couldn't have understood it. As long as power meant violence to take down the enemy, none of this would have made sense. And if we're honest it still doesn't make sense. The reason we accept it, this incarnation, this embodiment of God in human flesh, is that we no longer see it as the *skandalon,* the scandal it really is. What kind of god would have the patience, not to mention the love, to work with creatures who resolutely kill everyone who offers them hope?

"The central miracle asserted by Christians is the Incarnation," said C. S. Lewis in *The Joyful Christian.* "They say God became Man . . . Every particular Christian miracle manifests at a particular place and moment the character and significance of the Incarnation."[2]

This is where it begins for us. It doesn't really matter if we can't figure out the biological status of a virgin birth or even if *parthenos* means a young girl of marriageable age versus a woman who has never had sex. What matters is that we accept this gift of God become human, scandal and all.

---

2. Lewis, *The Joyful Christian,* 52.

Advent for me means the coming of the Christ-child into this world, through the back door of the world, under the silent stars of the world, for the world. It always catches me off guard, which is good, because we should always be surprised at Advent. Surprised that the kingdom begins in such a quiet way; surprised that at least once during the year we can say in all honesty, that we were blind, but now we see; surprised that silence carries a deeper truth than we could think of on our own.

After surprise comes wonder, since Christ comes to us in every breath we take, every person we meet, in the dust on the road to Emmaus, in the waves we sink into, in the beauty of communion with one another. All of these are Advent moments; they give us a way to live inside the saying, "Lo, I am with you always, even to the end of the age."

55

The Edge of Innocence

You learn somehow to be confident in a presence, an 'other' who does not change or go away. You realize ... there is a presence that does not let you go. And that is faith, I would say, in a very deeply biblical sense.[1]

I HAVE BEEN THINKING about the story of the Mount of Transfiguration. It features in the Gospels of Matthew, Mark, and Luke, and it is a story that somehow connects heaven and earth, faith and doubt, God visible and God hidden, the past, the future, and the present—and so it is a subject for a New Year's Day.

On New Year's Day we come the closest to innocence that we are capable of as adults during the cycle of seasons in the year. We are done with the old year and its failures. We've shed that year like a snake sheds its skin, and we look to the new year with a touching naiveté, believing that if we want to fly we can make it so. We will make new beginnings; we'll have a breakthrough; all our false starts will fade away. Never mind all the home gym equipment that was set up in the basement with such resoluteness the day after Christmas, only to appear on the curb in March with the rest of the trash.

And so we keep at it, this starting again and making promises to ourselves, because we absolutely must have a way to break up the surge of time and divert it at intervals. If December 31 is the lowest trough of

1. Williams, *Being Disciples*, 25.

the year, then New Year's Day is the wave crest. End and beginning curve back to touch each other like one of Einstein's sinkholes in time.

At the bottom of the worn-out year, scraping the barrel as it were, all the social norms for many ancient civilizations could be reversed or at least suspended for one night. Kings could be dissed without fear, peasants could don kingly robes. For a few hours, in a bacchanal celebration, all the fears and anxieties of the year could be discarded like old rags. It was a time for the expulsion of sins, for starting afresh, for the regeneration of time itself.

Recently, I read a news article about a dairy farmer who was finally selling off his cows after four decades of running the family farm. "It is said that farmers get forty chances," he wrote in conclusion. "I've had my forty and I'm getting out." Forces beyond his control had made it impossible to carry on, despite the efforts of him and his family. The plight of small family farms only highlights how important it is to us that we have a chance to start over.

Our lives are played out in an arena of paradoxical claims, as we try to unite opposing elements. "Be ye therefore perfect" sniffs at "All our righteousness is as filthy rags." "Why has thou cast us off, O God? Is it forever? Why art thou so stern, so angry with the sheep of thy flock?" gapes in disbelief at "The Lord's love never fails those who fear him." For those who search for God with all their hearts, the wry observation of R. S. Thomas, the Welsh poet-priest, rings true:

> . . . He is such a fast
> God, always before us and
> leaving as we arrive.[2]

We may be breathless to keep the back of God within sight, but the time between Christmas and New Year's offers a chance to catch one's breath. It is a fertile field of both regret and promise, of challenge and joy, of surrender to the incarnation and determination for the year ahead. The story of Jesus' transfiguration reveals the poles-apart thinking of the disciples; we see his glory revealed even as his compassion drives him deep into the common suffering of the world, and he is shadowed by the ordeal to come.

He had taken three of his disciples, Peter, James and John, to the top of what might have been Mount Tabor or maybe Mount Herman, leaving

---

2. Thomas, *Collected Poems*, 364.

the other disciples at the foot of the mountain, where they soon attracted a crowd. The three accounts in the Synoptic Gospels of Matthew, Mark, and Luke are substantially the same, with Matthew and Luke drawing from Mark's core story but adding significant details of their own.

Maybe Jesus anticipated what was in store for him on the mountain, or maybe he just needed to get away for a bit with his three good friends. In any case, there is an eerie resemblance to his night of sorrow in Gethsemane. The same three disciples are close to him while Jesus has a divine encounter; in Luke's Gospel account the disciples grow heavy with weariness and fall asleep, and Peter—bless him—speaks and acts in ways that Jesus must reject or risk losing his focus.

The outlines of the story are simple enough. Jesus and the disciples are on the mountain, when Jesus is suddenly radiant with light, his robe so white that it is almost blinding. Two resplendent figures appear and the three of them speak together.

The symmetry is arresting: Moses and Elijah, the Law and the Prophets, bookend Jesus with support just as he is growing into the conviction that he will die violently at the hands of authorities, religious and political, in Jerusalem. (An aside: How did the disciples *know* who they were? Were there introductions all round?) The disciples are both awed and terrified, so much so that Peter is babbling giddily about constructing three shelters when a voice thunders from heaven, "This is my beloved son. Listen to *him*." The disciples fall to the ground, overcome, and the apparitions vanish, leaving Jesus to touch the disciples: "Stand up," he says, "do not be afraid." And when they raise their heads, they are alone with Jesus.

What were they talking about? Luke tells us they "spoke of his departure, the destiny he was to fulfill in Jerusalem." On the way down the mountain Jesus tells the three not to talk of what they have seen until he has been raised from the dead. Ah, they say, apparently unfazed by talk of Jesus' impending death and resurrection. In Matthew's account the disciples raise a question on a technicality. Wasn't Elijah's appearance supposed to precede all this? Yes, responds Jesus, Elijah has already come, but nobody recognized him. "Then the disciples understood that he meant John the Baptist." What remains unremarked upon by the disciples is that this future event, Elijah preceding the Messiah, *is already in motion*. John the Baptist is dead, the Messiah is Jesus, and he is going to die.

When they reach the bottom of the mountain, they see a commotion in the crowd gathered there. A man has brought his epileptic son to the disciples to be healed—and they can't do it. The father implores Jesus to heal his son and Jesus explodes: "What an unbelieving and perverse generation! How long shall I be with you and endure you all? Bring your son here." There is a final convulsion as the boy writhes on the ground, the demon departs, and Jesus hands the boy back to his father. Mark up another victory against the forces of darkness. All's well that ends well, right?

If we were filming this episode, we would have used tight shots on the contorted face of the boy, close-ups on Jesus as he casts out the demon, and then a slow zoom out to encompass the crowd, ecstatic at the miraculous healing, filled with admiration and awe for the power of Jesus. Luke says that after this Jesus went indoors and the disciples, those who had remained at the foot of the mountain, had a private word. "Why couldn't we cast out the demon?" they ask. "Well," says Jesus, "this kind takes prayer."

***

Pull the cameras back into a high, wide shot stretching to the horizon, high and behind a group of tiny figures making their way south on the Jerusalem road. *We* know that Jesus has set his face like flint toward the holy city and that ahead of him lies the final conflict and his approaching death. Nothing is scripted here; no one's hand is being forced; each actor in this drama sets his own lines and actions, according to his will. The events jerk and tilt toward their bureaucratic finality in a way that seems, in retrospect, foreordained, but for those caught up in it the outcome is realized too late.

***

For us, poised on the cusp of the new year, the transfiguration offers us a way to into the times ahead. The incarnation has been our transcendental experience on the mountaintop, our unexpected blessing coming out of the darkness; we would like to remain there—if only for a few more days. It's a time when people seem to set aside their egos and think of others. If they—we—can do that consciously for several days, why can't we continue? Perhaps we can keep that going for a week and then New Years' can act like a slingshot to keep us in orbit above the earth.

"At some moments we experience complete unity within us and around us," says Henri Nouwen in *Bread for the Journey*. "But whenever and however it happens we say to ourselves, "This is it . . . everything fits . . . all I ever hoped for is here." This is what Peter, James, and John experienced on the mountain with Jesus. "This is the experience of the fullness of time," writes Nouwen. "These moments are given to us so that we can remember them when God seems far away, and everything appears empty and useless. These experiences are true moments of grace."[3]

But we can't remain on the mountaintop, up there in the glorious light with revered figures from our past. Down below, back in the world, there are the constant reminders that suffering continues and that we are not complete. "This kind takes prayer," says Jesus.

Up ahead are trials, but also moments of transcendent joy, communion, beauty. We are blessed by the Spirit, by the epiphanies granted to us that open us to a steadfast courage. There are crosses up ahead, no doubt, but spring is coming and there is a resurrection.

---

3. Nouwen, *Bread for the Journey*, loc. 4011.

56

Unveiling Reality

What in Greek was called epiphaniea meant the appearance, the arrival of a divinity among mortals ... Epiphany thus interrupts the everyday flow of time and enters as one privileged moment when we intuitively grasp a deeper, more essential reality hidden in things and persons.[1]

IN SAUL BELLOW'S HENDERSON *the Rain King,* the blustering, bumbling, red-faced, and violently suffering protagonist confides to us that "when things got very bad I often looked into books to see whether I could find some helpful words, and one day I read, 'The forgiveness of sins is perpetual and righteousness first is not required.' This impressed me so deeply that I went around saying it to myself."[2]

    This is an insight that arrives unexpectedly, cracking open his hard and aching heart, and setting him on a picaresque journey of self-discovery to Africa, where he learns humility and wisdom—and where he finally feels that his spirit is no longer slave to his body. It's an *epiphany*, a moment when he understands his reality in a way that he never could have before.

---

1. Milosz, *A Book of Luminous Things,* 3.
2. Bellow, *Henderson the Rain King,* 7.

It is reminiscent of another story, one that Jesus told, in which a young man, impatient and strident in his demands, took his inheritance and left for a far country, breaking his father's heart and setting ablaze a fire of resentment in his older brother. Later, after his money has burned up in moments of profligacy that have begun to blur and fade, he takes whatever work he can to sustain himself. One day, while mucking out the pig pen of a farmer outside the city, he "comes to himself," a telling phrase that both reveals the split within himself as well as the potential of reintegration. It's an *epiphany* that wells up within him while he is up to his knees in pigs, proving that a life-transforming moment can break in on us no matter where we find ourselves.

Czeslaw Milosz calls an epiphany "an unveiling of reality" in his international anthology of poetry, *A Book of Luminous Things*. He writes of ancient cultures in which streams were inhabited by the naiads and forests by the dryads, and the gods sometimes walked among humans. "Not rarely, they would visit households and were recognized by hosts." Abraham entertains God in the guise of three travelers and later, "the epiphany as appearance, the arrival of Christ, occupies an important place in the New Testament."[3]

We are living, says Milosz, in a world that has been deprived of clear-cut outlines and has been drained of color. This deprivation is not much helped, he continues, by theology, science, and philosophy. While they try to provide cures for nihilism, they are not usually effective, and instead give us descriptions that simply confirm our condition.

Poetry, however, looks at the singular rather than the general; it focuses on the leaf, not the forest, and thus it cannot help but see the variations, the diversity, the abundance of throbbing, colorful life. A poem, by describing a particular moment of present reality, illuminates the human experience and brings the divine into the mundane. A poem bears epiphanies.

***

Epiphany, from a Greek word for "manifestation" or "appearance," is for Christians the season after Advent and Christmas in which we celebrate the unveiling—just for a moment—of the divine nature of Christ, that moment in which a young Jewish carpenter arises from baptism in

---

3. Milosz, *A Book of Luminous Things*, 3.

the waters of the River Jordan, as the heavens split open above him and the voice of God declares him to be his beloved Son.

It is just a breath, a heart's beat, a hummingbird's jeweled flash of winged light, a disturbance in the space-time continuum, but it is gratefully grasped by Jesus. John the Baptist hears it too; they share a look between them, John all fire and sword and Jesus with a muscular tenderness.

We who watch from the riverbank twenty-one centuries later may only hear thunder in a cloudless sky and shrug.

John, with his fierce, hooded hawk's eyes, understands the moment: it reverberates in his chest like a bell. This is the moment he has prepared for all his life; it is here now, and he gives himself to it without hesitation. John had disciples, followers, people who revered him and did not shrink from his shouts into the desert wind. "He must increase, and I must decrease," he thinks. A gate, sensed but hidden, swings open behind his eyes and he steps through and knows somehow, beyond a shadow of a doubt, that he will not live to see this king crowned.

***

You wonder if these epiphanies can be prepared for. If they add to the quality of life, then shouldn't we figure out a way to generate them? Yet, they come when we need them and not before. They are gifts and as gifts we accept them or misuse them. But, faith, like poetry, cannot be duplicated: every experience is a new reading of meaning.

> If we could get the hang of it entirely
> It would take too long;
> All we know is the splash of words in passing
> And falling twigs of song,
> And when we try to eavesdrop on the great
> Presences it is rarely
> That by a stroke of luck we can appropriate
> Even a phrase entirely.[4]

Milosz shows us that epiphanies are the inbreaking of the divine in unexpected ways and places. They are "aha" moments, flashes of intuition that reveal an eternity in a grain of sand. Poems may carry epiphanies for

---

4. MacNeice, *Collected Poems*, 171.

us; nature may as well. We learn to see with our hearts as well as with our heads.

> Cease to dwell on days gone by
> and to brood over past history.
> Here and now I will do a new thing;
> this moment it will break from the bud.
> Can you not perceive it?[5]

The season of Epiphany is also a time to reflect on the experience of the magi, the travelers from another land, who searched with mind and heart for the Christ-child, leaving behind their familiar ways and traditions for something or someone they could not be sure would accept them.

Thus, it is a season to reflect on and seek out what unifies all Christians. Michael Mayne, the former dean of Westminster Abbey, wrote in *Responding to the Light*, "We Christians are as diverse and varied as the colors of the rainbow . . . Though at one level we are divided and have been divided by history into our separate traditions, yet there is a deeper truth, for those with eyes to see . . . All who believe that in Jesus we see God and put their faith in him are at the deepest level already *one* in Christ."[6]

An epiphany is a manifestation, an appearance, perhaps of something that was always there but overlooked or excluded out of habit and tradition, brushed aside in our haste—only to become, when revealed, so compelling that we can't take our eyes off it.

That which changes us from the inside may be the outside seen through new eyes.

---

5. Isa 43:18–19.
6. Mayne, *Responding to the Light*, 87–88.

57

Jonah's Bad Trip: A Lenten Meditation

> *Lent is a time set aside to reorient ourselves, to clarify our minds, to slow down, recover from distraction, to focus on the values of God's kingdom and on the value he has set on us and on our neighbors.*[1]

As prophets go, Jonah went—as far away as he could from this thunderous, all-seeing, lion of a God who could pick him up and shake him like a rag doll. It was no use; he'd taken a ship to Tarshish, roughly in the opposite direction from Nineveh, which was picturesquely situated far out on the burning plains of what would much later become Iraq.

Most prophets decidedly did not want the job; long hours, no benefits, one's very presence tended to make the children cry and the dogs bark. And it could get you killed. The killing part is what Jonah objected to the most.

So, he rushed down to the docks, paid the captain, and went aboard without so much as an overnight case. This raised suspicion. Most of the passengers on ships out of port were merchants. Jonah looked like a fugitive, but he paid up front, so the captain took him aboard. He told the first mate to keep an eye on him though. There was something fishy about him.

---

1. Guite, *Word in the Wilderness*, ix.

The first day out a tremendous storm came up. The wind roared and cracked through the rigging and the deck was slippery with foam. The crew flung the cargo over the rails to keep the ship afloat and it was all they could do to keep the bow headed into the waves. Being a multiethnic and polytheistic crew, they were desperately calling on their gods for relief when someone thought to search out their odd passenger.

He was found deep in the hold, asleep in a fetal position. Finding this both unnerving and insulting under the circumstances, the captain shook him awake and forced him topside. "What are you doing asleep! Get up, call on your god! Perhaps the god will spare us a thought so that we do not perish."

Since all the usual gods had been accounted for and the storm still raged on, the sailors cast lots to see who was at fault. When the lot fell to Jonah, the men rounded on him. "What's your business? Where do you come from? Who are your people?"

"I'm a Hebrew," he replied. "I serve the God who made the sea and the dry land." At this the crew gasped and drew back. "What did you *do*?" they demanded. And as the storm increased in fury they screamed, "What should we do to *you* to quiet this storm?"

"Throw me overboard," he cried out. "It's my fault this storm is upon us."

Let us pause here a moment to consider Jonah's plight. He is a prophet on the run from the God who controls all of the world. Perhaps it was simply a reflex to run, to escape a frightful duty. But it was a duty imposed by a God whose reach extends over the globe and who controls heaven, the sea, and the earth. A prophet on the run from a God like that is the living embodiment of futility, and Jonah knows it.

To their credit, the crew see flinging a man overboard in a whiplashing storm as a last resort. They row for shore, even though if they succeed they will crash on the rocks. But they row anyway, without progress, in the teeth of this blinding gale until, at last, exhausted and fearful, they pray for mercy from Jonah's god for throwing him overboard, and then over he goes. No doubt they see it as a sacrifice to a capricious god who can be appeased by a human sinking down into the cruel depths.

Does Jonah think the same way? In his state, confused, angry, bitter, and afraid, he may have felt he had nothing left, that his flight from the all-seeing God was a sure sign of his guilt, but that somehow, some way, this was all God's fault. But Jonah would get even. He'd die in the waves and *then* God would be sorry.

At this point the story takes a wild turn. In fact, it becomes a fable, replete with a fantastic animal. Scholars are unsure of when this story was written, although it was most certainly long after Nineveh had vanished into history. As a historical event it doesn't meet the bar, but as a story with a point, how could it be better?

A fugitive on the lam from God gets swallowed by a big fish, spends three days and three nights in the depths of both the ocean and the fish's innards, and, after a heartfelt prayer for salvation, is vomited (the Hebrew here is precise) up on the beach, dazed and slimy. It's a perfect setup for comedy and drama.

Onward, then! No time to lose! There's a whole city of wicked people to be warned, after which Jonah (he imagines) will be ceremonially cut into pieces and fricasseed over an open fire, all for the glory of the all-seeing God. Let's get this over with.

We can't fault Jonah too much for a grim outlook. He stood in a long line of prophets who understood that their messages, however compelling, would usually fall on deaf ears, and that at the very least they would be mocked and scorned. He had also grasped, with a singular clarity, that while most of the top tier of Hebrew prophets risked derision only from their own people, he, Jonah, was compelled to thrust God's warning under the noses of their ancestral enemies, a people wholly given over to unholy practices and unvarnished blasphemy. In the history of Israel, the Ninevites were the ultimate bogeymen, renowned for dragging their prisoners by hooks through the nose. And that was tender and thoughtful compared to what lay ahead for those who survived the long trek back to the city. No, there was nothing for it: he had been singled out by God for this exquisite punishment. "Pardon me," he thought bleakly, "if I go to my death stinking of fish and short on manners."

"And the word of the Lord came to Jonah a second time, saying, 'Get up, go to Nineveh the great city, and call out to it the call that I speak to you.' And Jonah got up and went to Nineveh according to the word of the Lord. And Nineveh was a great city of God's, a three days' walk across"[2]

Robert Alter's commentary on Jonah in his magnificent three-volume translation, *The Hebrew Bible (2019)*, cheerfully informs us that doing the math for a three-day walk across a city would give us a metropolis larger than Los Angeles, a sprawl no city in the ancient Near East could achieve, but if we regard it symbolically we see that just as Jonah was in

---

2. Jonah 3:1–3.

the belly of the fish for three days, so he will have three days to proclaim the message throughout Nineveh.

And it also appears that Nineveh, that great city, belongs to God, just like the sea, the mountains, donkeys, figs, and Israel. Jonah should feel right at home. Off he goes, then, striding a day's walk toward the center, shouting as he went, "Forty days more, and Nineveh is overthrown." And the people, the story says, trusted God and donned sackcloth and ashes and repented, just like that, from the greatest of them to the least.

The news travels like an invisible tsunami from the periphery to the center of the city where the king resides, and when it reaches him he stands up, throws off his mantle, covers himself in sackcloth, and sits down upon ashes (an observer wonders, did they keep sackcloth in the linen closet for just such an occasion?). The king makes a proclamation, remarkable in its force and comprehensiveness. Immediately, everyone, even the cattle and sheep, are commanded not to eat nor to drink water. "And man and beast shall cover themselves with sackcloth, and they shall call out to God with all their might . . . Who knows? Perhaps God will turn back and relent and turn back from His blazing wrath, and we shall not perish."[3] There is an echo here of the ship captain who tossed out a similar hope that God might tamp down his wrath in order that they might live.

Cattle and sheep wearing sackcloth, an entire city wearing sackcloth, no one eating or drinking, everyone (even the animals) repenting of the evil they had done? It's safe to say that no evangelist since has scored so complete a victory as Jonah. It's a record that will stand for all time.

But of course, it wasn't him. In fact, he did not take it well. "And the thing was very evil for Jonah, and he was incensed." He was incensed enough to pray to God in complaint, virtually fizzing in anger. Isn't this what I said when I was back home? he yells. *I knew* you would pull a trick like this! "For I knew that You are a gracious and compassionate God, slow to anger and abundant in kindness and relenting from evil." So, put me out of my misery—just kill me; I'm better off dead than alive. "And the Lord said, 'Are you good and angry?'"

Yes, yes, you could say that, muttered Jonah bitterly. He retraced his steps, trudging out of the city up to a hill to the east, where he made himself a shelter and sat down to watch what would happen. He wanted fire from heaven, napalm and howitzers, the mother of all bombs to flatten

---

3. Jonah 3:8–9.

this great city. Maybe that would make him feel better, salve his bruised ego and lower his blood pressure.

And God, smiling quietly to himself and compassionate to a fault, "set out a *qiqayon* plant, and it rose up over Jonah to be a shade over his head to save him from his evil plight. And Jonah rejoiced greatly over the *qiqayon.*" And despite the long arms of the sun as it sets on that day, Jonah finds comfort in the shade and passes the night thankfully and well.

And in the morning, as the sun rises, God sends a hot wind to wither Jonah's precious plant. Immediately, the bile rises in his throat, his blood pressure shoots skyward, and again he prays to die. The city, that great city, lies peacefully spread out below him, its inhabitants hungry but redeemed, its cattle and sheep bewildered by their sackcloth outfits and vaguely aware of how quiet it is.

"Are you good and angry over the *qiqayon*?" chuckles God. Jonah sighs, "I am good and angry, to the point of death." We can almost hear the shake of the divine head and a hint of exasperation because of this child. You cared more about the plant than the people, says God. "And I, shall I not have pity for Nineveh the great city, in which there are many more than one hundred twenty thousand human beings who do not know between their right hand and their left, and many beasts?" And there the fable ends.

***

We don't know how Jonah got home again or if he did. The story leaves us with questions, like all good stories do. Did the animals get to go naked again? Is Jonah like the prodigal son's elder brother? Can we drop our resentment at God's forgiveness? Does God really love our enemies? Are we good and angry over his compassion? Can we forgive ourselves as he has forgiven us?

Can we go home again?

58

Planks and Sawdust

How rare is the person who would be willing to accept the forgiveness of sins on condition of being willing to undergo the punishment of becoming entirely revealed to others, so that they could see right into the soul and all its secret guilt![1]

IN DANTE'S *INFERNO* THE damned in the sixth circle of hell are allowed to see far into the future, but in a remarkable detail in God's plan they know nothing of the present nor can they see what is happening right in front of them. In life, consumed by ambition and the grasp for power, they ignored those closest to them, while they schemed and strategized against their enemies. In the chess game that was thirteenth-century Florentine politics, these men planned out their deadly moves against their opponents, while they could not see clearly how their actions affected their own families. In Dante's hell the sinners are cursed to suffer the symbolic effects of the sins they committed in life. Because they did not see on earth, they *will* not see in hell.

Luke 6 is about the relationship between our intentions, our character, and our actions, and how those actions reverberate throughout the circles of our relationships. In contrast to Matthew's sermon given from the mountain, Luke's version has Jesus coming down from the hills at

---

1. Kierkegaard, *Spiritual Writings*, 261

daybreak and choosing twelve out of the crowd of disciples (in Greek *mathetas*, "those who follow") and designating them apostles. Then he stands at the foot of the hill, "on level ground," and addresses the hundreds who have come from Jerusalem, and from as far away as Tyre and Sidon, to hear him and to be healed.

It's a message that exactly reverses what we might expect. We've skimmed it so many times that we no longer see how radical it is, how the good news it proclaims is bad news for some, how confounding it must have been for those who thought Jesus was launching his messiahship.

He begins with the punchline, the message that was most pointed, which like an arrow pointed to the largest group listening to him that day: "How blest are you who are poor; the kingdom of God is yours." The words that follow are paradoxical: those who weep now will laugh; those who are hated will dance for joy. Then, with a hinge that shows Luke's literary skill, the reversals are stated. The rich have had their fun; now they face hardship. The well-fed will be hungry; those who laugh will be weeping.

The clincher is that those who mourn now stand in a long line of people who have suffered unjustly, including the true prophets of old, and those who garner all the praise now should know that people spoke well of the false prophets back in the day too.

Jesus then turns to such reliably off-putting sayings as "Love your enemies; do good to those who hate you" and "Turn the other cheek" and "Treat others as you would like them to treat you." His disciples must go beyond the reciprocal manners of doing good to those who do good to them; that is just standard social courtesy. What the kingdom expects has a much deeper meaning, one that transforms relationships and begins with self-awareness and humility.

Jesus' social communication skills reveal a person who challenges us to exceed the minimum in social interaction. "Pass no judgement and you will not be judged," he says. "Do not condemn and you will not be condemned." That's the minimum. Just as "sinners" (those who flout the finer points of the law or whose professions place them outside the community) love those who love them, most people know they'll get back what they dish out to others. There is a common ethic that most people subscribe to, an enlightened self-interest that expects some give-and-take and is willing to give some leeway to others until pushed to defend oneself. In that way we can claim to be as good as we are expected to be.

But to be disciples, those who follow Jesus, there is a higher standard that comes from love. Duty does the minimum, but love attempts the maximum. Duty follows the rules, but love seizes opportunities. Duty does what is required and no more, but love acts spontaneously. Duty wants a receipt; love says, "Don't worry about it." The "sons [and daughters] of the Most High" will be compassionate toward the ungrateful and the wicked, just as God is compassionate.

He offers them a parable about the blind leading the blind and both falling into a ditch, and then follows with a swift right uppercut about self-awareness and humility. "Why do you look at the speck of sawdust in your brother's eye, with never a thought for the great plank in your own? How can you say to your brother, 'My dear brother, let me take the speck out of your eye', when you are blind to the plank in your own? You hypocrite! First take the plank out of your own eye, and then you will see clearly to take the speck out of your brother's."[2]

As metaphors go, this is vintage Jesus—heavy on the hyperbole, vivid in imagery, delivered with a twinkle in his eye. But he is serious. The disciples learned that no matter where they stood in the social register, they were to be leaders in ethics. They are followers of Jesus now; they *will* be teachers of others, and a teacher cannot teach what he has not learned. Character makes influence a live possibility, and influence, in turn, helps shape character. We're known by what we produce, by what people around us can see of us in our behavior. "By their fruits you shall know them" is not just a biblical saying; it's how we navigate our relationships and place our trust in others. As such, it's the foundation of a society. Out of the abundance of character the fruit of the heart is grown.

Are disciples to be silent about evil and injustice then? "The ban on speck-hunting," notes G. B. Caird wryly in his commentary *Saint Luke*, "does not, of course, mean that Christians must condone evil or refrain from forming moral judgements . . . Pseudo-religion, which Jesus calls hypocrisy, is for every trying to make other people better; and the cure for it is a mirror."[3]

---

2. Luke 6:41–42.
3. Caird, *Saint Luke*, 106.

✳✳✳

Most college and university teachers I know have at times suffered from "imposter syndrome," that dread feeling that students will see right through you to the vast, empty, and echoing interior of your knowledge warehouse. If you teach ethics, as I did for many years, you feel the pressure even more. I wondered, at times, how I had the nerve to stand up in front of students who demanded at the very least that I always knew what I was talking about, and who expected, in varying degrees of interest, that I flawlessly practiced what I preached. But there is some comfort in the very realization of how much we lack; if we can see our condition we can, at least, do something about it.

In order to follow Jesus, we need to see where we're going. It also helps to be aware of how much we don't yet know nor do. Planks in the eye get in the way of that. What I have noticed is that if you pray for help to remove your plank, God may send you someone with clearer vision than your own, someone with a speck of sawdust in her eye. Plank removal may begin when you see that person's speck and then realize your own condition. This ordinance of humility can have the effect of deepening our self-reflection as we learn through observation. For all of us have something in our eyes that clouds our vision.

"If we are humble," writes Thomas Merton, "and if we believe in the Providence of God, we will see that our mistakes are not merely a necessary evil . . . they enter into the very structure of our existence. It is by making mistakes that we gain experience, not only for ourselves but for others."[4]

Jesus once restored the sight of a blind man by putting saliva on his eyes and then touching him. "Can you see anything?" he asked. "I see people," said the fellow, "but they look like trees, walking." Jesus touched his eyes again, and the man looked intently, and this time he saw everything clearly.

Some commentators note that Matthew and Luke did not use this story from Mark, perhaps because they were embarrassed that it took Jesus two tries to heal the man. But I think the story is meant for all of us for whom seeing clearly does not happen all at once.

---

4. Merton, *No Man Is an Island*, 128.

59

The Doubtful Pilgrim

[D]oubt wisely; in strange way
To stand inquiring right, is not to stray;
To sleep, or run wrong, is.[1]

IF THERE IS ONE thing I should like to give up for Lent, it would be impatience. I do not look like an impatient fellow to my friends, but that is because I have perfected an expression of benign composure that covers a roiling sea of clashing thoughts and enough second-guessing to keep me dithering in place. Rarely do I accelerate down the golden road of certainty without fishing in the glove compartment of my memory for maps of alternate routes.

Usually people give up something they like for Lent, such as chocolate or the movies or donuts. The idea is that such a sacrifice, however provisional, will concentrate the mind long enough to focus on more serious things. Somehow that seems off-point to me, not really weighty enough to bend the needle on the spiritual Change-O-Meter. And one of the unintended consequences is the flagrant growth of spiritual pride. So, I would hope to give up something that will make a difference, something I don't like.

Although I have come lately to a fuller awareness of Lent, I understand it to be a season for introspection, for searching ourselves for our motives and attitudes. It is a way to examine spiritual habits, those

---

1. Donne, "Satire III," 74.

engrained neural pathways that can free us up for deeper thought or can dull our sensitivities. We may also liken Lent to a pilgrimage of the spirit, a way to cast a look backward along our path and then forward to where we hope to go.

Impatience isn't all wrong; it can spur us to cut through our hesitation over things that are trivial. Sometimes it really doesn't matter which brand of chips you buy in an aisle with dozens of slight variations on a theme. But most of the time impatience makes us cut corners, disregard the context, and nullify the nuances.

Sometimes impatience is a form of intellectual laziness. We don't want to think a thing through; it's easier just to jump the gap to the closest conclusion and hope to find a handhold. People who are good at math and actually like it assure me that finding the solution to the problem is as much about the steps in the process as it is about cresting the mountain to find—surprise!—the summit. There's an elegance there, they say, a beauty in the way the symbols lead one through the maze to the fountain at the center.

I just wonder what fiend thought it would be fun to make x stand for something unknown. "What are they trying to hide?" I wondered in math class. "If I can see the solution, why do I have to go through all the steps to prove I got there?"

There is a saying that I've begun to find irritating, partly because I've used it myself, since it was cheap and available, but mostly because it doesn't square with my experience. The saying is: "Getting there is half the fun." We usually cite this phrase when it is manifestly untrue, when getting there was an unconscionable slog, only redeemed by the fact that ultimately we prevailed and finally did get there.

I feel this way about flying these days. A journey of two hours of actual flying time inevitably becomes six or even eight hours of travel time (there's the unknown x in the equation), once you factor in getting to the airport two hours early, trudging shoeless through TSA, suffering the delay while the airline waits for a missing part to be delivered through rush-hour traffic, and then the final half-hour on the tarmac while we gaze at the airport terminal. No, getting there is not half the fun. It's not even an eighth of the fun. It is *not* fun.

There is a related phrase that I *do* appreciate, however, despite my struggle with impatience. That is, "It's not the destination, it's the journey." Granted, it might seem too similar to pass inspection, but there is a difference—context matters.

I am thankful to have come from a religious tradition that regards our passage through this life as a pilgrimage. It teaches us that pilgrims have their eyes set on a future home and thus, in this journey one must travel light, unencumbered by the excess of having that ties one down. It is part of our traditional hope in the Second Advent of Christ, that portal through which we imagine justice and peace just beyond the foreground of the breakup of all things on this earth.

An image that captured this for me as I studied the philosophy of Gabriel Marcel was his description of us as *Homo Viator,* humans as wanderers and wayfarers, whose provisions for our journey are indeed "pro-visions," those acts of imagination and faith that stimulate us before we set out and which sustain us on the journey.

We are restless beings, says Marcel, forever longing for transcendence and fulfillment. That hunger lures us onward, what C. S. Lewis called *Sehnsucht,* the longing for a joy that will never be completely satisfied on this earth. We have choices to make, implies Marcel, between resigning ourselves to the absurdity of traveling without meaning until we die or rising to the risk of faith that we shall discover ourselves in God through hope and trust while on the road.

Here is where patience must play its part and where doubt becomes the handmaiden of faith. "Doubt wisely," advises John Donne in the epigram. "To stand inquiring right is not to stray." We have no need to rush on the way; our journey toward the kingdom yet to come does not hasten or prevent its coming. What matters is that we find our way forward in faith, remembering experience but not hampered by it, attentive to our reasonable doubts.

Donne continues with the famous metaphor:

> On a huge hill,
> Cragged and steep, Truth stands, and he that will
> Reach her, about must and about must go,
> And what the hill's suddenness resists, win so . . .[2]

Some of the really important things in life must be approached indirectly. Doubt can foster patience, the willingness to traverse that huge hill around and around, climbing higher as we go, learning in the journey toward the truth as it is in Christ.

---

2. Donne, "Satire III," 74.

If we will it so, our capacity to doubt will be matched by our desire for truth. Ironically, we doubt because we want authentic faith, the kind to sustain us through our doubt.

And so, it seems that after all, now would be a good time for a pilgrimage of the heart.

60

Cross-Purposes

Salvation is a child and when it grows up it is crucified. Only he who can see power under weakness, the whole under the fragment, victory under defeat, glory under suffering, innocence under guilt, sanctity under sin, life under death can say: Mine eyes have seen thy salvation.[1]

WHEN I WAS A child, I discovered that when I crossed my eyes I could see the world in very different ways. Instantly, my left eye invaded the territory of the right eye and the result was a disorienting Escher-like amalgam of images, as if Spock and Kirk had gotten their body parts reversed going through the transporter device. It was an ersatz Picasso lens for budding cubists. Ignoring the taunts of older children that one day my eyes would stay crossed, I enjoyed these brief forays into alternate reality.

Standing on my head was another way to reimagine the world. Although I couldn't sustain the full upright position for long, I could live for a few moments in a world with a limitless blue airiness underfoot beneath a ceiling of trees, streets, and buildings.

It's good for us to see the world from odd angles from time to time. It reminds us that ours is just one of many viewpoints. And it gives us insight into primitive Christianity, which abounds with paradoxes and upside-down values.

---

1. Tillich, *New Being*, 95.

Christianity often seems to be at cross-purposes with standard operating procedures. In the Genesis story, creation is the high point, but after sin everything is downhill from there, whereas with evolution everything begins with the humble one-celled organism and climbs to the top of the food chain, which is us. In the darkest, coldest month of the year, Christianity says the light came into the world. In the spring, when everything in nature is waking up and blooming, Christians celebrate a death.

"I am come that they might have life, and that more abundantly," claims Jesus, but then he also proclaims the poor to be blessed. The Beatitudes are all about opposites. Blessed are those who mourn, for they shall be comforted. Blessed are those of a gentle spirit; the world shall be theirs. Everywhere you look in the Gospels there are these cross-eyed, headstand ways.

Don't kill each other, says Jesus, but in the next breath he pushes it way back behind actions to intentions. Don't nurse anger toward others, because anger nursed can then be weaned to murder. Without denying the front-facing commandment, Jesus goes back to the root of the outward action.

It's easy for us to love those who love us—or at least to avoid conflict with most people. But what about those who get in our face? Jesus tells us to love our enemies and to pray for those who flame us on Facebook or who lie about us at work. This is how God sees us as children of his family. After all, Jesus reminds us, God makes the sun to shine upon the good and the bad alike and sends rain for both the liars and the honest. You're all in the family, he says. Do you think I'll treat you unequally?

It takes a while to get used to this radical way of thinking. Actually, we don't get used to it. It doesn't become habitual and it certainly isn't instinctual; it is something that must be relearned and practiced daily. It's as if our brains were developed to float in our skulls just so, vertically aligned in such a way that stimuli reaching us from the external world hit their receptors precisely, with no tolerance for wavering or misalignment. The world shot in portrait mode only, the landscape view constrained to fit only through distortion and elongation. Only when we stand on our heads does any of it begin to make sense.

Why does so much of what Jesus says sound so alien? Lest we think that two thousand years and a clash of cultures has created this great divide, we can take some rueful comfort in that his mother and his brothers thought him a stark lunatic and his own disciples could not grasp his simplest commands. "Who is the greatest in the kingdom of heaven?" they ask. He calls over a child, sets him down in the midst of them, and responds, "Unless you turn round and become like children, you will never enter the kingdom of heaven."[2] The meaning is unequivocal: what part of "never" don't we understand?

Yet, when one door slams, another opens. "Let a man humble himself till he is like this child, and he will be the greatest in the kingdom of heaven."[3] In this new economy of virtues only the humble survive. In one stroke, Jesus flattens the social hierarchy based on status and power and spreads it horizontally. If we want to see this kingdom as it is, we shall have to look in landscape mode, turning and turning in the widening gyre 360 degrees, until we return to this little child.

Paradoxes and reversals abound. Paul is shipwrecked, beaten, imprisoned, and starved. He has to light out of town more than once under cover of darkness, and who could calculate the miles he put in walking, sailing, riding for the gospel of the kingdom? Yet all these things he counts as nothing, save for the cross of Christ and the glory to come. "Our eyes are fixed," says Paul, "not on the things that are seen, but on the things that are unseen." [4]We can imagine him, stripped for thirty-nine lashes, with a gaze that penetrates to heaven.

What do we see? What are we looking at? Even after the hundreds of miles he walks and the beatings he endures, there is a certain bounce in Paul's stride. "Therefore, we never cease to be confident," he writes. "Faith is our guide, we do not see him."[5] He looks at the world with eyes wide open, seeing himself as he is, but more importantly, how God sees him. Living as an exile in this world, Paul knows that those who play by the rules of the world may succeed in the ways of the world—although they will lose their lives—but those who take up their cross and follow Jesus will gain their lives. In the midst of death there is life.

"Sin is our refusal to become who we truly are," writes Michael Mayne in *Pray, Love, Remember*. When we confess our sins, we may think of all the moments we tripped up in our daily walk, all the unthinking ways we brushed others aside, the petty grievances we took into foster care, the blindness to our effect on others that caused them pain. But

2. Matt 18:3.
3. Matt 18:4.
4. 2 Cor 4:18.
5. 2 Cor 5:6–7.

Mayne is looking deeper than just sins. "Chiefly I am aware of a much more subtle temptation," he writes, "to settle for less than I might be. To choose the lesser good. To lack curiosity and wonder. To miss the mark because my sights are fixed too low. Not to perceive that I am 'fearfully and wonderfully made' in God's image."[6]

At all times, but especially at Lent, if we ask it of God, we are blessed to see ourselves as we are and what we may become. Seeing thus is to see the world turned upside down, and yet to walk confidently.

It may all seem to be at cross-purposes with how the world works. Yet, in the end, all our purposes *begin* with the cross, the cross that brings life, the death of Death, and, most wonderfully, resurrection.

---

6. Mayne, *Pray, Love, Remember*, 46.

Bibliography

Alighieri, Dante. *The Divine Comedy*. Translated by John Ciardi. New York: Penguin, 2003.
Armstrong, Karen. *The Bible: A Biography*. New York: Atlantic Monthly, 2007.
———. *The Case for God*. New York: Knopf, 2009.
Augustine, Saint. *The Confessions*. Translated by Maria Boulding. Hyde Park, NY: New City, 1997.
———. *Confessions*. Translated by Garry Wills. New York: Penguin, 2006.
———. "Sermon 256." In *Essential Sermons*. Hyde Park, NY: New City, 2007.
Bellow, Saul. *Henderson the Rain King*. Greenwich, CT: Fawcett, 1958.
Berger, Peter. *The Sacred Canopy: Elements of a Sociological Theory of Religion*. New York: Anchor, 1969.
Brueggemann, Walter. *The Practice of Prophetic Imagination: Preaching an Emancipated Word*. Minneapolis: Fortress, 2012.
Caird, G. B. *The Gospel of Saint Luke*. New York: Penguin, 1963.
Camus, Albert. *The Rebel*. New York: Vintage/Random House, 1991.
Carroll, Lewis. *Alice's Adventures in Wonderland and Through the Looking-Glass*. Everyman ed. London: J. M. Dent, 1993.
Charon, Joel M. *Symbolic Interactionism: An Introduction, an Interpretation, an Integration*. 7th ed. Upper Saddle River, NJ: Prentice Hall, 2001.
Crossan, John Dominic. *The Power of Parable: How Fiction by Jesus Became Fiction about Jesus*. New York: HarperCollins, 2012.
Donne, John. "Satire III." In *John Donne's Poetry: Authoritative Texts, Criticism*, edited by Arthur L. Clements, 74. 2nd ed. New York: Norton, 1992.
Emerson, Ralph Waldo. "The American Scholar." In *The Essential Writings of Ralph Waldo Emerson*, edited by Brooks Atkinson. New York: Modern Library, 2000.
———. "Nature." In *Selected Essays*, edited by Larzer Ziff. New York: Penguin, 1982.
Epictetus. *The Art of Living: The Classic Manual on Virtue, Happiness, and Effectiveness*. A new interpretation by Sharon Lebell. New York: HarperCollins, 1995.
Frost, Robert. "Mending Wall." In *The Road Not Taken*, edited by Louis Untermeyer. New York: Holt, 1985.
Fry, Christopher. *The Dark Is Light Enough: A Winter Comedy*. Oxford: Oxford University Press, 1954.
Frye, Northrop. *The Great Code: The Bible and Literature*. New York: Harcourt, 1982.
Gallagher, Winifred. *Rapt: Attention and the Focused Life*. New York: Penguin, 2009.
Goodman, Nelson. *Ways of Worldmaking*. Indianapolis: Hackett, 1978.

Guite, Malcolm. *The Word in the Wilderness: A Poem a Day for Lent and Easter.* London: Canterbury Press Norwich, 2014.
Gunderson, Gary. *Deeply Woven Roots: Improving the Quality of Life in Your Community.* Minneapolis: Augsburg Fortress, 1997.
Heschel, Abraham Joshua. *God in Search of Man: A Philosophy of Judaism.* New York: Farrar, Straus and Giroux, 1955.
———. *Moral Grandeur and Spiritual Audacity.* Edited by Susanna Heschel. New York: Farrar, Straus and Giroux, 1996.
Hillman, James. *Kinds of Power: A Guide to Its Intelligent Uses.* New York: Doubleday, 1995.
Holloway, Richard. *Doubts and Loves: What Is Left of Christianity?* Edinburgh: Canongate, 2001.
Housden, Roger. *For Lovers of God Everywhere: Poems of the Christian Mystics.* Carlsbad, CA: Hay House, 2009.
James, William. *Psychology.* Cleveland: Fine Editions, 1948.
———. *The Varieties of Religious Experience.* New York: Modern Library, 1999.
———. *The Will to Believe and Other Essays in Popular Philosophy, and Human Immortality.* New York: Dover, 1956.
Jobs, Steve. "'You've Got to Find What You Love,' Jobs Says." Transcript of Stanford commencement address delivered June 12, 2005. https://news.stanford.edu/2005/06/14/jobs-061505/.
Julian of Norwich. *Revelations of Divine Love.* Translated by Clifton Wolters. New York: Viking Penguin, 1966.
Jung, Carl. *The Undiscovered Self.* Boston: Little, Brown, 1958.
Kierkegaard, Soren. *Papers and Journals: A Selection.* Translated by Alastair Hannay. New York: Penguin, 1996.
———. *Spiritual Writings: Gift, Creation, Love: Selections from the Upbuilding Discourses.* Selected, translated, and with an introduction by George Pattison. New York: Harper Perennial, 2010.
La Rochefoucauld, François, duc de. *Maxims of La Rochefoucauld.* Translated by John Heard Jr. Mineola. New York: Dover, 2006.
Lattimore, Richmond, translator. *Acts and Letters of the Apostles.* New York: Farrar, Straus and Giroux, 1982.
———, translator. *The Four Gospels and the Revelation.* New York: Pocket, 1962.
Lewis, C. S. *The Joyful Christian.* New York: Simon and Schuster, 1996.
MacNeice, Louis. "Entirely." In *Collected* Poems, edited by Peter McDonald. Winston-Salem, NC: Wake Forest University Press, 2013.
Mannheim, Karl. *Ideology and Utopia: An Introduction to the Sociology of Knowledge.* Translated by Louis Wirth and Edward Shils. New York: Harcourt, Brace, 1936.
Maslow, Abraham H. *Religions, Values, and Peak-Experiences.* New York: Penguin, 1976.
May, Rollo. *Love and Will.* New York: Dell, 1969.
Mayne, Michael. *Pray, Love, Remember.* London: Darton, Longman and Todd, 1998.
———. *Responding to the Light: Reflections on Advent, Christmas, and Epiphany.* Edited and introduced by Joel W. Huffstetler. London: Canterbury Press Norwich, 2017.
McAdams, Dan P. *The Stories We Live By.* New York: Guildford, 1993.
Merton, Thomas. *The New Man.* New York: Farrar, Straus and Giroux, 1961.
———. *New Seeds of Contemplation.* New York: New Directions, 1961.

———. *No Man Is an Island*. New York: Harcourt Brace Jovanovich, 1955.
———. *Seeds*. Edited with an introduction by Robert Inchausti. Boston: Shambala, 2002.
———. *Turning Toward the World: The Pivotal Years*. Edited by Victor A. Kramer. New York: HarperCollins, 1997.
Miles, Jack. *Christ: A Crisis in the Life of God*. New York: Random House, 2001.
Milosz, Czeslaw. *A Book of Luminous Things: An International Anthology of Poetry*. San Diego, CA: Harcourt Brace, 1996.
Moltmann, Jürgen. *The Crucified God*. Translated by R. A. Wilson and John Bowden. New York: Harper & Row, 1974.
Neiman, Susan. *Evil in Modern Thought: An Alternative History of Philosophy*. Princeton, NJ: Princeton University Press, 2002.
———. *Moral Clarity: A Guide for Grown-Up Idealists*. Orlando, FL: Harcourt, 2008.
Niebuhr, Reinhold. *Beyond Tragedy: Essays on the Christian Interpretation of History*. New York: Scribner, 1965.
Nouwen, Henri. *Bread for the Journey: A Daybook of Wisdom and Faith*. Ebook ed. New York: HarperCollins, 2007.
———. *The Spiritual Life: Eight Essential Titles by Henri Nouwen*. San Francisco: HarperOne, 2016.
Oakley, Mark. *The Splash of Words: Believing in Poetry*. London: Canterbury Press Norwich, 2016.
O'Connor, Flannery. *Wise Blood*. New York: Farrar, Straus and Giroux, 1990.
Orwell, George. "The Spike." In *Facing Unpleasant Facts: Narrative Essays*, edited by George Packer. Boston: Houghton Mifflin Harcourt, 2009.
Pascal. *Pensées*. Translated with an introduction by A. J. Krailsheimer. Harmondsworth, UK: Penguin, 1966.
Pearson, Mike. "A Long Time in Politics." *Pearson's Perspectives* (blog), January 18, 2019. https://www.pearsonsperspectives.com/single-post/2019/01/18/A-long-time-in-politics.
Pelikan, Jaroslav. *Jesus Through the Centuries: His Place in the History of Culture*. New York: Harper & Row, 1985.
Peters, John Durham. *Speaking into the Air: A History of the Idea of Communication*. Chicago: University of Chicago Press, 1999.
Peterson, Eugene. *The Message: The New Testament in Contemporary English*. Colorado Springs: NavPress, 1993.
Riley, Gregory John. *One Jesus, Many Christs: How Jesus Inspired Not One True Christianity, but Many: The Truth about Christian Origin*. San Francisco: HarperSanFrancisco, 1997.
Rilke, Rainer Maria. "Gott spricht zu jedem nur, eh er ihn macht." In *Rilke's Book of Hours: Love Poems to God*, translated by Anita Barrows and Joanna Macy. New York: Riverhead, 1996.
———. "Ich glaube an Alles noch nie Gesagte." In *Rilke's Book of Hours: Love Poems to God*, translated by Anita Barrows and Joanna Macy. New York: Riverhead, 1996.
———. *Letters on Life*. Translated by Ulrich Baer. New York: Modern Library, 2006.
———. *The Selected Poetry of Rainer Maria Rilke*. "The Spanish Trilogy." Edited and translated by Stephen Mitchell. New York: Random House, 1989.
Rohr, Richard. *Falling Upward: A Spirituality for The Two Halves of Life*. San Francisco: Jossey-Bass, 2011.

Sanford, John A. *Evil: The Shadow Side of Reality*. New York: Crossroad, 1982.

Simon, Paul. "Slip Slidin' Away." On *Still Crazy After All These Years*. Sony Music, 1975.

Steindl-Rast, David. "The Shadow in Christianity." In *Meeting the Shadow: The Hidden Power of the Dark Side of Human Nature*, edited by Connie Zweig and Jeremiah Abrams. Los Angeles: J. P. Tarcher, 1991.

Stevens, Wallace. *Collected Poetry and Prose*. New York: Library of America, 1997.

Tao Te Ching. Translated by Stephen Mitchell. New York: Harper & Row, 1988.

Taylor, Barbara Brown. *An Altar in the World: A Geography of Faith*. New York: HarperCollins, 2009.

———. *The Seeds of Heaven*. Louisville: Westminster John Knox, 2004.

———. *Learning to Walk in the Dark*. New York: HarperCollins, 2014.

Taylor, Charles. *A Secular Age*. Cambridge, MA: Harvard University Press, 2007.

Taylor, James. "Watchin' Over Me." On *Before This World*. Concord Music, 2015.

Teresa of Avila, Saint. *Santa Teresa, an Appreciation: With Some of the Best Passages of the Saint's Writings*. Transcribed from the 1900 Oliphant, Anderson & Ferrier edition by David Price. Amazon Kindle ed. Amazon Digital Services, 2011.

Thomas, R. S. *Collected Poems 1945–1990*. London: Orion, 1993.

Thoreau, Henry D. *Walden*. New Haven, CT: Yale University Press, 2006.

Tillich, Paul. "The Good That I Will, I Do Not." In *The Eternal Now*. New York: Scribner, 1963.

———. *On the Boundary: An Autobiographical Sketch*. New York: Scribner, 1966.

———. "To Whom Much Is Forgiven." In *The New Being*. New York: Scribner, 1955.

Tonstad, Sigve. *God of Sense and Traditions of Non-Sense*. Eugene, OR: Wipf & Stock, 2016.

U2. "When I Look at the World." On *All That You Can't Leave Behind*. Island Records, 2000.

Wallis, Jim. *The Call to Conversion: Recovering the Gospel for These Times*. San Francisco: Harper & Row, 1981.

Watzlawick, Paul. *The Language of Change: Elements of Therapeutic Communication*. New York: Norton, 1978.

Whitehead, Alfred North. *Aims of Education*. Free Press edition. New York: MacMillan, 1929.

Williams, Rowan. *Being Disciples: Essentials of the Christian Life*. Grand Rapids: Eerdmans, 2016.

Wilson, A. N. *The Book of the People: How to Read the Bible*. New York: HarperCollins, 2016.

———. *Jesus: A Life*. New York: Norton, 1992.

———. *Paul: The Mind of the Apostle*. New York: Norton, 1977.

Wiman, Christian. *Ambition and Survival: Becoming a Poet*. Port Townsend, WA: Copper Canyon, 2007.

———. *My Bright Abyss: Meditation of a Modern Believer*. New York: Farrar, Straus and Giroux, 2013.

Woodruff, Paul. *The Ajax Dilemma: Justice, Fairness, and Rewards*. New York: Oxford University Press, 2011.

Wright, N.T. *Evil and the Justice of God*. Downers Grove, IL: InterVarsity, 2006.

www.ingramcontent.com/pod-product-compliance
Lightning Source LLC
Chambersburg PA
CBHW060559230426
43670CB00011B/1889